# WHAT IS PROFESSIONAL SOCIAL WORK?

Malcolm Payne

Consultant editor: Jo Campling

Revised Second Edition

**Rawat Publications**

Jaipur • New Delhi • Bangalore • Mumbai • Hyderabad • Guwahati

ISBN 81-316-0165-X
**Indian Reprint, 2007**



This edition is published by arrangement with The Policy Press, University of Bristol, Fourth Floor, Beacon House, Queen's Road, Bristol BS8 1QU, UK. www. policypress.org.uk



*Published by*
Prem Rawat for **Rawat Publications**
Satyam Apts., Sector 3, Jawahar Nagar, Jaipur - 302 004 (India)
Phone: 0141 265 1748 / 7006 Fax: 0141 265 1748
E-mail : info@rawatbooks.com Website: www.rawatbooks.com

*New Delhi Office*
4858/24, Ansari Road, Daryaganj, New Delhi 110 002
Phone: 011-23263290

*Also at Bangalore, Mumbai, Hyderabad and Guwahati*

Printed at Chaman Enterprises, New Delhi

# Contents


| | | |
|---|---|---|
| List of tables and figures | | iv |
| Preface and acknowledgements | | v |
| Notes on the author | | vii |
| *one* | Introduction: the social work discourse | 1 |
| *two* | The identity of social work | 23 |
| *three* | Social work as a practice | 53 |
| *four* | Social work values: social justice and social care | 81 |
| *five* | Social work, management and the agency | 103 |
| *six* | Social work, power and society | 121 |
| *seven* | Social work: profession among professions | 141 |
| *eight* | Social works: global and local | 163 |
| *nine* | Social work: (inter)personal, political and professional | 181 |
| References | | 191 |
| Index | | 213 |

# List of tables and figures

## Tables


| | | |
|---|---|---|
| 1.1 | Terms referring to social work and related services | 4-5 |
| 2.1 | Internet search: define 'social work' | 27 |
| 2.2 | Definition of social work from the *Oxford English Dictionary* | 28 |
| 2.3 | IFSW international definition of social work | 28 |
| 2.4 | Department of Health information on social care | 30 |
| 2.5 | Social care and social work: official statements | 31 |
| 2.6 | Definitions of social work in the early 20th century | 33 |
| 2.7 | Definitions of social work and social casework (1930-70) | 35-8 |
| 2.8 | Definitions of social casework and social work from 1971 | 41 |
| 2.9 | The Barclay Report's social care planning and counselling | 46 |
| 3.1 | Usages of communication as a concept | 63 |
| 3.2 | TAPUPA framework standard for assessing knowledge | 73 |
| 4.1 | UK Social Care Councils: codes of practice | 87 |
| 4.2 | Difficulties with codes of ethics and practice | 88 |
| 4.3 | IFSW ethical problem areas | 89 |
| 4.4 | International conventions | 90 |
| 4.5 | Views of welfare and views of service users | 93 |
| 4.6 | Value complexities | 95 |
| 4.7 | Reamer's guidelines for thinking through value complexities | 99 |
| 5.1 | Management challenges: four formulations | 117-18 |
| 7.1 | Partnership working: New Labour policy | 154 |
| 8.1 | Social work education bodies' requirements for international understanding | 165-6 |
| 8.2 | International social work 'notables' | 169 |
| 8.3 | Fields and methods of international interest | 170 |


## Figures


| | | |
|---|---|---|
| 1.1 | Pathways to and through social work | 7 |
| 1.2 | Pathways analysis format | 9 |
| 1.3 | The three views of social work | 13 |
| 1.4 | Views of social work scale | 17 |
| 1.5 | Examples of views analyses | 19 |
| 7.1 | Networks of professions, knowledge and services | 156 |

# Preface and acknowledgements

The first edition of this book was written for the British Association of Social Workers (BASW) and was published by their publishing company, Venture Press, in 1996. I am grateful to Sally Arkley, the BASW publisher at the time, for her interest and support in the project, and to staff at BASW and The Policy Press for their help. I am also grateful to Barbara Monroe, the Chief Executive of St Christopher's Hospice, for facilitating the work of rewriting.

Although this second edition takes a similar (social construction) approach to the issues raised by examining the nature of social work, it is completely rewritten and extensively updated, with new case studies in many chapters. Much of the development of the book has arisen because of the teaching on this topic that I have done in many countries across the world and to courses and conferences in the UK. The analysis of the discourse among three views of social work is the same, but I have updated and developed the argument and provided more extensive evidence of the sources from which the argument is drawn. The discussion of welfare regimes as a way of analysing international variation in the organisation of social work is new, and the role of social work is more clearly placed within the context of multiprofessional services and the development of social care in the British context. Chapter Four on social work values and much of the argument in the conclusion (Chapter Nine) are completely renewed, looking forward into the 21st century.

The argument of this book connects with my books *Modern Social Work Theory* (3rd edn, 2005a) and *The Origins of Social Work: Continuity and Change* (2005c), both published by Palgrave Macmillan. Collectively, they examine the nature of social work by looking at theory that prescribes practice (*Modern Social Work Theory*), historical and value origins of the current state of social work (*The Origins of Social Work*) and, in this book, debate about the nature of social work. I gratefully acknowledge that this understanding of the interaction of the works, which I now make explicit in them, arose from discussion with Steven Shardlow. Material about the three views of social work in Chapters One and Two is written to connect and be consistent with *Modern Social Work Theory*, so readers familiar with both will find a few paragraphs that start from the three views in a similar way; this book provides a much more extensive analysis. Chapter Five is based on material first published in 'Managerialism and state social work in

Britain' by my late colleague, Steve Morgan, and myself, commissioned and published by the *Hong Kong Journal of Social Work*, 36(1/2): 27-44. I am grateful for permission to adapt this material to the present use. I also acknowledge the influential contribution of my collaborator in various other work on international aspects of social work, Gurid Aga Askeland.

# Notes on the author

Malcolm Payne is Director, Psycho-social and Spiritual Care, St Christopher's Hospice, where he is responsible for creative and complementary therapies, day care, mental health, social work and spiritual care. He has broad experience of social work, having worked in probation, social work, particularly with mentally ill people, and management in social services departments. He was Chief Executive of a large city council for voluntary service, where he worked on community development and projects to respond to unemployment, and Development and Policy Director for a national mental health organisation, where he worked on new housing and care projects across England. He has held various academic posts, and has acted as a consultant in teamwork and team development in local government, health and social care organisations. He was a member of the Wagner Committee (the Independent Review of Residential Care, 1988).

He was Head of Applied Community Studies, Manchester Metropolitan University, for many years, during which he was chair for four years of the Association of Professors of Social Work and was also involved in child and mental health service advocacy projects and research. Now Emeritus Professor there, he is also Honorary Professor, Kingston University/St George's Medical School, and docent in social work at the University of Helsinki, Finland. He has been extensively involved in international social work, leading and working on projects to develop social work and social policy in Russia, China and Eastern Europe. He has lectured and presented papers all over the world on social work education, theory and practice, teamwork and palliative care. Together with the Norwegian social work academic, Gurid Aga Askeland, and others, he has published a number of articles about the impact of globalisation and postmodern ideas on social work.

His main publications among 10 books and more than 250 shorter works, published in 13 languages, are: *Modern Social Work Theory* (3rd edn, Palgrave Macmillan 2005a), *Social Work: Continuity and Change* (Palgrave Macmillan, 2005); *Teamwork in Multiprofessional Care* (Palgrave 2000); and *Social Work and Community Care* (Palgrave, 1995). He co-edited a widely used series of social work texts on critical social work practice with Robert Adams and Lena Dominelli. Recently, together with colleagues at St Christopher's Hospice, he has been researching and publishing about social work, welfare rights, day care and other aspects of palliative care services.

His work demonstrates a commitment to the value of social work in society, and a strong emphasis on interpreting social work values and ideas in a way that makes sense to and is useful to practitioners. He uses ideas about social construction in his work that permit social work practice to be flexible in responding to the values, wishes and needs of the people that social workers serve. For him, social work has to be seen and practised within an understanding of its organisational and social contexts, and must combat inequalities in society that mean that many people cannot live fulfilling and satisfying lives.

ONE

# Introduction: the social work discourse

Social work makes a claim. It is this: that social improvement can be achieved by interpersonal influence and action, that social change can be harnessed to individual personal development and that carrying out these two activities together should be a profession. Social workers seek social betterment, but mostly they do it by helping individuals, families and small social groups as part of their professional work. Societies change, and people mostly have small concern for others who struggle with how that society is organised, but social work seeks to adapt social movement and change so that it is more manageable by, and more help to, individuals, particularly those who are poor and disadvantaged.

No other professional group makes this claim: doctors, teachers, nurses, psychologists and counsellors focus on their patient, student or client's concerns and interests. To them, social order and social change is the context, and they help people within that context. Politicians, economists, journalists, planners and campaigners seek beneficial social change, but do not seek to work with individuals, families and groups to connect change and the person. They expect people to respond rationally and personally to meet their needs and achieve their desires, responding to social forces. Social work's claim is unique, and many people think it is impossible to make that connection, or disagree with trying to make it.

People disagree about what social work is (Asquith et al, 2005), and they are unclear about it. Sometimes this is a cause for complaint. Social workers often find that they cannot describe what is involved in it, so the people they serve and work alongside can understand what they do. Politicians, civil servants and managers want a practical servant for their social change, which in any case they think should happen by people's own response to their laws and organisations. The people that social workers help want a result from social change that benefits them personally. So, social workers are in the middle of an interaction between the social and the personal that people find hard to understand and believe in.

This disagreement and uncertainty about the nature of social work comes from its central claim to connect personal help, achieved by interpersonal relationships, with social improvement. Because social change cannot be wholly under control, because so many social and human currents swirl around in a constantly changing river of change, because individual human beings are infinitely various, the claim to connect all these things together requires flexibility in social work practice, when people and organisations want certainty of outcome. Yet most complex societies have found that social work or something like it arises within them. This is because groups in society that are responsible for broad social change need mechanisms for carrying out their social objectives, and because individuals find they cannot fit in with social movements. Therefore, social work plays its role. Even though it seems ambiguous, it has its uses. If this is so, people who become social workers and people who deal with them in various ways need to understand what social workers do and in what ways it might be useful.

This book argues that to do social work and to understand it in this constantly changing social world requires a particular approach to knowing and thinking about social work: a social construction approach. Instead of defining social work as one thing, one practice, one social system, I argue that social work constantly redefines itself as it is influenced by others, by social need and social change, and by its own internal discourse about its nature. There are continuities in social work: particular elements that operate together in a constantly changing balance to meet its central claim. To understand social work, we must explore and analyse: we must understand the continuities and analyse the social contexts that construct how they are played out in particular social or interpersonal situations.

One way of looking at this issue is to say that social work is what social workers do. This is an extreme form of the idea of social construction, that human beings 'construct' social phenomena like social work by their interactions; when they interact differently, the phenomena change. This view says that if you do social work in one way, and say: 'This is social work', so it is, in that situation. If someone claims to be doing it another way in another situation, then that is social work too. This draws attention to how any social situation offers an opportunity to be flexible and to achieve change. Human beings often have freedom to be different, and have power to construct situations in different ways. It also draws attention to 'claims-making', where what people say they are doing or even what they do 'makes a claim' about a social situation.

However, this extreme social construction view does not fit with what many people perceive as reality. In ordinary social interactions, there is a shared agreement about reasonable and appropriate ways to behave, and there are statements of these agreements such as dictionaries, textbooks and management guidelines to help us be clear. A less extreme view of social construction sees construction as the processes by which people arrive at these shared views and they become established as the norm in particular societies. This approach comes from the work of the originators of the idea of social construction, Berger and Luckmann (1971).

This does not mean that agreed views never change. They change from situation to situation and from time to time. I can remember when, as a young man in 1966, I took the decision that was to lead me into social work. I remember gazing at the notice about the new course in social work in the darkened, pine-clad corridor of one of our new universities thinking through what I wanted to do. I decided to go for it, in that corridor. It was the start of a pathway into and through a career in social work. Through my experiences on that pathway, I have formed conceptions of myself as a social worker. Everyone arrives, similarly, at their own view: of themselves within their occupation and of the occupation they follow.

Our occupational self-concept is not entirely personal, however. When I started out in the social services world, I acquired some ready-made concepts of what social work was about from the people who introduced me to their work. My social work degree provided an intellectual and academic basis for understanding the nature of social work and of my contribution to it. Both of these have been refined and developed by experience and learning throughout my career. So, my view of social work reflects and reacts to shared conceptions. These have come from social workers and others directly involved in the social services, and broader conceptions reflected in the news and media.

My view of social work is different now, decades later, as I work with doctors, nurses, chaplains, physiotherapists and other healthcare professionals in palliative care. When I chose to go on a social work course, the first modern hospice caring for dying people, St Christopher's, where I currently work, was only just being built: it opened in 1967. So, I work in a health and social care specialty that did not exist when I started out, and my view of social work is, of course, affected by my colleagues' understanding of their own work and mine. The time in history and the social environment in which I talk about social work now is different, and so, of course, social work is different.

## 'Social work' in the language

Yet the words 'social work' are the same, and they offer an occupational identity, which forms a bridge between then and now. The dictionary definition of them in the Oxford English Dictionary was not substantially changed between 1926 when it was first published and 1987, the latest edition. That identity is, however, different, because the words mean something slightly different. For a while, I was a probation and aftercare officer. The word 'aftercare' had recently been added to the job title, as government policy and legislation incorporated prison aftercare into the probation service. It was later removed, as the aftercare role of probation officers became taken for granted. Later, I worked in the 'social services'; more recently I am seen as part of 'social care', or 'health and social care'. My current job title includes the words 'psycho-social care'. These word changes recognise changing identities, even though there have also been continuities in my occupational identity. Table 1.1 defines these terms and some others that occur throughout this book, to explain briefly what I mean by them, but there are alternative views of them and shifts in meaning all the time, so, like all definitions, they are useful for finding a way through this book, rather than being absolutes.

Social construction ideas give an important place to language, because human beings interact using words, so the words they use have an important place in identifying social constructions. Shifts in words often indicate shifts in meaning. Even though words may mean similar

**Table 1.1:** Terms referring to social work and related services

| Term | Meanings |
|---|---|
| Personal social services | A British term, used in the Seebohm Report (1968), to refer to local government social work and personal welfare services, and to distinguish this provision from the social services. Usually abbreviated to 'social services' in everyday usage |
| Social assistance | A European term used, particularly in Germany, to distinguish the welfare and problem-solving aspects of social care from its educational and personal growth aspects |
| Social care 1 | Social work practice in residential, day care and other group care settings (eg the Social Care Association) |
| Social care 2 | Practice and training for practice focused on care for people, often in group care settings, as distinct from therapeutic social work designed to enhance personal growth and self-understanding |

*continued.../*

**Table 1.1:** contd.../

| **Term** | **Meanings** |
|---|---|
| Social care 3 | A British term referring to services, including social work, provided in the field of social welfare, in analogy particularly with the term 'healthcare'. By focusing on the range of services, it emphasises that providing effective services is a crucial aspect of social work, and that social work is part of social care |
| Social pedagogy | A European term, deriving particularly from German philosophy, used to describe social work, particularly in group settings and in work with young people, that uses educational, artistic, creative and cultural approaches to enhance personal and social fulfilment |
| Social security | Services to provide income and other financial help that help people to feel secure from extreme poverty |
| Social services | A broad term, used in the study of social policy and in political debate. It refers to state provision designed to enhance social solidarity and stability, and is usually taken to include education, healthcare, housing, the personal social services and social security. This usage is easy to confuse with the everyday usage of 'social services' to refer to the local government personal social services |
| Social welfare | Services, usually provided by the state, designed to promote well-being in interpersonal, family, social and community relationships that enhance solidarity and mutuality in society |
| Social work | A service and practice using social and psychological sciences in interpersonal interactions with people, especially from deprived social groups and experiencing practical and emotional difficulties in social relationships. Social work balances three objectives: maintaining social order and providing social welfare services effectively, helping people attain personal fulfilment and power over their lives and stimulating social change |
| Welfare 1 | The good fortune, health and happiness of people, families and groups |
| Welfare 2 | Services, usually provided by the state, designed to promote welfare, particularly basic physical or material well-being |
| Welfare 3 | Welfare services that provide welfare benefits |
| Welfare benefits/ rights | Welfare benefits are practical assistance, primarily financial, given, usually by the state, in accordance with rules to assist individuals or families in dealing with events that threaten their welfare; welfare rights exist where individuals or families are entitled by law or regulation to benefits |

things, a different word usually implies something slightly different. Sometimes we use words to emphasise that we are trying to make a difference. For example, at one time people who are now known as having 'learning disabilities' were termed in law 'idiots' or 'imbeciles'. These came to be stigmatising terms, so the term 'mentally handicapped' was in use when I became a social worker, deriving from the Mental Health Act 1959. This in turn became stigmatising, so people moved to 'learning disabilities' as a less negative term during the 1980s. This term emphasises that it is possible for changes in language to be used to try to change attitudes; here, this is done by emphasising the ambiguities in the word 'disability' and the wide application of the term 'learning'. The problem is that as people come to understand that a stigmatised condition is being concealed by the new title, the ambiguity disappears, and the new term is again stigmatised; this is what happened with 'mentally handicapped'. Ambiguity and uncertainty, therefore, are sometimes useful parts of our world. Often, we are asked to be clear and to avoid ambiguity, but if there are different ways of looking at someone or something, then what we say should reflect it.

This use of language to construct something, and making changes to language to change behaviour and attitudes is a characteristic of a set of social construction ideas. The argument is that if we can understand concepts as being constructed by shared agreement, we can try to develop agreement to make a change.

## Social work as pathways and networks

I owe to N. M. Tsang the idea that we can see social work (and any other occupation) as the place where a convergence of pathways forms a nexus of ideas. There people interact more closely and see themselves as 'together' in their work. They have been incorporated and socialised into social work. Each of them will have converged on that point; some will stay there; others will diverge towards other interests. They become more specialised, diverse or may modify their conception of social work or reject it altogether. Tsang drew a diagram that I have adapted (see Figure 1.1) to show this description of social work as a profession. The pale circle in the middle of the diagram represents a conventional boundary for social work, and the darkening patch in the middle represents an area of the field that many people would recognise as strongly 'social work'. They might define people within the boundary as social workers. They might be less sure of people just outside the boundary. The further a person has to travel to enter this

**Figure 1.1:** Pathways to and through social work

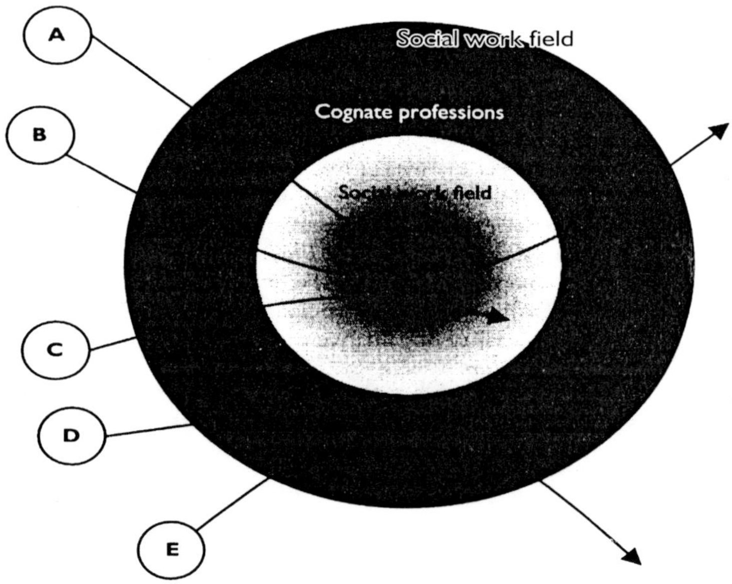


boundary, the less sure we would be of calling them a social worker. The circle defines what most people would think of as social workers; outside the circle, they might have more doubts.

The person who followed the path shown as A moved more or less to the centre of social work and stayed there, say, providing community care services in adult social services departments in local government. B moved through social work and ended up in an occupation related to it, perhaps as a clinical psychologist. The path of person C through social work moves from outside any relevant occupation, through a related job into the centre of social work and then away again to something, still in social work but a bit more peripheral, perhaps as a counsellor in a youth centre. D came into youth work, came close to social work as they worked with young offenders, but stayed in youth work, and now has less to do with social work. E was perhaps a teacher, who became involved in school counselling for a while, having a lot to do with child and family social workers and moved away again when they were promoted to head of department and had different duties.

Within social work, there are specialisms, a more complex identity. Some of these are wholly within social work, for example adoption social workers. Others are part of a multiprofessional specialty. Forensic social workers in the UK, for example, work in secure hospital or residential care units with people who have committed serious offences because of a severe mental illness; in the US, forensic social work refers to social workers who work in courts. The multiprofessional team of these specialists in Britain includes psychiatrists, psychiatric nurses, clinical psychologists, sometimes a range of other professions and also managers, clerical and administrative staff and people providing catering and living services to patients. Forensic social workers would regard themselves as part of social work, and also as part of forensic mental health. Similarly, hospice social workers are part of the multiprofessional speciality of palliative care, alongside nurses, doctors and spiritual care workers.

Figure 1.2 is a blank form of Figure 1.1 with two more people added. It offers an opportunity to analyse social workers' pathways; a team could do it together. There are seven blank lists for seven workers. The starting point of each worker might be the point at which they first thought of being a social worker. Perhaps you can identify it, as I can, picturing that university corridor. Perhaps, however, when you look back, you can identify some experiences that contributed to your progress towards being a social worker. Even before that corridor, I now think that my experiences of being an assistant youth leader as a teenager was an early indication of what would interest and motivate me. Then note down the major points in your life that form your pathway into social work. It might include particular experiences, or jobs, or organisations or people you came into contact with. When you each have your lists, the most valuable part of this exercise is to discuss with others how each should be plotted. Is that youth work experience in social work? Or on the borders? Or outside the box or circle? Experiences we have in our lives and interactions with others on our personal pathways intersect with other people's pathways and influence each other. By discussing this, you can enter into discussion about where the boundaries lie: you are becoming engaged in the discourse about the nature of social work.

## Discourse

The idea of discourse helps with definition and developing understanding through 'pathways'. Discourse theory proposes that social work is not one thing, but consists of a body of social actions and

**Figure 1.2:** Pathways analysis format

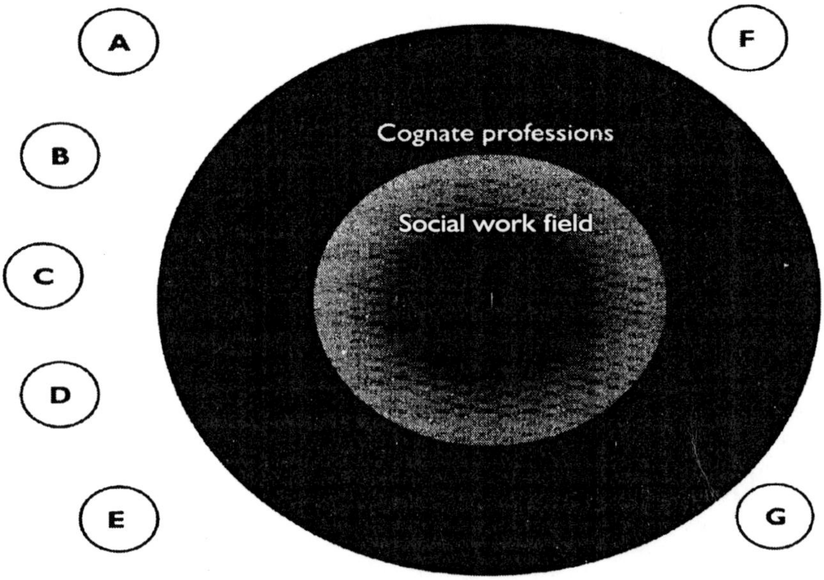


| Person | A | B | C | D | E | F | G |
|---|---|---|---|---|---|---|---|
| First thoughts of social work | | | | | | | |
| First relevant experiences | | | | | | | |
| Decision to move into social work | | | | | | | |
| Pre-qualification experiences | | | | | | | |
| Qualifying training | | | | | | | |
| First experience post-qualification | | | | | | | |
| Later experience and decision points | | | | | | | |
| Later experience and decision points | | | | | | | |

debates formed by people rubbing up against one another, acting together in concert or opposition and sharing or disputing their ideas about what they are doing and thinking. Their rubbing up against each other, a discourse, is the nature of the thing itself. Thus, the discourse 'social work' is formed by the actions, understandings, thoughts and arguments of the people involved in it; it is not separate from the people involved. Their thinking and actions, as they argue through what to do about a case, constructs what social work is, and because they are a collective, their pathways and shared experiences will have influenced their thinking and action.

If we accept that social work is contested and ambiguous, the best way to understand it is to rise above the different points of view and look instead at the areas that are contested; this tells us what their 'discourse' is about. Social workers often find themselves doing this in their work. For example, if the children in a family are arguing about which one of them is most helpful to their parents, a worker might look beyond this to see why they need to compete for their parents' approval in this way. Examining the discourse about social work tries to do the same thing. Many writers, for example, argue for one or the other of two forms of social work: social change and individual problem solving. They see them as competing for the most important role in social work, and they try to promote practice that focuses on one or the other.

To find the discourse, we lift ourselves up above the level of the debate to ask what the nature of the debate is about, to the 'metalevel'. In this case, people are really trying to emphasise one or other aspect of social work's claim, the social or the interpersonal. But the fact that we are constantly arguing about it and the issue never gets resolved suggests that 'you can't have one without the other', as the song has it. When we rise above a dispute like this, we often find that the metalevel is not the simplicity of an 'either–or' but the complexity of an 'also-and'. The dispute arises because of strong commitment to making sure one view or the other is included, and sometimes also because of the difficulty of putting the two elements together in practice. This is true of social work's claim; since it is tough to achieve, we are constantly in battle about the right approach.

Howarth (2000) identifies three main historical elements to the idea of discourse:

1. The idea of investigating 'language in use' and 'talk in context' as part of linguistics, particularly social linguistics.
2. Its extension by phenomenological sociologists, ethnomethodologists and post-structuralists, in particular Foucault (1972), to investigate wider social practices which at least in Foucault's later work include how discourses shaped by social practices in turn shape social institutions.
3. Its extension in investigations such as Fairclough's (1992: 12) 'critical discourse analysis' to non-discursive practices in a wider range of social relations.

The first approach focuses on and limits itself purely to linguistic practices. For example, in most conversations, people take turns to communicate and there are complex social rules about taking turns in conversations. People learn these rules as part of growing up in a society. Sometimes if we meet people from a minority ethnic group or in another country, we find that they have slightly different rules, and we find ourselves clashing, interrupting or thinking the other person is rude. Social workers learn about these communication rules as part of using talk to influence their clients. Ideas of rhetoric examine how we can use language to persuade others, in court reports and assessments, for example. Returning to the different views of social work, people who use language that talks about problems, individuals, and needs are likely to be of the view that competition is natural, while people who talk about inequality, oppression and division are likely to focus on radical change.

Foucault's approach, and others like it, still emphasise the importance of texts and talk, but go beyond this to examine the social relations created by discourses, particularly those concerned with power. In any social situation, if you examine how people behave towards one another, you can often see who is powerful or submissive. You can also examine patterns of behaviour in social institutions such as social work agencies or prisons to see patterns of social power. These patterns and the institutions that they are a part of reinforce social expectations and exert control over people to fit in with influential ideas in society. Thus, for example, social work, in helping people deal with problems in family relationships, reinforces powerful ideas about how people should relate to one another in families. The fact that it is necessary to help families resolve some of their difficulties through social work and other professional interventions also emphasises how important families are in social relations. You can see what these powerful ideas in society (the discourse about the family) are by seeing what social workers and other similar professions enforce. So, pursuing the example about social work, the problem-solving view favours using families to maintain the present social order. A radical change view, alternatively, suggests that families often oppress people within them, for example, children and women, by violence.

Critical discourse analysis takes these ideas further by using them to look at the social impact of all sorts of activities, and this includes social work practice. Fairclough (1992: 91) makes the point that:

> ... discursive practices ... incorporate significations which contribute to sustaining or restructuring power relations. Relations of power may in principle be affected by discursive practices of any type, even scientific and theoretical.

By 'discursive practices' he means activities such as social work practice that create and disclose discourses. These discourses are the sometimes obvious, sometimes hidden, power relationships between people as they interact. Relationships always represent particular ideologies about how society should be. 'Significations' are words or practices that represent important ideologies, for example appeals to the importance of the family or a kind of social work that sustains traditional family structures, or, on the other hand, they accept that families may include relationships between gay and lesbian couples or single-parent families.

All these types of discourse analysis connect together, because looking at language in written texts and in practice in an organised way through research into the use of language in texts and in practice can reveal power relations and the ideas that lie behind them. In this book, I look at written texts about social work as a technique for revealing the ideas about social work that lie behind everyday statements. I use professional documents, textbooks, articles, internet searches and government and official statements. I also look at social work practices, by examining examples of practice or organisation.

## Social work's three-way discourse

The argument in this book is that social work is a three-way discourse; every bit of practice, all practice ideas, all social work agency organisation and all welfare policy is a rubbing up of three views of social work against each o .her. I argue that this discourse plays out the struggle about the claim: these three views are different ways of dealing with the claim. Figure 1.3 shows them at the corners of a triangle; the triangle represents the discourse between them, a field of debate that covers all social work. When I first described these three views, in the first edition of this book, I used complex names for them, but more recently, people have used simpler terms, so in this edition, I concentrate on the simpler terms, and give the complex names in this figure for reference. The important differences between these views of social work connect with different political views about how welfare should be provided.

*Therapeutic views.* These see social work as seeking the best possible well-being for individuals, groups and communities in society, by promoting and facilitating growth and self-fulfilment. A constant spiral of interaction between workers and clients modifies clients' ideas and allows workers to influence them; in the same way, clients affect workers' understandings of their world as they gain experience of it. This process

**Figure 1.3:** The three views of social work

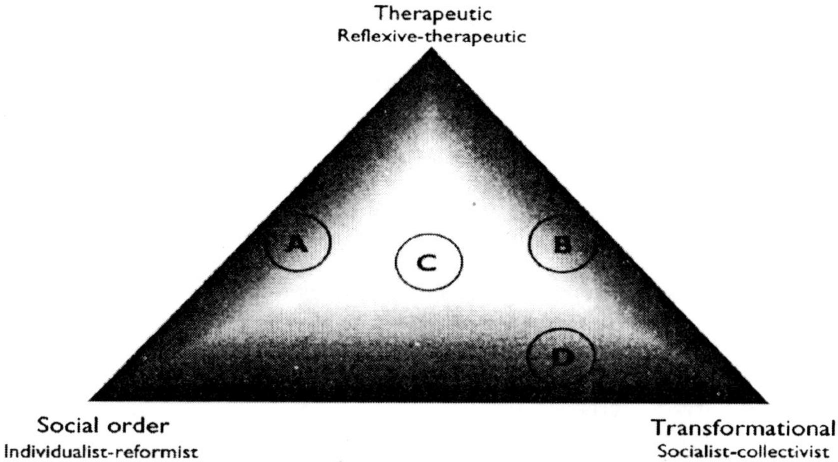


of mutual influence is called reflexiveness. Because it is reflexive in this way, social work responds to the social concerns that workers find and gain understanding of as they practise, and feeds back into society knowledge about these problems and how society might tackle them. Through this process of mutual interaction with social workers, clients gain power over their own feelings and way of life. Such personal power enables them to overcome or rise above suffering and disadvantage, so they experience the work to help them gain this power as therapeutic. I originally called this kind of social work 'reflexive-therapeutic'. This view expresses in social work the social democratic political philosophy that economic and social development should go hand-in-hand to achieve individual and social improvement.

This view is basic to many ideas of the nature of social work, but two other views modify and dispute it.

*Transformational views.* These views (for example, Pease and Fook, 1999) argue that we must transform societies for the benefit of the poorest and most oppressed. Social work aims to develop cooperation and mutual support in society so that the most oppressed and disadvantaged people can gain power over their own lives. It facilitates this by empowering people to take part in a process of learning and cooperation, which creates institutions that all can own and participate in. Elites accumulate and perpetuate power and resources in society for their own benefit. By doing so, they create the oppression and disadvantage that social work tries to supplant with more egalitarian relationships in society. Transformational views imply that disadvantaged and oppressed people will never gain personal or social empowerment unless society makes these transformations. Value statements about social work, such as codes of ethics, represent this objective by proposing social justice as an important value of all social work. This view expresses the socialist political philosophy that planned economies and social provision promotes equality and social justice, and I originally called it 'socialist-collectivist'.

*Social order views.* These see social work as an aspect of welfare services to individuals in societies. It meets individuals' needs and improves services of which it is a part, so that social work and the services can operate more effectively. Dominelli (2002) calls these maintenance approaches, reflecting the term used by Davies (1994); I originally called them 'individualist-reformist'. They see social work as maintaining the social order and social fabric of society, and maintaining people during any period of difficulties that they may be experiencing, so that they can recover stability again. This view expresses the liberal or rational economic political philosophy, that personal freedom in economic markets, supported by the rule of law, is the best way of organising societies.

Each view says something about the activities and purposes of social work in welfare provision in any society, and so they are each different implementations of social work's claim. Therapeutic social work says: 'Help everyone to self-fulfilment and society will be a better place'. Social order social work says: 'Solve people's problems in society, by providing help or services, and they will fit in with general social expectations better; promoting social change to stop the problems arising will produce all-round improvements'. Transformational social work says: 'Identify and work out how social relations cause people's problems, and make social changes so that the problems do not arise'.

Each view criticises or seeks to modify the others. For example, seeking personal and social fulfilment, as in therapeutic views, is impossible to transformers because the interests of elites obstruct many possibilities for oppressed peoples, unless we achieve significant social change. They argue that merely accepting the social order, as therapeutic and social order views do, supports and enhances the interests of elites. To the transformer, therefore, the alternative views involve practice that will obstruct the opportunities of oppressed people who should be the main beneficiaries of social work. To take another example, social order views say that trying to change societies to make them more equal or create personal and social fulfilment through individual and community growth are unrealistic in everyday practice, and inconsistent with the natural organisation of societies in competitive markets. This is because most practical objectives of social work activity refer to small-scale individual change, which cannot lead to major social and personal changes. Also, stakeholders in the social services that finance and give social approval to social work activities mainly want a better fit between society and individuals. They do not seek major changes. That is why social order views prefer their approach.

However, these different views also have affinities. For example, both therapeutic and transformational views are centrally about change and development. Also, therapeutic and social order views are about individual rather than social change. Generally, therefore, most conceptions of social work include elements of each of these views. Alternatively, they sometimes acknowledge the validity of elements of the others. For example, transformational views criticise unthinking acceptance of the present social order, which is often taken for granted in social order and therapeutic views. Nevertheless, most people who take this view of social work accept helping individuals to fulfil their potential within present social systems. They often see this as a stepping-stone to a changed society by promoting a series of small changes aiming towards bigger ones.

So these different views fit together or compete with each other in social work practice. Looking at Figure 1.3, if you or your agency were positioned at A (very common especially for beginning social workers), your main focus might be providing services in a therapeutic, helping relationship, as a care manager (in managed care) or in child protection. You might do very little in the way of seeking to change the world, and by being part of an official or service system, you are accepting the pattern of welfare services as it is. However, in your individual work, what you do may well be guided by eventual change objectives. For example, if you believe that relationships between men and women should be more equal, your work in families will probably reflect your views. Position B might represent someone working in a refuge for women suffering domestic violence. Much of their work is helping therapeutically, but the very basis of their agency is changing attitudes towards women in society, and you might do some campaigning work as part of your helping role. Position C is equally balanced; some change, some service provision; some therapeutic helping. My present job is like that: to promote community development so that communities become more resilient about and respond better to people who are dying or bereaved, but I also provide help for individuals and I am responsible for liaison with other services so that our service system becomes more effective. Position D is mainly transformational but partly maintenance. This reflects the reality that seeking social change is not, in the social services, completely revolutionary, but will also seek to make the service system more effective. Many community workers, for example, are seeking quite major change in the lives of the people they serve by achieving better cooperation and sharing, but they may act by helping local groups make their area safe from crime, by providing welfare rights advocacy or by organising self-help playgroups in the school holidays.

You can assess your position in social work by trying out the exercise in Figure 1.4.

First, you complete the three scales at the top. You circle one figure on each line; the 0 means your job is equally balanced between these two points of view, whereas a 3 would mean that your job is very strongly oriented towards one view or the other. When you have completed the scales, you can plot your position on each of the three sides of the discourse triangle; 0 will be in the middle of the triangle side, and 1 or 2 a proportional step towards the relevant corner; a 3 will be at the corner. Now connect up the three points you have identified. Often this will form a triangle, perhaps a fairly flat triangle. Your job is positioned in social work discourse at the fattest part of the triangle. If you have a straight line, your position is one third along the line away from the strongest point. Figure 1.5a-c gives some examples drawn from exercises I have done with different social workers.

By copying Figure 1.4, you can get people who know you or your supervisor to make their own assessment of your territory, and you can plan; for example, you can go on to identify the position you would like to be in. By carrying out these exercises, you are again involving yourself in the discourse around the nature of the social work that you have constructed for yourself. It is also possible to do this for agencies and their policies, or the welfare regimes of different countries and the priorities that social work has in that country.

This process of engaging in the discourse about your own role can help to clarify the range of objectives in your work and contributions that you make. Figure 1.5 offers some examples, which are composites of people from different areas of social work that I have discussed this with. A palliative care social worker (Figure 1.5a), for example, might start out by seeing themselves as primarily doing therapeutic work

**Figure 1.4:** Views of social work scale

Consider the balance between each pair of views of social work, as explained in the text, within your present practice. If it is equally balanced between the pair, circle 0; if your practice is strongly biased towards the left-hand view, circle 3; indicate less strong biases by circling 1 or 2. You can only circle one number for each pair.

| | | | | | | | | |
|---|---|---|---|---|---|---|---|---|
| Therapeutic | 3 | 2 | 1 | 0 | 1 | 2 | 3 | Social order |
| Therapeutic | 3 | 2 | 1 | 0 | 1 | 2 | 3 | Transformational |
| Social order | 3 | 2 | 1 | 0 | 1 | 2 | 3 | Transformational |

When you have finished, transfer the scores to the triangle. Start with the first scale on the left side of this triangle (social order to therapeutic). If you circled 0, mark the midpoint of the side; each corner represents a 3: 'therapeutic' at the top or 'social order' on the far left. If you circled 2, put a mark about a third of the way from the corner to the midpoint; if you circled 1 put a mark about two thirds of the way to the midpoint. Repeat for the other two scales: scale 2 on the right, scale 3 along the bottom. Connect the marks to create a triangle that represents the territory of your view of your practice.

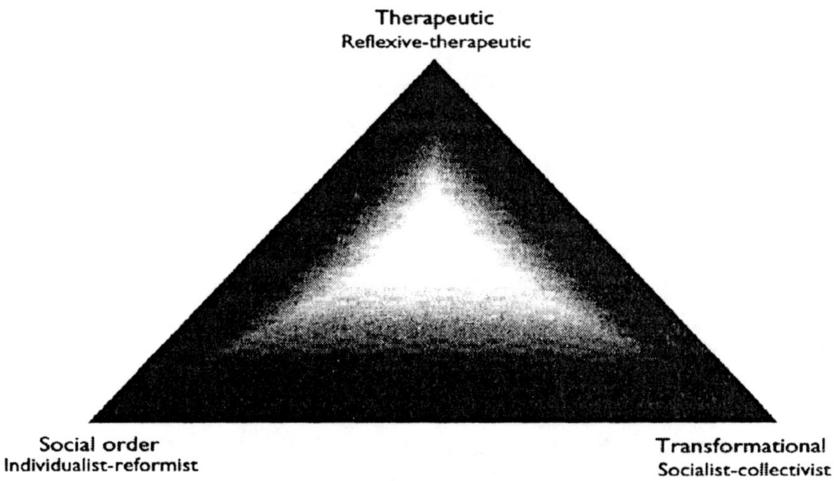


You can repeat the exercise by getting your supervisor or a colleague who knows your work to work out their view of your practice. You can also work out what your ideal combination might be. Comparing these with your present analysis can help you to see how you might want to change your practice.

with their patients, in fact, almost as a straight line from the therapeutic corner to the mid-point of the opposite side, between social order and transformation. However, they often arrange services for their patients and their families, and might persuade patients not to commit suicide because of their illness. Providing or organising services is clearly a social order activity: it is about maintaining the fabric of society through the provision of social services. The question then arises: how far is therapeutic work on patients' family relationships also a service? One might see it more as helping people achieve happiness by fulfilling the potential of their relationships and preventing difficulties in bereavement, but others might see it as an element in a package of caring services that also includes, for example, practical help at home and with physical needs. Persuading people not to commit suicide might be a therapeutic process, enabling people to come to terms with their impending death and to use their time to achieve other social objectives. However, it might also help to maintain a social convention against suicide. A palliative care social worker's actions also connect with ethical objectives to value the experience of dying and to avoid preventable early death. Thus, they are also part of the hospice movement's mission to change attitudes to death in society.

Our own social work territory does not remain the same. Every case and every social work action contain elements of all three views, which interact and sometimes conflict with each other. We can look at each situation, and at each action we take to adjust the emphasis of our work. Social workers in an Asian youth project (Figure 1.5b) might see themselves as being on the side of mainly Muslim young people who feel marginalised and disadvantaged in a large public housing estate. Therefore, they might see a large element of transformation in their work: to change the practice of other agencies and social attitudes among the white people on the estate. Most of the work with the young people themselves might be therapeutic. However, in discussion with such workers, they talked about helping several young women to decide whether they would agree to take part in arranged marriages proposed by their parents, and also about a young man who decided that he would ask his parents to do so. In this way, they contributed to social order, by helping young people and their families adjust their wishes to social structures, helping the social structures to change to fit new circumstances. While this did not fit with their own political views, as social workers dealing with troubled individuals, they had to remain open to the alternatives that they were considering. So, some of the work was more therapeutic or social order influenced than much of the community work activity.

**Figure 1.5:** Examples of views analyses

**Figure 1.5a:**
Palliative care social worker

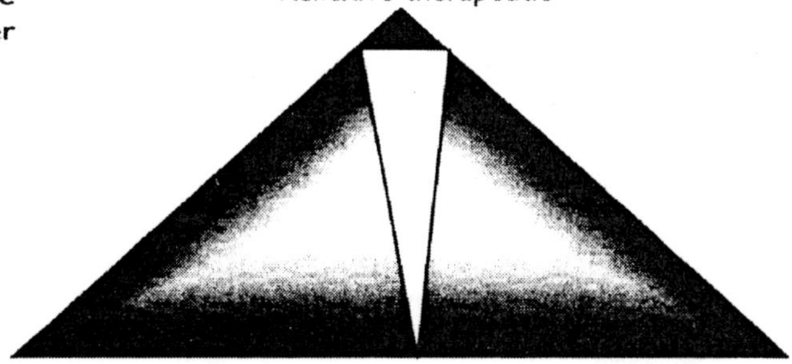


**Figure 1.5b:**
Asian youth project social worker

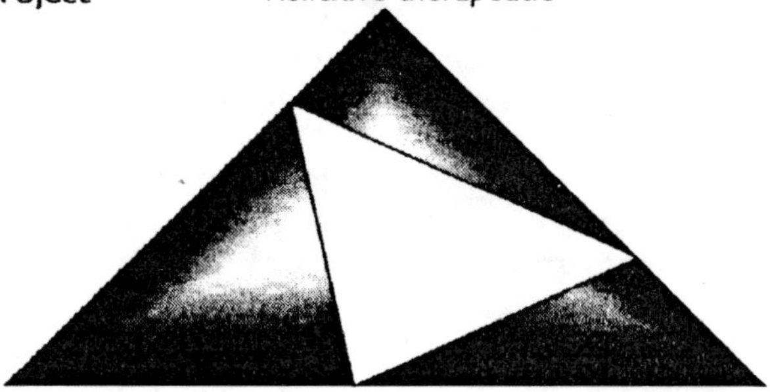


**Figure 1.5c:**
Youth offending team social worker

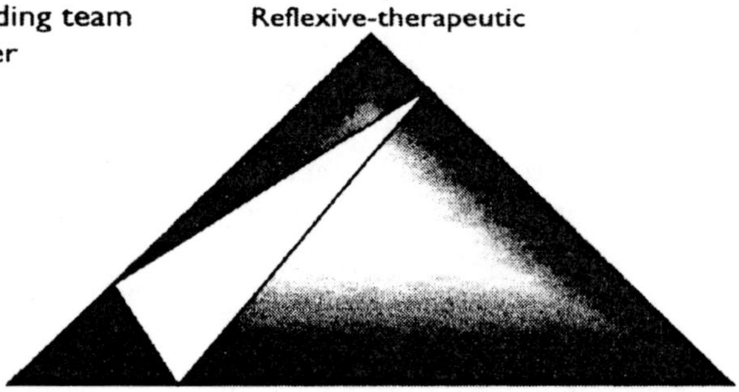

Views analysis also enables us to look at agencies and welfare systems. The youth offending team social workers (Figure 1.5c) were committed to therapeutic help for the young offenders they worked with. They were active in working to change the criminal justice system to recognise the social pressures on young offenders and avoid punitive approaches to their needs. Their agency, where they cooperated with police officers and others in the criminal justice system, limited the range of possibilities for flexible practice, compared with a community youth agency that might enable a worker to have an impact on the same issues with the same people; the triangle was quite restricted. However, working in the agency meant that they gained access to young people and helped them in the youth offending system in a way that was not possible in the voluntary sector.

All these workers faced directly some of the challenges of social work's claim to bring together social change and individual help. They came to their own construction of practice, sometimes unwittingly incorporating these three elements. However, views analysis shows us the process of social construction for individuals, in agencies, in particular cases, and in particular social work actions in response to the struggle to meet the claim. It can also apply to welfare systems. Some welfare systems focus more on therapeutic work, less on transformation. Sometimes, policies affect welfare systems to create a period of transformation.

Political aims in welfare, views of social work and social work practice thus link in complex ways, and are constantly interacting to create the particular discourse that social work is at any one time. Views analysis is a way of examining that discourse, either as we practice, or as we analyse how the agencies and welfare systems that surround us deal with the problem of the claim.

## The plan of this book

This book aims to examine elements within current discourses about social work. The claim to combine social and personal improvement in an interpersonal professional practice is difficult to work out in practice within the social work profession. Chapter Two explores the identity social work tries to create for itself, and that is created by public policy and perception, by using evidence from official and professional definitions of social work and the related concept of social care. The discussion points up how the three views are constantly present in both contemporary social work debate and throughout its history. Chapters Three and Four focus on how social work practice, values and ethics incorporate elements of the discourse, and attempt to deal with the difficulties of social work's claim, through the discourse on the three views within interpersonal activity in practice. Chapters Five to Eight discuss how social work interacts with the forces surrounding it by considering successively social work management and agency, the use of power and authority in society, the role and character of social work as a profession including its education and research, and the interaction of social work with current issues about globalisation and postmodernism. Chapter Nine brings together these different strands of the construction of social work as a profession, and discusses how in everyday practice social workers can work towards achieving social work's claim in the context of today's society and its social movements and policies.

## Conclusion: the claim and the perspectives

Social work's claim, unique among similar professions, is to combine in a professional role both social transformation and also individual improvement through interpersonal relationships. Because the social world is constantly in flux and individual humanity is infinitely variable, the only valid approach to understanding social work is to examine its social construction. However, a completely relative social construction, premised on constant variation in response to social and human contexts, does not reflect the world that most people experience. There are many continuities in social work, which is constructed in a shared language of concepts about its nature, contained in a discourse among three views of it: therapeutic, social order and transformational views. Social workers construct their own social work practice by following pathways towards, through, and sometimes away from, a nexus of ideas and debate that is the centre of social work. Thus, any particular social work act, any case, any social work role, any agency, any welfare system reflects a constantly changing balance among these three views about how to meet the claim. However, the three views are consistently present.

TWO

# The identity of social work

Intake and assessment (I&A) teams receive, investigate and try to resolve problems that arrive in social work agencies. If they cannot do so, they pass on the work to long-term teams, which provide more extensive help over a longer period. The B Area I&A team had run into relationship problems with its long-term childcare team. The complaint was that important childcare work was closed down with only cursory assessment and without giving priority to the best interests of the child. It looked like a typical conflict of attitude between teams of these types. Intake teams get into the habit of looking for ways to deal with things quickly. They often dislike giving up work they have started. Long-term teams, on the other hand, look for broader and deeper issues. They are often slow to take on work. So, intake teams get in the habit of closing cases and holding onto work to keep the waiting list down. Then, when there is space, all the long-term work seems impossible to transfer, or it has vanished through interim measures.

On investigation it turned out that the teams had completely different views about working with 'at-risk' children. The I&A team had a policy of helping parents to deal with practical problems to relieve stress on them. Abuse had to be gross and obvious before they would act to remove the children. They described the long-term team as 'child-snatchers'. The long-term team thought that indications of abuse should be referred immediately to them. This was necessary because they would need specialised, long-term work. The children, for their own safety, should be removed immediately, while an investigation took place. An apparently commonplace dispute, about an intake team not being prepared to give up work, turned out to require a detailed analysis and resolution of attitudes to social work and childcare practice.

Most of the time, everyday practice does not require us to think about and define the purposes of social work. We can take a rough approximation for granted. Sometimes, as in the intake and long-term dispute, this take-it-for-granted approach comes adrift and we find we really are talking about different things. Social work therefore occasionally faces practitioners with the need to review their ideas about the nature of their activity, and seeing what underlies taken-for-granted daily assumptions is useful. This example also makes it clear that within social work, there are identifiable different groups such as 'intake workers', 'childcare' and 'long-term' teams.

Identifiable groups like this share an 'identity'. Social workers are not doctors, teachers or nurses. How do we understand the differences between these groups?

## What is identity?

Identity is a complex idea; I have drawn this account from Jenkins (1996), Craib (1998), Archer (2000), Alcoff and Mendieta (2003) and Hockey and James (2003). The word is connected with 'identical', which means 'exactly the same'; so things or people sharing an identity are alike or the same in some important way. It also connects with 'identify', finding out what something is and deciding how it is different from other things. 'Identify' in psychology also means the process of seeing ourselves as similar to, modelling ourselves on and valuing another person. We often think about what factors make us the same as other people, for example, being part of a particular family or community. However, feeling the same as some people inevitably involves others being excluded. Therefore, thinking about identity also concerns factors that make us different from others, for example gender, ethnicity and nationality (Craib, 1998). There are also social consequences of sharing an identity. Does a Muslim behave in the same way as all other Muslims, and is this different from the way Christians behave? In a simple way, this may be so: Muslims pray in mosques, Christians in churches. However, some may not pray at all. As human beings, we all represent a variety of characteristics. Seeing people in groups with a particular identity is a shorthand. This leads to a concern for social divisions, that is, how the way people form into groups or the groups that we think of them as being part of creates social limitations on them and us, because one identity may exclude or limit them from taking on another. This may be true in their own view and in the view of others, and those views may conflict. So a particular Christian may feel that they have a lot in common with Muslims, and many people might agree with that, but a particular Muslim might not.

Personal identity develops through our experience of others. As we come to understand that we are different from others, we identify to ourselves what the differences are and explain them in an internal commentary or debate with ourselves. Directly connected with this is the idea of agency, the capacity to have an impact, make changes or get things that we want in the world.

Different stages of the life-cycle provide examples of how identity and agency are built up. When a baby is born, everything is a jumble of experience. If babies are hungry, they naturally cry to express discomfort; as a consequence, discomfort is reduced, because they are fed. This enables babies to differentiate themselves from others: the food comes from outside. Over time, babies realise that they have agency: crying enables them to achieve results, although sometimes the consequences may be good and bad, rather than just what they intended. The person who brings food is different from other people; people who love and provide are different from people who take no interest. The physical experiences, reactions and emotions provide an inexplicit commentary on what is going on in the outside world around a baby, so that particular behaviours and characteristics are associated with particular experiences. Another example is young people's experiences of others. They see what other people's parents are like, the different approaches teachers take to teaching, the different ways their friends and peers behave when something goes wrong. They can test themselves against this experience of others, and say 'no, I don't want to be like that,' or 'I wish I was more like her'. This is an explicit internal dialogue, which encourages people to model themselves on others, or on their dislike of others' traits. An older person redefines their identity in relation to others. At one time, you may see yourself as a young mother; later you may become a grandmother and your relationship with your daughter and her daughter defines you as a mother in a different place in life. Towards the end of life, your daughter may become your carer, responding in part to a social expectation that as you cared for her, now she will take responsibility for you.

These experiences that create personal identity are social: we gain our identity and sense of agency by interacting with others, and by our social roles interacting with their social roles. In the process, we also develop social identities. Children have relationships with parents, brothers and sisters and see themselves as part of a family. If the parents divorce and remarry, the children may have variable feelings about whether step-parents, brothers and sisters are part of the same family. The child will be part of a class at school, a social group of peers and perhaps some formal organisations like a youth club. We are all affected by this involvement with collectivities, that is, social institutions that collect people together according some features of their personal identity. We represent the collectivity and it represents us. So the people in the I&A and long-term teams did not want, as professional groups, to be like each other in how they dealt with children, and this became part of their social identity and in turn affected how they behaved socially; in the end it affected the organisation.

The assumption behind these ideas of identity is that we have a single continuous personality; that our identity reflects our human nature and the characteristics that we have built up through our experience of social interactions. Personality is a commonplace way of understanding how people are. However, our involvements change over our life-cycle and we can make active decisions about the kind of collectivities that we want to be part of, and how we want to behave. So personal and social identity is influenced by our social experience and our own preferences and rational decisions.

What does it mean when we talk about the identity of 'social work' and our personal identity as a 'social worker'?

## Present identities of social work

People might understand the identity of social work in different ways. Sometimes this will be a personal experience. I once sat next to a woman at a formal dinner, and early in the conversation, she asked about my job and I said I was a social worker. She was obviously disconcerted, and turned away, unable to speak to me. At the end of the dinner, as we were getting ready to leave, she apologised and said that she had had a difficult experience with social workers as an adoptive parent, and never expected to meet one socially. There are, of course, people who have had a good experience of social workers. But not everyone has had that personal experience, so how do they acquire a view about them? Often this will be from the press, television or other public images. In this section, I look at a number of different identities that we can find in fairly formal sources.

An ordinary person, not knowing anything about social work, might look it up on the internet or in a dictionary. What they would find provides a starting point: both a representation of how educated people might understand social work, and a definition that would influence anyone trying to find out about social work from a position of ignorance or uncertainty. To check what they would find, on 15 May 2005 I typed 'Define "social work"' into the commonly used internet search engine, Google, from a UK computer. As 'web definitions of social work', the first entry in the list, it came up with the four responses in Table 2.1. The first definition is part of a glossary to help users of a North American healthcare service understand different services. The

**Table 2.1:** Internet search: define 'social work'

| | |
|---|---|
| 1 | Specialized treatment of mental or emotional disorders, including substance abuse (www.century-health.com/glossary.asp) |
| 2 | Applied to books intended for social workers or students of social work. Services can be educational, psychiatric, nursing, services to the disabled, etc (lib.ucr.edu/depts/acquisitions/ YBP%20NSP%20GLOSSARY%20EXTERNAL%20revised6-02.php) |
| 3 | Any of various services designed to aid the poor and aged and to increase the welfare of children (www.cogsci.princeton.edu/cgi-bin/ webwn) |
| 4 | A **social worker** is a professionally trained person employed in the administration of charity, social service, welfare, and poverty agencies, advocacy, or religious outreach programs. Social workers may also work with community health agencies. In developed countries a large number of social workers are employed by the government. Other social workers work as psychotherapists, performing individual counseling, frequently working in coordination with psychiatrists, psychologists, or other physicians. Additionally, some social workers have chosen to focus their efforts on social policy (en.wikipedia.org/wiki/Social_work) |

*Source:* Google UK (2005)

second is part of a glossary used by a library to decide whether a book is useful to readers interested in social work. The third is from the internet equivalent of a dictionary, Word Net. The fourth is from the internet equivalent of an interactive encyclopaedia that allows people to contribute amendments. All these are examples of what people might find if in some walk of life they suddenly needed to think about what a social worker is.

Dictionaries provide brief definitions of a term, while encyclopaedias provide more complex information about how a term is used. The many dictionaries across the world all define 'social work' slightly differently. The *Oxford English Dictionary* seeks quotations from writers to illustrate how they used a term, and then creates definitions that incorporate all the usages they have found. The present edition offers only one definition, covering the period from 1890, the earliest quotation they found, to the late 1980s, when the research was completed. This definition is set out in Table 2.2.

Looking at these entries, then, a layperson would find social work to be an activity associated, particularly on the internet, with healthcare, especially psychiatry, and also perhaps education. It would aid poor and elderly people and children, and also be concerned with 'welfare'.

**Table 2.2:** Definition of social work from the *Oxford English Dictionary*

**Social work ...**Work of benefit to those in need of help, especially professional or voluntary service of a specialized nature concerned with community welfare and family or social problems arising mainly from poverty, mental or physical handicap, maladjustment, delinquency etc. Hence social worker, one who undertakes social work, especially someone professionally trained....

*Source: Oxford English Dictionary* (Simpson and Weiner, 1989)

The *Oxford English Dictionary* definition also focuses on these elements of service to particular groups, and refers to disadvantage and need.

The next main response in the Google search, and a definition also quoted by several other websites in its top ten, is the 'International Definition of Social Work' adopted by the International Federation of Social Workers (IFSW), in 2000 (IFSW, 2000), and agreed by the International Association of Schools of Social Work (IASSW) in 2001 (IASSW, 2001). This is presented (minus its commentary) in Table 2.3. It is an authoritative definition created by people representing social work, and, as we might expect, it presents a more complex picture than internet and dictionary definitions. There are three elements of social work identified: social change (transformational objectives), individual problem solving (social order perspectives) and empowering and liberating people and enhancing their well-being (therapeutic objectives). Two areas of knowledge and understanding are integral to social work: both psychological and social understanding. Two areas of concern about values are relevant: human rights and social justice. The implication of this definition is that these elements are inseparable from each other: a social worker must be involved in all three elements, must use both psychological and social understanding together, not just psychology or just sociology, and be committed to both individual human rights and social justice.

Another powerful stakeholder in understanding social work is the state, since, as some of these definitions suggest, the state is an important provider of social work. The main UK government department

**Table 2.3:** IFSW international definition of social work

The social work profession promotes social change, problem solving in human relationships and the empowerment and liberation of people to enhance well-being. Utilising theories of human behaviour and social systems, social work intervenes at the points where people interact with their environments. Principles of human rights and social justice are fundamental to social work.

*Source:* IFSW (2000)

concerned with social work is the Department of Health; examination of its website reveals use of the term 'social care'. Table 2.4 presents information offered on its website about how social care is delivered. This reveals that the term refers to a range of services, covering those groups mentioned on the internet and dictionary definitions; the term social work is absent. Table 2.5 presents three official statements, two from the Department of Health website and one from a related site, designed to encourage people to take up careers in social work. The first of these defines social care as the services discussed in Table 2.4; the second indicates that the official view is that social workers are a small (14%) part of the workforce providing those services, whose responsibilities are particularly concerned with assessment and decisions affecting the rights of individuals and the protection and safety of individuals and the public. It is not clear what rights or what risks are involved. The third excerpt describes how social workers work. This statement connects a counselling role helping individuals to solve their problems with liaison and coordination between official agencies. As might be expected from a government department, this presents a social order perspective on social work.

If we put all these statements about the current identity of social work together, we can see certain features. First, it is associated with a range of social or welfare services, now called 'social care' in UK official terminology, and in particular healthcare and mental health issues. Second, the services are for people defined as 'deprived' or 'in need' and in particular categories; they are not universal. Third, social work involves problem solving for individuals by including counselling and similar activities and through liaison and coordination with official agencies. Fourth, it concerns individual human rights, protection and safety for people. Fifth, in some understandings, it also involves social change and human empowerment. Finally, it involves both psychological and social knowledge.

## Development of social work's identity discourse

In this section, I discuss a range of texts, reprinted in the tables that follow, that have sought over the years to define social work. Examining debate about these, I also quote some of the discussion in the 20th century about the identity of social work. I try to show:

- Concern about social work's identity is not just a modern phenomenon; it has been going on for as long as the term 'social work' has been in use; indeed 'social work' was regarded as an unsatisfactory term from its start.

**Table 2.4:** Department of Health information on social care

**Delivering social care**

Social care covers a wide range of services that can help people to carry on in their daily lives and is one of the major public services. At any one time, up to 1.5 million of the most vulnerable people in society are relying on social workers and support staff for help.

There are now 25,000 employers with over one million staff providing social care services for:

- elderly people, through residential care homes, nursing homes, home carers, meals on wheels, day centres, lunch clubs;
- people with physical disabilities or learning disabilities;
- people with mental health, ranging from support for those with mild mental illness, up to exercising legal powers for compulsory admission to psychiatric hospitals of potentially dangerous people;
- people who misuse drugs or alcohol and ex-offenders who need help with resettlement;
- families, particularly where children have special needs such as a disability,
- child protection, including monitoring of children at risk;
- children in care, through fostering, accommodation in children's homes and adoption;
- young offenders.

Social services are the responsibility of 150 councils across England. They provide services that meet an individual's or an area's circumstances and needs. Councils decide if an individual in their area needs care and support (called an assessment) and, if they do, arranges for that care and support. They also work closely with others including the NHS, voluntary and private organisations as well as with the education service, the probation service, the police and other agencies who share the responsibility to provide this care and support.

The aims of all services are to:

- support independence and respect dignity
- meet the individual's specific needs
- organise and finance social care services in a fair, consistent manner
- ensure that children in care get the same opportunities as other children
- ensure that every user is safeguarded against abuse
- provide a skilled, trained workforce
- provide care to the highest standards.

*Source:* DH (2005)

- The texts demonstrate a struggle to define social work in reconciling the elements of what, in Chapter One, I called the claim of social work: to achieve general social improvement through interpersonal help.
- The texts demonstrate the interaction of the three perspectives, therapeutic, social order and transformational, throughout the period; none ever displaces the others; one gains emphasis for a while and that emphasis is questioned in a critique from other perspectives.

**Table 2.5:** Social care and social work: official statements

**1. About social care**

The term 'social care' covers a wide range of services, which are provided by local authorities and the independent sector. Social care comes in many forms, such as care at home, in day centres or by way of residential or nursing homes. The term also covers services such as providing meals on wheels to the elderly, home help for people with disabilities and fostering services.

*Source:* www.dh.gov.uk/PolicyAndGuidance/HealthAndSocialCareTopics/SocialCare/AboutSocialCare/fs/en (accessed 20 February 2005)

**2. 'Notes to editors'**

**Radical reforms to social work training to raise social care standards.**

1. Social workers make up 14% of the social care workforce. They are required to make key assessments and decisions affecting people's lives, and so it is particularly important that they are properly equipped to do the job. Many of the decisions they are required to make affect the rights of individuals and their safety and protection, as well as the safety and protection of the public.

*Source:* www.dh.gov.uk/PublicationsAndStatistics/PressReleases/PressReleasesNotices/fs/en?CONTENT_ID=4010557&chk=A9sHY5/ (accessed 20 February 2005)

**3. What is social work? The role**

Social work is all about people.

Social workers form relationships with people. As adviser, advocate, counsellor or listener, a social worker helps people to live more successfully within their local communities by helping them find solutions to their problems. Social work also involves engaging not only with clients themselves but their families and friends as well as working closely with other organisations including the police, NHS, schools and probation service. Social workers tend to specialise in either adult or children's services.

*Source:* www.socialworkcareers.co.uk/ (accessed 19 March 2005)

When did the term 'social work' come into use? The *Oxford English Dictionary* (see Table 2.2) recognised the emergence of the term in the 1890s and early 1900s, starting from the US, but being rapidly assimilated into the UK.

However, in the first 20 years of the 20th century, social workers shifted their understanding of what they were doing from 'charity' towards 'social work'. After this, there are frequent attempts to struggle with the complexity of the social work identity. Table 2.6 shows excerpts from some early discussions of social work, obtained by searching the British Library catalogue for books with 'social work' in the title published between 1900 and 1930. Many writers of the time did not attempt a clear definition. Social work was changing: Tufts (1923), observing the North American field, suggests that the term is unfortunate, but more generally in use than terms such as social economics and social engineering. Richmond's *Social Diagnosis* is often considered to be the first social work practice text, and sees diagnosis as being at the centre of social work. Thus, her first (1917) definition in Table 2.6 focuses on social work as investigation and understanding. These examples demonstrate a social order perspective, but this on social work method was an innovation.

Early discussion of social work was transformational, seen almost as a generic term for people who were actively concerned with social issues; thus there was no attempt to distinguish it in a definition as a separate professional field. This is how it is used by Patten and Attlee. Patten is important because, as a North American professor of social economics, he gave an influential series of lectures in 1905 at the New York School of Philanthropy. These became his best-selling book, and ended with a 'programme of social work'. He said: 'The aim of social work is democracy rather than culture; energy rather than virtue; health rather than income; efficiency rather than goodness; and social standards for all rather than genius and opportunity for the few' (Patten, 1906: 213). Attlee, the future UK Prime Minister, wrote the first UK text on social work while he was the first social work lecturer at the London School of Economics. He saw social service as the right and duty of a citizen, and emphasised the breadth of the idea of social work, although as a profession it had a narrower interpretation. It incorporated the idea of charity, and social reform, now displaced by better knowledge and more effective democracy: 'formerly social work was done *for*, now *with* the working class' (Attlee, 1920: 19; emphasis original).

**Table 2.6:** Definitions of social work in the early 20th century

| **Definition** | **Date and source** |
|---|---|
| Social diagnosis needs to '... make as exact a definition as possible of the situation and personality of a human being... in relation to the other human beings upon whom he in any way depends or who depend upon him and in relation also to the social institutions of his community'. | Richmond (1917: 357) |
| 'The narrower object of social work is (I) the care of those who through misfortune or fault are not able under existing conditions to realize a normal life for themselves or who hinder others from realizing it – dependent children, aged poor, sick, crippled, blind, mentally defective, criminals, insane, negligent parents, and so on – and (2) the improvement of conditions which are a menace to individual welfare, which tend to increase the number of dependents and interfere with the progress and best interests of others who may be in no danger of becoming dependent.' | Devine (1922: 3) |
| 'Social casework consists of those processes which develop personality through adjustments consciously effected, individual by individual, between men and their social environment.' | Richmond (1922: 99) |
| '...social work includes all voluntary attempts to extend benefits which are made in response to a need, are concerned with social relationships, and avail themselves of scientific knowledge and employ scientific methods.' | Cheyney (1926: 24) |
| 'It is defined in various ways, each definition expressing as a central idea service to an individual as the first consideration, always with the underlying purpose of promoting the welfare of the group.... Three characteristics appear to distinguish social work from other vocations. The first is that *social work takes account of the multiple needs of the individual and treats them as a unit....* A second characteristic lies in the fact that *flexibility of program is an essential of social work....* A third characteristic is found to be that *social work is usually financed by society and not by the individual benefited.'* [emphasis original] | Walker (1928: 19-21) |
| 'Social casework deals with 'the human being whose capacity to organise his own normal social activities may be impaired by one or more deviations from accepted standards of normal social life....' | AASW (1929) (Milford Conference Report) |

Table 2.6 shows how the use of the term narrowed. Signs of this shift, which came about as the field expanded massively in the First World War, were the change in title from the US National Conference of Charities and Correction to the US National Conference of Social Work in 1916 (Alden, 1929), and the change in role of the American National Social Worker's Exchange to the American Association of Social Workers in 1921 (Dubois and Miley, 1999: 47). Social work became less a social movement, more a job; less a 'cause' for activism and more a 'function' of an increasingly organised society and state, as the famous paper by Porter R. Lee (1929) described it.

Almost as soon as this happened, there was a shift in focus in definition to a concern with 'social casework', as we see in Richmond's (1922) definition, showing how much more important psychology and individual change had become to her since 1917 and as compared to Devine, writing a major teaching text in the same year. This shift was solidified by the influential Milford Conference of the American Association of Social Workers (AASW) (Table 2.6). These definitions are largely social order definitions of casework; they are about the provision of services and the solving of problems, even in the Milford Conference statement.

Casework became the dominant approach to practice, strongly influenced by developments in the US, in the period 1920-70; Table 2.7 sets some of these out. The shift to a therapeutic focus in casework, and away from a social order focus, arose from the impact of the mental hygiene movement, which aimed to deal with social problems by improving mental health and psychoanalysis in the US during the 1920s (Payne, 2005c: 210). Enthusiastic embrace of psychoanalysis in the 1930s produced mystical statements, such as:

> After Mary Richmond came a psychiatric deluge. It overtook case work from without in the shape of theories about human development, explanations of human behaviour and relationships, and methods for changing human feelings and conduct.... New material was brought into use, this time material more directly and authentically related to psychoanalytic experience and knowledge. The observations of case work were noticeably sharpened and deepened by attention to data the significance of which had been established by psychoanalytic enquiries. The findings of case work were subject to improved understanding supplied by psychoanalytic discoveries about the structure, development, and functioning of the human

psyche. The case work method of study and treatment underwent inner corrections inspired by psychoanalytic experience with methods of studying the mind. (Marcus, 1935: 126)

**Table 2.7:** Definitions of social work and social casework (1930-70)

| Definition | Date and source |
|---|---|
| 'Social work concerns itself with human beings where there is anything that hinders or thwarts their growth, their expanding consciousness, their increasing co-operation. Social case work is that form of social work which assists the individual while he struggles to relate himself to his family, his natural groups, his community... we shall use no methods that in themselves hamper the growth of the human spirit.' | Reynolds (1935: 136-7) |
| 'Social work... always finds its focus and its object in the helping of individual human beings, who face in their social relationships all sorts of disturbing inadequacies, frictions, limitations, that frustrate the full realization of their own capacities and wants as persons. Its philosophy and its practice are rooted in a profound respect for individual personality, for the significance of the individual as such and in his own right. Its service is directed primarily, therefore, to freeing and helping individuals to find and to fulfil themselves – their own unique selves – within the society of which they are a part. The service is made available through social agencies, organized by members of the community who become aware of, and especially sensitive to, certain problems that confront their fellows, and who believe that community well-being, as well as individual humanitarian feeling, requires that this help shall be made available to those who want and can use it.' | Pray (1942: 18-19) |
| 'A professional social worker is one who is employed to provide some social service for individuals or groups of individuals. The aim of the service should be to work in co-operation with the individual in such a way that his or her potentialities are given the fullest possible scope in relation to the community of which he or she is a member. In performing that service, it is the function of the social worker to interpret the existing social service to the individual or group of individuals. He should also be ready to suggest changes in the social services where experience shows them to be desirable.' | Simey Report (1947: 10) (the constitution of the British Federation of Social Workers) |

*continued.../*

**Table 2.7:** contd.../

| **Definition** | **Date and source** |
|---|---|
| 'Social casework is an art in which knowledge of the science of human relations and skill in relationship are used to mobilize capacities in the individual and resources in the community appropriate for better adjustment between the client and all or part of his total environment.' | Bowers (1949:317) |
| 'The basis of all case work is the natural human response of one individual to another in some need which he cannot meet alone.... If the starting point is [this] ... either because society has not allowed for provision for his wants or then the simple elementary process of social work is to give the individual's need an individual remedy; and similarly to help such other individuals as may subsequently happen to be in the same straits. Sometimes the difficulty is seen to beset, not one solitary individual at a time, but such a number of people and in such a manner that collective action is necessary and the appropriate activity to meet it can only be social reform. In some cases, again, it begins to appear that the individual is suffering not from any single need that can be supplied separately but from a poverty of social life, the lack of opportunity for certain social experience...; and the remedy is then by means of group or community work....There is the fundamental unity of one whole process underlying all these different activities, springing from the natural human situation and the natural human response to it in which it all originates.' | Cormack and McDougall (1950: 16-17) |
| 'Social work rests ultimately on certain assumptions ... without which its methods and goals can have no meaning. The axioms are, for example: human betterment is the goal of any society; ... the general standard of living should be progressively improved; education for physical and mental health and welfare should be widely promoted; the social bond between man and man should lead to the realisation of the age-old dream of universal brotherhood. The ethic derived from these and similar axioms leads to two nuclear ideas which distinguish social work as one of the humanist professions. The first is that the human event consists in person and situation which constantly interact, and the second that the characteristic method of social work incorporates within its processes both scientific knowledge and social values in order to achieve its ends.' | Hamilton (1951: 3) |
| 'Social casework is a process used by certain human welfare agencies to help individuals to cope more effectively with their problems in social functioning.... The nucleus of the casework event is this: A *person* with a *problem* comes to a *place* where a professional representative helps him by a given *process*.' | Perlman (1957: 4; emphasis original) |

*continued.../*

**Table 2.7:** contd.../

| **Definition** | **Date and source** |
|---|---|
| 'The practice of social work has as its purposes:<br>• To assist individuals and groups to identify and resolve or minimize problems arising out of disequilibrium between themselves and their environment.<br>• To identify potential areas of disequilibrium between individuals or groups and the environment in order to prevent the occurrence of disequilibrium.<br>• In addition to these curative and preventive aims, to seek out, identify, and strengthen the maximum potential in individuals, groups, and communities.' | Bartlett (1970: 221-4) (the NASW 'Working Definition' of 1958) |
| 'Social work seeks to enhance the social functioning of individuals, singly and in groups, by activities focused upon their social relationships which constitute the interaction between man and his environment. These activities can be grouped into three functions: restoration of impaired capacity, provision of individual and social resources, and prevention of social dysfunction.' | Boehm (1958: 275) |
| 'Social work would be ... all efforts carried out in order to achieve welfare and this can be done by any person, whether professional or not. Social service would be the same efforts indicated above, but carried out in an organised form by a competent professional who carries out her work through the application of methods and techniques supported by a philosophy and by the fundamental principles of human rights.' | Chilean Committee of Social Work (1961: 7) |
| '... social work is an independent field of work existing side by side with the social insurance and pension system whose competence, substance and scope are settled by political legislation. The special character of social work is constituted by the fact that it gives or procures help to individuals or groups in distress, who are:<br>• not provided for under social security<br>• do not receive the necessary help for development from either family or society<br>• handicapped mentally or physically, socially or because of an abnormal disposition.<br>Social work's guiding principle is to give help to enable people to help themselves.... The term 'social worker' is ... applied ... only to full-time experts who have received their training at recognized technical schools and have passed a state examination....' | German Council on Social Welfare (1961: 8-9) |

*continued.../*

**Table 2.7:** contd.../

| **Definition** | **Date and source** |
|---|---|
| 'The Japanese translation of 'social work' is *Shakai-jigyo* or literally, 'Social Enterprise' ... the term usually implies organized welfare activities.... The purpose of social work... is not only to give help to rehabilitate individuals with dependency, ill-health, and maladjustment problems but also to promote actively the welfare of the community as a whole by various measures.' | Japanese National Committee on Social Welfare (1961: 30-1) |

The words 'authentically' and 'corrections' are examples of uncritical acceptance of these ideas, although both in the US and in Britain, psychoanalysis had little influence in everyday practice in state services (Lees, 1971; Alexander, 1972). In the US, it was heavily used in a few elite voluntary sector family service agencies and in training courses that few took. Elsewhere people were more pragmatic. In Britain, the influence was two decades later in the 1940s and 1950s (Yelloly, 1980). However, elites write the definitions, and individualised work influenced by psychological and psychoanalytic ideas became routinely incorporated into accounts of social work.

This view also dominated agencies that were able to maintain independence from pressures to be more pragmatic and convert therapeutic personal growth into individualised service provision. Butrym (1976: 2-3) argued that the continuing role of statutory responsibility in British services prevented workers from having the professional independence to follow such trends. This represents a view that state provision focused on social order is likely to restrict wholesale influence for therapeutic ideas.

The definitions by Reynolds (1935) and Pray (1942) are striking: shortly after the Milford Conference definitions, they are extremely therapeutic in approach. This is also true of the British Federation of Social Workers' constitution, reported by the Simey Report (1947): here social order style social provision takes a second place to therapeutic approaches. There was a transformational critique committed to a social change view of social work, particularly at the time of the 1930s recession. Lurie, famously in the 1930s (Schriver, 1987), maintained a consistent critique. He focused on the tendency to use psychological techniques to exclude promoting practical help from the community:

> The concrete value of the social case worker in the past has been the possibility of using available resources in the community.... Helping individuals to obtain relief, to register for and obtain employment ... to obtain health, educational and recreational services on some decent level have been important contributions made by the social agency to social welfare. At present, we must recognise the fact that all of these services, economic, vocational, health and cultural, are less and less available in relation to the needs of the masses of the population ... with the depression there are evidences that they are deteriorating in quality. (Lurie, 1935: 617)

In a very significant paper, Bowers (1949) identified 34 definitions of casework from what he claims is the earliest (by Mary Richmond in 1915) to one by Charlotte Towle in 1947. From these he devised the widely quoted omnibus definition (Table 2.7). This definition juxtaposes art, scientific knowledge and skill. It sees social work as an artistic activity that incorporates scientific knowledge and interpersonal skill. The knowledge used is about human relations, which might include the social, but seems to emphasise the psychological. It connects the social with the individual by seeing them as two aspects of life that social workers seek to adjust to each other, by mobilising individual capacities and community resources.

The definitions by Cormack and McDougall (1950) and Hamilton (1951) are important as presentations in major British and North American textbooks at the beginning of the period in which social work was becoming an established element of Western welfare regimes. Hamilton, the major writer in her generation on 'diagnostic' casework theory, develops the concept of 'person' and 'situation' from earlier ideas such as Richmond's adjustments between 'man and his social environment'. This concept is reaffirmed in Hollis's psychosocial casework of the 1960s and 1970s:

> The major system to which diagnosis and treatment are addressed is the person-in-situation gestalt or configuration. That is to say, to be understood, the person to be helped – or treated, if you prefer – must be seen in the context of his interactions or transactions with the external world; and the segment of the external world with which he is in close interaction must be understood. (Hollis, 1970: 35-6)

The definitions created by the (American) National Association of Social Workers (NASW) in their 'working definition' and by Boehm for the North American association responsible for the control of social work education (the Council on Social Work Education, CSWE) in the mid-1950s reflect a common reason for developing definitions, as organisational and political structures change. In this case, North American social work was unifying from previously specialised groupings and there was a need to establish over-arching definitions. A similar response to similar changes nearly two decades later led to further definitions established by working parties of the British Association of Social Workers (BASW) and the British education body, the Central Council for Education and Training in Social Work (CCETSW) in Table 2.8.

## Continuing discourse from the three perspectives

During the late 1950s, a social order critique of the therapeutic perspective on social work emerged. An example was Wootton's (1959: 271) famous attack: '... modern definitions of "social casework", if taken at their face value, involve claims to powers which verge upon omniscience and omnipotence', and 'It might well be thought that the social worker's best, indeed perhaps her only, chance of achieving aims at once so intimate and so ambitious would be to marry her client' (Wootton, 1959: 273). Wootton accepts that social work focuses on individuals, and sees reform or improvement of the existing system as a matter for politics. She argued for restricting social work to practical advice, in the same way that the American radical Lurie had in the 1930s (see above):

> The range of needs for which public or voluntary services now provide, and the complexity of the relevant rules and regulations have now become so great, that the social worker who has mastered these intricacies and is prepared to place this knowledge at the disposal of the public, and when necessary to initiate appropriate action, has no need to pose as a miniature psychoanalyst or psychiatrist: her professional standing is secured by the value of her own contribution. (Wootton, 1959: 296)

In 1961, the International Council on Social Welfare (ICSW) (see Chapter Eight for information about international organisations in social work) collected and published definitions of social work from

**Table 2.8:** Definitions of social casework and social work from 1971

| Definition | Source |
|---|---|
| 'Social work is the professional activity of helping individuals, groups, or communities enhance or restore their capacity for social functioning and creating societal conditions favourable to that goal. Social work practice consists in the professional application of social-work values, principles, and techniques to one or more of the following ends: helping people obtain tangible services; counselling and psychotherapy with individuals, families, and groups; helping communities or groups provide or improve social and health services; and participating in relevant legislative processes. The practice of social work requires knowledge of human development and behaviour; of social, economic, and cultural institutions; and of the interaction of these factors.' | NASW (1973: 4-5) (the 'interim definition') |
| 'Social work is a form of social intervention which encourages social institutions to respond to individual needs, enabling individuals to use their resources and in turn to contribute to them. It holds that the capacity and dignity of the individual are enhanced by participation in the life of the community. To achieve this end, it contributes to adjustments in the distributions of power and resources and attempts to help people, whether as individuals or groups, to have sufficient control over their lives to increase their opportunities for personal choice and self-realisation.' | CCETSW (1975: 17) |
| 'Social work is the purposeful and ethical application of personal skills in interpersonal relationships directed towards enhancing the personal and social functioning of an individual, family, group or neighbourhood, which necessarily involves using evidence obtained from practice to help create a social environment conducive to the well-being of all.' | BASW (1977: 19) |
| 'The purpose of social work is to promote or restore a mutually beneficial interaction between individuals and society in order to improve on the quality of life for everyone.' | NASW (1981: 6) |
| 'Social work is an accountable professional activity which enables individuals, families and groups to identify personal, social and environmental difficulties adversely affecting them. Social work enables them to manage these difficulties through supportive, rehabilitative, protective or corrective action. Social work promotes social welfare and responds to wider social needs promoting equal opportunities for every age, gender, sexual preference, class, disability, race, culture and creed. Social work has the responsibility to protect the vulnerable and exercise authority under statute.' | CCETSW (1991: 8; original edition, 1989) |

around the world, and three examples show how different conceptions arose through the adjustment of social work to the welfare regime in each country. Germany's definition, for example, reflects the primacy of the social insurance system and the European principle of subsidiarity, that at the primary level, social provision should be in the family and local community, rather than by official services.

Social work began to change again in the 1970s, and this is reflected in the definitions in Table 2.8. These start in the early 1970s, with attempts to incorporate transformational objectives into the 1950s' and 1960s' emphasis on therapeutic perspectives. Radical social workers saw the therapeutic perspective as '... a skill which was rewarding to the social worker, who felt helpless before problems which were the results of political decisions and material deprivation' (Bailey and Brake, 1975: 6). This subsequently began to incorporate concerns about broad social divisions emerging from feminist thinking (for example, Wilson, 1980), and concern about racism (for example, Husband, 1980) and discrimination against gay and lesbian people (Milligan, 1975; Hart, 1980). Radical social work claimed: '... that it questioned conventional practice in terms that pushed the interests of the client to the fore....' (Langan and Lee, 1989a: 7). However, it did so in a way that focused on collective social change, using such techniques as welfare rights and community work, in Bailey and Brake's (1975) original book.

Social order perspectives continued in their influence. Brewer and Lait (1980) explicitly followed Wootton in arguing for a more practical, less therapeutic conception of social work. Another example is Davies (1994: 4), who promoted a view of social work as maintaining itself by providing for and managing '... people in positions of severe weakness, stress and vulnerability'.

Therapeutic perspectives also continued in their influence. Writers from this position reject technological, scientific conceptions of social work. Personal and interpersonal helping relationships and the associated values of respect for others and caring should be at the centre of social work. Wilkes (1981) argued that an essential feature of many of the people social workers help is that they are undervalued by society. Social work primarily aims to increase their valuations of themselves, by acting intuitively, and seeking meaning within their lives as part of valuing them. This view plays down the importance of service provision or social change in favour of emphasising the mutual interaction and influence of worker and client (hence reflexivity) and personal growth objectives. Krill (1990) argues that we should concentrate on subjective experience. England (1986) recognises the difficulties of trying to define social work's claims, as would a postmodernist. Although they can all be criticised, they reveal something of the nature of social work because:

> The source of social work's potential strength ... is the very fact that it does not separate the world experienced by those in need of help into component segments. Such experience is always a complex, composite experience, it is always a unique synthesis; yet it cannot be impossible to construct such a synthesis, because the client – and everyone – does so all the time. The strength of the able worker lies in his ability accurately to join the client in the construction and experience of this synthesis. It is only through such sharing that people sometimes say to others (and should say most often to social workers) 'you seem to understand' – and we know that to be understood by others is a necessary and a therapeutic experience. (England, 1986: 6–7)

Brandon and Jordan's (1979) account of 'creative social work' lies in this, radical therapeutic, tradition. It gives some idea of what this view of social work consists of. First, it rejects the institutional pressures on social work:

> Powerful social forces push social workers into restricted roles. There is a strong public expectation that they should be nicely and inoffensively helpful, never angry and disturbing. Some clients paralyse social workers' imagination and creativity with threatening and disruptive demands, but most see them as low-ranking officials of whom little is to be expected. (Brandon and Jordan, 1979: 1)

Second, it identifies qualities that characterise 'good' creative social work:

> ... self-confidence ... of the kind that comes from security of identity, from knowing one's own boundaries and limits as a means of recognizing and respecting others' ... positive use of feelings he previously feared as damaging and destructive, and to rely more on intuition.... Closely linked with greater trust of self is an increased respect for clients ... enjoy his contacts with most clients, to like them better and so share more of himself with them ... enter into more

> of a partnership with clients, recognizing their strengths and developing them ... sharing, sometimes to the point where there is a kind of fusion between client and social worker ... the importance of flexibility in what they are as well as in what they do ... respond less predictably to clients' needs ... a substantial element of self-discipline.... (Brandon and Jordan, 1979: 3–4)

## Critical practice

Critical practice, in the early 21st century, is a development of radical ideas (Payne, 2005a), incorporating postmodernist and feminist ideas that suggest that interaction and reflection provide flexible and interpersonal ways of knowing. Fook (2002: 17) presents five main elements:

- Oppression is structural in origins, but experienced personally – radical theory neglected the personal experience and responses to it.
- False consciousness recognises that oppressive social relations are constructed by social experience and therefore might potentially be transformable – radical theory proposed that working-class people's lack of awareness of oppression, once dispelled, would itself promote change.
- Positivism as an ideology of knowledge encourages fatalism about social forces that create social divisions and oppression – radical theory itself assumed that social relations were determined.
- Using critical theory raises awareness of the connections between structural oppression and everyday experience, so that we are free to break the connection in our daily experience – radical theory assumes that the connection is determined and difficult to break.
- Knowledge is constructed by people, derived from empirical reality, so that the constructions made may be changed, even if empirical reality cannot – radical theory emphasised how understanding social forces restricted people's options.

Healy (2000: 123) emphasises how critical theorists '... emphasize the 'pragmatic, ad hoc, contextual and the local' and in doing so challenge the priority accorded to the social totality in contemporary approaches to activism'. Thus, critical theory shifts the basis on which we treat people holistically. Social systems are complex, with every element influencing every other element, thus making it seem impossible to create change. Critical theory identifies the complexity of the stream of development in social contexts as offering possibilities for change in a local and ad hoc way, which will benefit the individual and also add an element to the stream, which may push it in a new direction.

Critical theory, thus, struggles with social work's claim, trying to connect the interpersonal with the social in a new way. It continues radical theory in rejecting the assumptions of social order views that the task of social work is to help people within an existing social order. However, it also seeks a new flexibility in which individual change is less constrained, and social transformation is made more possible, by the availability of individual change.

## Self-determination, participation and advocacy

As radical ideas emerged and developed into critical practice, the therapeutic idea of self-determination also began to change, as social workers reconsidered the role of 'clients' in therapy. Self-determination (see Biestek, 1961) was necessary to a therapeutic approach to social work because to help a client change, the worker needed to engage their commitment to the process by helping them understand and agree with the objectives. However, it began to acquire an ethical dimension: something that social workers should do to respect and value their clients (McDermott, 1975; Payne 1989).

Radical social work emphasised the importance of advocacy on behalf of clients (Moreau, 1990), broadly in the welfare system (Rose, 1990; Ezell, 1994) and also in ensuring that they received their entitlements in the social security system (Bateman, 2000). This then led to a development of advocacy services for many excluded groups, such as people with learning disabilities, children in care, survivors of mental illness, and disability, using a variety of models of practice, but crucially involving people who used the services themselves, rather than professionals acting on their behalf (Brandon et al, 1995). Alongside this, there was a movement for client participation in decisions affecting them (Jordan, 1975; BASW, 1980). This had a significant effect on services. For example, after considerable campaigning by childcare professionals in the UK, the Children Act 1989 established in law the importance of considering the wishes and feelings of children in making decisions and formal involvement in decision-making processes (Gomes, 1995). It became common practice that children and their parents should be present at case conferences discussing their care (DH, 1999).

More recently, partnership between service users, a term first arising in services for people with learning disabilities and now more widely employed to replace 'client' with its therapeutic assumptions, has become an important service objective and maintaining greater equality of respect between professionals and users has become an important professional objective. These developments seek to establish that participation should be part of the objective of achieving empowerment rather than merely consultation (Grant, 1997). However, such partnerships are inevitably complex. The client, like the patient in healthcare, may be only one focus of attention.

## Emergence of social care

The idea of social care as an element of the social services also emerged during the 1980s, and in the UK contests the identity of social work. The most obvious source was the Barclay Report (1982) on the role and tasks of social workers, and its formulation of the two aspects of social work in Table 2.9. This distinguished the service provision element of social work, a social order objective, from a therapeutic element, although it expresses therapeutic work primarily from a social order perspective, focusing on clients tolerating or changing aspects of the world affecting them, rather than seeking personal growth. This form of social care was given impetus by the NHS and Community Care Act 1990, which established care management as an important aspect of social services provision, care managers, who were often social workers, creating 'packages of care' (Payne, 1995; Lewis and Glennerster, 1996).

**Table 2.9:** The Barclay Report's social care planning and counselling

| Social care planning (paras 3.2-3) | Counselling (para 3.4) |
|---|---|
| '...social workers are needed to carry out two different but interlocking activities. The first is to plan, establish, maintain and evaluate the provision of social care.' | 'The second activity which social workers are needed to provide is that of face-to-face communication between clients and social workers, in which social workers are helping clients to tolerate, or to change, some aspect of themselves or of the world in which they are living.... [T]his activity is now very often called counselling, and the client may be an individual, a family or a community group.' |

*Source:* Barclay Report (1982: 33-4)

Another aspect of social care is what Clough (2000) calls 'direct care' and Ainsworth and Fulcher (1981) 'group care', in residential homes or day centres. Clough identifies three purposes:

- parenting or 'tending';
- controlling residents' behaviour;
- changing behaviour (Clough, 2000: 54).

These are carried out in special places, where people are residential or go for the day. People live together or spend time together in groups. The provision may offer:

- caring services, where people are unable to manage the tasks of daily living, perhaps through illness or disability;
- assistance in planning and organising daily life and relationships with the outside world, perhaps through learning disabilities;
- for holding and refuge, to establish boundaries for oneself or one's behaviour, to reflect, recover past coping strategies and learn new ones;
- for holding and healing, because of disturbance or addiction (Clough, 2000: 55).

Social care and its tasks often seem to be a selection of roles in social work that focus on social order. For example, Bland (2002) describes two contrasting regimes in old people's homes, and comments that the local authority's 'social care' approach leads it to take responsibility and independence away from residents, because of its public accountability. However, to achieve either regime still requires therapeutic work in helping people to higher levels of personal achievement and fulfilment, or transformational approaches that seek to change ways of living together, as therapeutic communities have sought to do (Kennard, 1998).

As these two elements of social care provided a focus for service provision, the concept of partnership has seemed more relevant to service provision rather than therapy, and has strengthened its impact, in two different ways:

- partnership with service users to allow them as wide a choice as possible in the services they receive, and to enable their definition of their needs to have an impact on agency decision making;

- partnership with adjacent services, so that 'joined-up' services meet needs more effectively.

The consequences for the identity of social work of the new policy emphasis on participation produce a tension. While partnership builds on important social work values such as self-determination by clients in social casework, and client and citizen participation and advocacy in 1970s' radical social work, in the early 21st century it is more concerned with managing professional discretion. The concern is that professions seek to extend their span of control, perceiving problems within their own knowledge framework, rather than the view that service users or members of the public might have (Chapter Seven); this connects with the economic and political development of managerialism (Chapter Five). For example, criminal justice professionals, concerned with prevention and rehabilitation of offenders, may provide services that benefit offenders in a way that morally seems to condone the crime or ignore the suffering of the victim. Similarly, the hospice movement started from a criticism of healthcare professionals that they ignored people who did not respond to treatment, rather than seeking to make their death more comfortable. Social work expertise has often focused on therapeutic work, rather than caring. Partnership with service users thus seeks to balance professional objectives, which may reflect their own therapeutic assumptions, with users' objectives, which may be concerned more with effective service provision.

## Social work's claim and discourse in different welfare regimes

So far, because of the focus of this book on social work, I have been looking at the identity of social work through its internal discourse about identity. I have argued that the discourse between therapeutic, transformational and social order perspectives on social work define the social and conceptual territory of the claim to achieve social improvement through interpersonal work and personal development by implementing social change. The continuities in all social work, I have argued, arise because it all incorporates an interplay of these ideas in pursuit of these aims. However, identity involves understanding both how things are the same, and how they differ from other similar or related things.

Two issues arise in looking at related actions and professions:

- Social work is divided in a variety of ways and it is often unclear whether these different forms of social work are separate activities, or divisions within social work. Is residential work a form of social work, for example?
- There are a number of 'social services' which are not regarded as social work, but which have connections with social work practice. Where do we make the division?

To help in discussing these issues, I use the idea of a 'welfare regime', which I have adapted from the work of Esping-Andersen (1990). He analyses how different countries provide welfare according to the way in which roles of the state and the market connect to create a particular pattern of provision. This provides a set of social assumptions that form how the welfare services are organised. Social work, as part of those services, is divided differently in every country, to fit that country's social assumptions and welfare regime. There is a range of 'social professions', occupational groups that operate in the territory of responses to identified social issues.

This allows us to look at divisions within social work and related ideas and see how they connect together. Table 1.1 (see Chapter One) contains a number of broad ideas about welfare and the social services. We can see various explanations of the term 'welfare', from a very broad statement about people's happiness to everyday usages that refer to particular kinds of service. One everyday meaning of welfare, for example, is services that provide welfare benefits, and another part of the table describes what these are. Social security is a set of services that provide welfare (in the everyday sense), and some welfare benefits. Are these social services? A look at the description of this term suggests that they are, but there is an everyday usage of this term that refers to personal social services, which refers to local government social work services. This leads us on to social work.

The description of 'social work' in Table 1.1 expresses in a short compass the account given in this book. Also contained in this list are other manifestations of social work: social assistance, social care, social pedagogy and welfare benefits and rights. They are forms of social work, rather than related services, because they all involve the fundamental claim: interpersonal work for social improvement, social improvement implemented through interpersonal work. The idea of 'social care' is a current British one with a number of different strands, focusing on the caring and service delivery aspects of the social services system in the UK, rather than the therapeutic or transformation approach. It is, therefore, a social order implementation of social work.

The idea of 'social pedagogy' is found in Germany, the Netherlands, some Nordic, east European and southern European countries. It incorporates elements of residential and day care, that in Britain are part of social care, and youth and community work with a caring aspect, that in Britain is part of informal and adult education. The move to associate social work with families and children and education departments in British local government reflects a perception that many aspects of social work are about education, personal and community development, without incorporating the philosophical and practice approach of social pedagogy. These ideas also vary in the extent to which they focus on transformational or therapeutic development. Perhaps youth work is mainly keeping youngsters off the street, or preventing delinquency. Or perhaps it is a form of personal social development to enhance the lives of young people. Perhaps day care using the creative arts for people who are dying is a social order service to distract and occupy people who are too disabled by their illness to carry on with ordinary life, in which case it is a form of social care and mainly reflects a social order perspective. Alternatively, as Kennett (2001) argues, it aims to enhance dying people's lives, so that they can feel they are achieving greater self-fulfilment until the point of death; this is more a therapeutic perspective. Either would, in Denmark, be social pedagogy.

The idea of 'social assistance', in Germany and in France, where a group of social workers is called *assistants socials*, reflects an intuitive conception of the social aspects of a range of helping services, and connects with the idea of the more practical assistance afforded by welfare benefits and rights work, or the 'find-your-way-around-the-complex-welfare-state' social order perspective of Wootton (1959). This does not exhaust the range of possible practices (for example, cultural social work in the Netherlands, a conception that connects to the community arts in the UK). All of these activities are regarded as part of social work in the US.

A number of practices are shared between social work and other professions, in two different ways. One approach to sharing involves a shared practice, in which different professions use the same techniques, and often work together using similar techniques, often receiving the same advanced training and with very little differentiation of role. Examples might be counselling, family therapy, community work, groupwork and social development. Another approach is multiprofessional specialties, often healthcare specialties that involve care or help with the social and disabling consequences of the illness as well as active medical treatment, or criminal justice specialties such as youth offending or drug action team work. These lead to a practice in which different professions, often including medicine, nursing, psychology and social work, use their different skills, experience and knowledge together. Forensic psychiatry, palliative care, renal care or motor neurone disease services are examples.

## Conclusion

I have argued, here, by examining the social professions in different welfare regimes, that the identity of social work can be interpreted with different emphases in different welfare regimes, which can be plotted by examining the interaction of the three perspectives on social work, social order, therapeutic and transformational views. Partnerships make it possible to work in a shared way as part of related services and related professions, as well as with service users, their carers and their social network, and with colleagues such as foster carers. However, partnerships may constrain the flexibility of social work's focus on social improvement through interpersonal work and the interpersonal facilitation of social change.

We saw in Chapter One that different social work practitioners, different agencies and different instances of practice reflect different emphases in the discourse on social work. In doing so, they are a particular representation of social work within a particular welfare regime. In this chapter we have seen that the identity of social work has incorporated the three perspectives of social work as, at different times and in different places, it has struggled with the claim to connect interpersonal work with social improvement. The identity of a social profession in a particular welfare regime reflects the struggle between the three perspectives in interpreting the claim for that particular time and place. Each individual social worker embodies in their person, demonstrates in their practice and represents within interagency and interprofessional relationships an identity that reflects the claim and the struggle to act on in that welfare regime.

From the earliest stages of social work's development, people have been challenged by understanding and justifying its claim: to achieve social change by interpersonal work, to give social direction to interpersonal work. This still challenges us today. Throughout the 20th century, social workers have tried to integrate the three perspectives on social work as a way of meeting the challenge, creating different balances and priorities. Social order, transformation or therapeutic work to achieve social control, change and caring are always present. They are counterposed, but also in alliance as part of the same social processes. Social work is a product of industrialisation, secularisation and municipalisation in Western states in the 19th century (Payne, 2005c). It emerged to deal with major social change, moral and ethical challenges and problems of structuring and managing complex societies. We see social work as having a complex identity, because it was created in a time of ferment to respond to increasing diversity and complexity. In the 20th century, social work developed through two major world wars, the creation of welfare states and global economic and political movements. In the 21st century, major demographic changes and ecological and economic changes are clearly on the horizon. It is fortunate that social work is complex, because to achieve its claim it will need to cope with a lot in the future.

THREE

# Social work as a practice

## The screaming woman

When people ask me what social work is like, I often tell them the narrative of the screaming woman. Many social workers have similar anecdotes about their practice, and what they mean by 'practice' is what they do in interpersonal interactions with other people. Thus, seeing social work as a practice asserts the first element of social work's general claim of the value of interpersonal work as an element in the whole package that is social work. Interpersonal activity is what social workers observably do. It is easy to understand and explain as valuable to the people that social workers serve. Interpersonal work also connects well to the other professions working around social workers: they do interpersonal work as well. So, it is central to the identity of social workers as they represent themselves to the public and professional colleagues. Our early pathway through social work usually involves understanding experiences of social work as a personal activity and integrating it into the wider claim of interpersonal social work as a form of social improvement. Narratives like that of the screaming woman codify and classify the important parts of social work as a personal experience.

I was on emergency duty overnight for a social services department. The telephone call from the police, asking if I was covering mental health emergencies, came at 10 o'clock. 'We've got a problem here: there's this screaming lady.' 'How do you mean – screaming?' I asked. 'Well she's screaming. You'll see when you get there.'

The public housing estate, on the edge of the city, was arrayed down a hillside, and I entered the estate from the top. Laid out below was a wide sweep of low-rise housing, encasing several blocks of flats surrounded by tatty lawns. I could see the centre of a disturbance. Around the entrance of the most-distant block was a crowd of fifty or sixty people, with a police car parked nearby. As I drove down the hill, through the window piercing screams were coming from one flat. A young, anxious police officer emerged from the crowd and came across. 'It's this Mrs Woods,' he explained, 'She's just sitting up in bed and screaming.' Another screech rent the air. Answering my questions, he said that, aside from the name, he could find out little about her. She did not have many dealings with the neighbours; there was a husband, but he was absent. Neighbours had tried to get her to stop screaming; he had tried reasoning with her; all useless. We began to push through the growing crowd and, as we did so, the police officer concluded his account of the situation by saying: 'She's hysterical'.

My mind was already racing and the event was so unusual that I can still remember how my thoughts picked up on his comment. As a technical diagnosis of mental illness, the police officer's comment was inaccurate: hysterical behaviour refers to avoidance of reality by unconsciously mimicking behavioural or physical symptoms. Also, it was probably a sexist comment, attributing emotional behaviour to irrational characteristics assumed to be associated only with women. Still, it set me thinking. At school, I had won a prize. As one of the books, I chose a study of hypnosis, which described how most people could be hypnotised, that is, put into a form of sleep. The person is relaxed through being spoken to slowly, calmly and monotonously. People are more or less suggestible; that is, more or less responsive to this technique.

As I walked through the typical council flat into the bedroom where a late middle-aged woman was sitting up and periodically letting out a loud scream, my mind leapt to the man who taught me psychiatry. He was a tall, black-suited beetle of a man, who smoked dark cheroots. Talking about people who exhibited hysterical behaviour (in the technical psychiatric sense described above) I remember him saying: 'They are very suggestible'. My mind made the connection. If Mrs Woods had been hysterical in the technical sense, she was likely to be suggestible, and therefore easily subject to hypnosis. The police officer's comment might be inaccurate psychiatrically, but his common-sense theory of her behaviour might offer a way of beginning. I was not about to try hypnotism as such (not having any need to or being remotely qualified) but I could defuse the immediate situation by putting her to sleep.

I decided on this and sat on the edge of the bed. I leaned across Mrs Woods and took her hand, so that she could see me and be in contact with me. I explained who I was and why this strange man was in her bedroom. She continued to scream. I then said, in a low, slow voice: 'You are feeling very tired, your eyelids are heavy, you want to go to sleep...' and she keeled over to one side and went to sleep. I was the hero of the hour. Within moments of entering the flat, the disturbance that had kept everyone excited for some while was resolved, as far as the neighbours and the police were concerned. The skills of social workers were at a premium that night; every previous effort had failed, and I had instantly succeeded. The officer started to disperse the crowd. A more complex narrative would include Mr Woods' return home from the pub. It would describe a history of domestic violence, of depression, anxiety and dread as a loved family left home and an empty old age loomed, and of need for personal and family change to offer fulfilment again. These matters occupied the social services in the future, as they dealt with Mrs Woods, and they connect with the wider claim of social work to offer social improvement.

However, this one brief and unusual incident contains many elements of interpersonal social work, as social workers often describe and analyse it:

- Intervention in the personal aspects of people's lives on behalf of the public's interest.
- Human communication within a relationship as the basis of social workers' actions.
- Social work is a process; that is, all events in a social work activity are joined and progress from one point to another helped by relationships among the people involved.
- Specific values lie beneath all social work activities.
- Knowledge reconstruction – I used knowledge and skills drawn both from my academic learning and from my personal experience and life interests and reconstructed it in a package that was relevant to this particular situation.
- I used myself. The use of self in relationships within social work meant that my self-confidence in the face of demands from police and neighbours, my self-control in the face of anxiety about what to do, my mental energy in the face of an unknown situation, and my personality and ability to interact with a stranger in a personal way were all brought into play.

I embodied, in this small piece of practice, social work, myself and my life. So does every social worker, every time they are doing social work: they represent social work, they become, embody, incorporate, they *are* social work. This chapter explores accounts of most of these aspects of carrying out social work activities. One, the area of social work values, is so complex and important to an understanding of social work that I reserve it to the next chapter.

## Practice as performance

The social work narrative describes interpersonal work as a practice: this means more than 'what social workers do'. Practice is at least two things. It is, first, *a* practice, a convention, standard or approach to the things that social workers do; we say 'it is our practice to…'. This conveys that social work has continuity, certainty and accepted standards. However, practice is also provisional (Payne et al, 2002: 6); it is like a musician rehearsing, or a jazz player improvising. The screaming woman was an exceptional situation and no prior prescription told me what to do, so I improvised and if my suggestion to her to sleep had not worked, I would have tried something else. One of the ways in which social work and its relationships with the people it serves come to be valued is by sticking with it and trying again. This is also a good model for people in difficulties. It is hard to try again when things do not work out in adversity, but the social worker sticking with it is likely to be more valued than someone who tries once or twice, then washes their hands of the situation.

To offer both the certainty of accepted practice and yet also to offer the flexibility of being provisional seems inconsistent, and this inconsistency is one of the things that concerns people, both social workers and non-social workers, about social work. It would seem better to be clear what social work does. Managers would like to be able to prescribe procedures to be followed on all occasions; academics would like to see evidence that social work techniques are effective in particular situations; social workers themselves would like to be clear what to do next, and seek guidelines or practice models that will help them. But yet, humanity and social context in all its variety demands flexibility of us. Many social work techniques have a basic underlying idea, such as 'task' or 'crisis', but as these are elaborated for explanation, we arrive at social work textbooks with their complicated lists or diagrams, that we cannot readily hold in our head, even though they are still too generalised to apply to the situations we have to deal with.

However, to see certainty and flexibility as inconsistent is to misunderstand the nature of social work and of humanity. What social workers do, and how they interact with others, is flexible and variable, because it reflects human and social variability. But their instruments of practice – knowledge, skill, understanding and value objectives – these are capable of clarification, coherence and consistency.

Goffman's (1968, 1972a, b, c) dramaturgical role theory suggests that we respond to human situations by acting out roles that are appropriate to the situation and the others involved. We change how we present ourselves to others according to the situation. Social work can be seen as a performance, in which we do things that represent something of ourselves as individuals, and our role as social worker, and this interacts with other people acting out their roles as troubled or sick people, parents, spouses, members of a community. This troubled role is not the whole of them, as the helping role is not the whole of us. They take from the set of roles that connect with parts of their lives those that are relevant to the moment and use them in the interaction with us. As soon as we begin to generalise from these particular situations, consistency and coherence begin to take over. Thus, Mrs Woods presented herself as extremely troubled to the point of needing emergency action. Attempting careful assessment and thoughtful therapeutic interaction as the social work therapeutic literature would suggest, or providing a supervisory home care support worker as social order views of social work propose, would not deal with the present situation of escalating anxiety and disturbance in the growing crowd around Mrs Woods' door. It was a fair guess that poverty, ageing and gender relations in her life would be contributing to her distress, but it was no time to raise these transformational concerns. No, 'calm things down' was the necessary intervention. And Mrs Woods, no doubt tired by her troubles, having ignored the ministrations of kindly neighbours and the intervention of social control in the form of the police, probably recognised the arrival of officialdom in a form that might have the potential to help her. She reacted by accepting the need to do what she would eventually have to do anyway. This joint performance of roles represented only part of the complexities of her life and my profession.

However, as soon as this had taken place, the arrival of her husband from the pub and her removal to psychiatric hospital added complexity to the situation, but permitted me to take up some of the other roles of the social worker. This included assessing some of the underlying factors in her disturbing behaviour and starting out on a process dealing with the social issues that she faced in a more complex way, and completing a form for the local team to pick up the next day. Included in that, eventually, was the provision of practical services to help her and her husband.

So, although infinitely variable performances are required to deal with the human and social, these fall into a well-established and professional process. Even the performance on this occasion illustrated the importance of establishing communication, official courtesies and a helping, if temporary, relationship. This single incident illustrates many of the principles of social work as a practice, and my own personal self and life experience as elements in it. It also begins to establish social work as other things: it incorporates the official role, the use of knowledge and research, the social values that social workers seek to achieve. I was called and acted as a public official, part of the machinery of social control. I also carried out a crucial value objective of social work: I assumed that there would be social factors that affected this bizarre behaviour, that they could be resolved. I carried the authority of my agency, the expectations of professional knowledge and self-confidence from police and neighbours. I call this the 'wise person' role. People assume when you intervene that you will be 'wise' in the ways of situations like this, you will have the necessary knowledge and some experience and self-confidence. Not knowing or caring where it comes from, not expecting it to be in undigested gobbets of knowledge, they look to, expect, your wisdom. As a consequence, you may be able to act, they may be able to join the performance, something local and personal may happen. Then, as a result, minor changes in gender relationships and responses might be gained, part of social work's mission for social justice and empowerment. All of this was contained within a single brief interpersonal performance.

This focus on practice, therefore, is a limited perspective. The interpersonal aspect of social work is often the first we get involved with and describes well what social workers do on a daily basis. However, it only *includes* the full claim of social work to achieve social improvement as well; it does not *reveal* it. But the interpersonal claim for social work is also that whatever it achieves is worthwhile to clients as participants in the endeavour. This is so, even though social work fulfils other social purposes by its activity and presence in the world as a profession. The personal and interpersonal narrative attempts to provide a coherent analysis and valuation of important aspects of social work. It centres on the public and everyday understanding of social work as an activity, as we saw in the dictionary and internet views of social work considered in Chapter Two. The additional aspects of social work both as an activity and as a profession require analysis and development from a basic understanding of social work in its personal and interpersonal form.

## Intervention

According to the personal/interpersonal narrative, social workers intervene in other people's lives and social situations. A loose meaning of 'intervention' is virtually anything that a social worker does with or on behalf of clients. This treats 'intervention' as a synonym for what in other texts (for example, Germain and Gitterman, 1996) is called 'helping' or 'practice' (for example, Fook, 2002). A second, tighter, usage of 'intervention' focuses on activities intended to affect clients' lives. In the following account, I give some examples of how the term is used in these different ways. Ng and Chan (2005: 68) are a good recent example of an 'anything you do' approach; they describe intervention: '... as a proactive means of enabling people to empower themselves to take action to improve their situation. The holistic approach proposed integrates the physical, cognitive and spiritual aspects of the person, with a view to develop strengths and enabling well-being rather than focusing on pathological problems'. Here, they present a therapeutic perspective on social work. By contrast, Dominelli (2004: 81) describes a transformational view of intervention as '... the processes whereby change occurs', and is concerned in her account with how social workers engage their clients, depending on their values, which help workers to be aware of conflicts in the values underlying practice; the conflicts help them to understand how and where to transform. She contrasts hierarchical and egalitarian processes. Hierarchical values 'drown out' (2004: 82) users' voices and limit the range of alternatives that clients may be offered. In this, she is referring to intervention as the whole character of the worker's relationship interactions with clients.

Compton and Galaway (1999: 309) provide an example of the more restricted use of intervention to describe '... activities undertaken subsequent to the development of a service agreement and directed toward the achievement of goals specified in the service agreement'. They identify a range of interventive roles, such as social broker, enabler, teacher, mediator and advocate. Following on from these, they focus on 'interventive methods to mobilise clients' power'. These include securing resources for clients, increasing clients' self-awareness, strengthening clients' communication skills, providing information, assisting clients to make decisions and assisting clients to find meaning in life. Similarly, Mattaini (2002: 175), introducing 'practice with individuals' in a major North American text, says that practice '... generally moves from assessment into intervention in a relatively seamless way...'. Dorfman (1996: 93) refers to '... a broad sampling of concepts and techniques (drawn from various models) that are commonly incorporated into eclectic social work practice'. Evans and Kearney (1996) refer to beginning, engaging, convening, assessing and planning before intervention starts. They argue that service users want an 'activist' approach, where there is evident activity on their behalf, but balance this with a focus on user control, very much a social control perspective. A 'fundamental principle' (Evans and Kearney, 1996: 116) for them is to maximise the user's control, starting from a voluntary approach before using statutory powers and promoting self-help and mutual support. Workers contribute optimism about change, knowledge of and access to resources and interpersonal skills in working with and acting for service users.

Here, interventions are formally stated sets of actions with environments, transactions and patterns of behaviour, and are what the worker does, rather than something shared. One widely used theory of social work explicitly contains 'intervention' in its title: crisis intervention. Recent leading texts in this perspective do not discuss intervention as such in detail. James and Gilliland (2001), for example, discuss 'basic crisis intervention skills' and 'crisis case handling', while Roberts's (2000: 2) seven-stage model of crisis intervention focuses on assessment, establishing rapport, dealing with emotions, finding alternatives and planning action, at which point 'crisis resolution' takes place. Rapoport's (1970) important early account of this theory rarely uses the word. She prefers 'crisis theory' or 'crisis-oriented brief treatment'. At one point, she makes a distinction between intervention and prevention: '... principles applicable to modes of intervention and prevention' (Rapoport, 1970: 269). Parad (1965: 1) makes the same distinction between preventive and crisis intervention in his classic book. He defines crisis intervention (1965: 2) as '... entering into the life situation of an individual, family or group to alleviate the impact of a crisis-inducing stress in order to help mobilize the resources of those directly affected, as well as those who are in the significant 'social orbit'...'. Brewer and Lait (1980: 121), in their social order polemic, apply the preventive/interventive distinction more widely in social work: '... evidence of the effectiveness of preventive casework is even more tenuous than in the case of intervention'.

Among the implications of seeing social work as an intervention is, first, that it asserts that social work tries to create a balance. The altruism of caring and helping is counterposed against the authoritative imposition of involvement against the conventions of the social worlds in which social workers act. In this way, the social order requirement for invoking social control is incorporated into the basic therapeutic approach of personal and interpersonal social work. Second, it makes claims for its scientific and authoritative nature. Such claims support social work against criticism of its invasive nature. In this way, the idea of intervention connects with social work's claim: to intervene in the personal requires the invasion of the public. All involvements with other human beings or other organisations necessarily imply intrusion on those individuals or organisations, their freedom to act as they wished and their privacy of decision making (Payne, 1993). Workers create a balance of advantages between intruding too much and getting involved enough to have an effect. These views imply that the normal situation where we give help is a closed social world in which official or professional helpers do not take part. Moreover, it sees social life as ordered. People go along in their social world until some invasion changes that. If we accept this as normality, seeking or receiving help from outsiders is a socially less preferred option than receiving help within the social circle. This conception of social work activity is not necessary. Transformational views of intervention, such as Dominelli's (2004), say that a better description of social life is of constant social change. Social work activities then become one part of the continuing experience of change, and consequently are not an invasion from another social order, but an interaction between different social orders in a continuing process of change. Looking at intervention closely, therefore, draws attention to its political and social implications. Seen from a social order perspective, politically, it implies that providing welfare services is not a natural way of providing help. It questions political assumptions that providing help should be a normal role of the state in welfare societies. Socially, it places burdens on those who are seen as the natural carers within social circles: often we assume that these are women, or close relatives. Thus, the situation in which social workers are assumed to be outsiders also assumes a gendered order of caring and the role of families, communities and others in the closed social circle in the welfare of its members. Taking for granted that social workers intervene may carry many of these hidden political and social assumptions. The therapeutic perspectives quoted above assume that invasion may be balanced with the benefits of the achievement of problem solving and personal growth. Dominelli's (2004) transformational view, in contrast, claims that, to be justified, the invasion must be a shared endeavour.

## Human communication within a relationship

However we see its invasiveness, social work is always carried out by communication between the worker and others involved. The communication takes place within a relationship or relationships. As Parton and O'Byrne (2000: 11; emphasis original) put it, commenting on studies of users' views of social work: 'This is not simply saying that good social work is about establishing a 'relationship', important though that is, but that the way we understand and come to terms with difficult and painful experiences is through talk. *Talk* and *language* are key to making sense and taking control'.

Communication conveys meaning between human beings by using symbols. A symbol is a device that 'stands for' something else. Sometimes the symbols are words, which may be conveyed in speech or writing or by sign languages. Sometimes the symbol is a piece of behaviour, such as touch, closeness or attitude. Sometimes the symbol is a situation that may be interpreted in particular ways. Examples are where someone is disabled or possesses the characteristics of a particular ethnic group. Communication carries wide implications. Table 3.1 sets out the range of theoretical usages of the concept of communication. This reflects how communication constructs social life, how we influence one another and take action. We can use communication to create a new understanding of something, or to express what is unexpressed. Contextualising, politicising and questioning are various ways of using communication to place present interpretations of a situation in a new light, for example politicising communications can call attention to the ways in which power is being used in the situation we are communicating about.

Trevithick et al (2004), in an authoritative literature review, identify three main groups of ideas underlying communication in social work:

- psychology and counselling theory
- communication and learning theory
- relational/cultural theory.

Counselling theory focuses on updated versions of Rogers' (1951, 1961, 1980; Fleet, 2000) 'core conditions' for an effective relationship in counselling – empathy, genuineness or authenticity and acceptance, unconditional positive regard or respect – and is therapeutic in approach. Communication and learning theory focus on the technical aspects of communication as a carrier of messages between human beings as a learned skill (Hargie et al, 1994); this is a social order approach. Relational/cultural ideas focus on engagement, mutuality and empowerment, and connect with feminist and transformational ideas about equality and dialogue to achieve social change through changing the relationships between social groups and recognising and responding to barriers in communication between different social groups. Pugh (1996), for example, discusses how the use of language in communication may communicate identity and power. Thompson (2003) draws attention to the way in which language use has political

**Table 3.1:** Usages of communication as a concept

| ***Making*** – *creating relationships and understanding* | ***Materialising*** – *understanding the unexpressed* | ***Contextualising*** – *allowing things to be understood in relation to others* | ***Politicising*** – *enabling people to achieve and use influence with other* | ***Questioning*** – *enabling ideas to be tested and developed* |
|---|---|---|---|---|
| Enables people to relate to one another | Allows collective memory to be recorded and invoked | Permits simultaneous differentiation and fusion through dialogue | Permits political participation | Permits Ideas to be disseminated and engaged with in public space |
| Creates patterns and rituals in life | Expresses a vision or intention of the future | Allows people to define and express themselves in their social context | Permits deliberation about experiences | Enables ideas to be articulated through debate |
| Allows people to experience themselves and others at the same time | Expresses the nature and style of individuals and their personalities | Allows people to create narratives to express their understanding of the world | Allows ideas to be diffused | Enables ideas to be translated and adapted into other contexts |
| Constructs people's understanding of relationships and activities | Reflects and expresses 'race' and ethnicity | Allows people to organise understanding in a complex way | Is a form or vehicle of social influence | Enables us to evaluate communications as effective or not |
| Is a social practice that people engage in | Expresses and represents social identities | Allows people to structure organisations and activities | Permits opposition and disagreement | Identifies where communication has failed or needs to be improved |
| | Is a practical art | | Permits argument | |

*Source:* Summarised and developed from Shepherd et al (2006)

implications, conveying cultural and social divisions, attitudes, identity and emotion.

The traditional formulation of the use of relationship is represented by Lee (2001: 66), in her book on empowerment, as follows: 'Basic to all social work processes and outcomes is the process of building relationships. Relationships form the bridge on which all work takes place'. Munro (1998) comments similarly, but emphasises the private character of this way of practising, and the tensions it sets up with the use of knowledge:

> Traditionally, the key feature of social work help has been the relationship with the client. Understanding and offering assistance to clients has been mediated through the social worker's private skills in relating. To most social workers, the helping relationship has seemed central to effective practice and also in direct conflict with the scientific approach. Although drawing on theories from the social sciences, most develop a personal and private style of working, relying on their own appraisal of their work and ignoring as irrelevant the findings of empirical research. (Munro, 1998: 26–7)

Similarly, Dorfman (1996: 93) represents this personal approach to practice as a relationship:

> The relationship between the worker and client is central to the helping process. Unlike friendship, it is not based on mutuality. Emotional support, services, gifts, and other intimacies are not exchanged. Although the client and worker may be partners in problem solving, the clinician alone is in charge of enhancing the therapeutic relationship. The clinical social worker creates a context in which change occurs (ie, where the client feels accepted, cared for, safe and respected). The social worker must radiate warmth, empathy, genuineness, and a sincere interest in the client's life situation (past, present, and future).

The fact that social work communication takes place in a relationship derives from an assumption that social work is a process. It continues over time. Therefore, the people involved have a period of continuing contact. The social work narrative is that the relationship does two things:

- Its special emotional nature has the capacity to 'move' and therefore influence clients.
- It creates an atmosphere of cooperation between worker and client. This forms the instrument through which communication takes place. Communication is also a factor in the worker's influence. Merely attaining effective communication is not enough to achieve changes in clients. It must be specially directed or organised to have its effects, and that special organisation is done through a relationship. Postmodern and critical views (Fook, 2002) suggest that only within interpersonal relationships can we reflect and develop a range of alternative ideas so that we can create knowledge and understanding of our situation and of how oppression, which has been created by past social relationships and experiences, affects us.

Therapeutic ideas are built up from two historic sources: the work of Biestek (1961) and Rogers (1961, 1980; Truax and Carkhuff, 1967; Carkhuff and Berenson, 1977), both of whom in different ways tried to formulate what therapeutic relationships were like and how they were effective; Rogers' 'core conditions' are referred to above. Recent interpretations build on these origins. Perhaps with the most traditional emphasis, Compton and Galaway (1999: 176–82) see the social work relationship as having a helping purpose in which worker and client work together. It contains the following elements:

- concern for the other
- commitment and obligation
- acceptance
- expectation or your own and the client's capacity to change
- empathy – the capacity to enter into others' feelings
- authority and power
- genuineness and congruence.

However, they also focus on the idea of partnership between workers and clients, in which there is respect for clients' dignity and uniqueness and decisions are negotiated; I noted in Chapter Two that 'client' might include a range of users, carers and others in their social network.

Dominelli (2004: 5; emphasis original), on the other hand, argues:

> Its interactive base makes social work a *relational profession*. In this, practitioners and clients become co-participants in elaborating other narratives in which new possibilities for

> action open up ... their 'new' narratives are formed through interactions between the worker(s) and client(s) and the worldviews to which they individually subscribe, as these shape the realm of the possible for them.

And similarly, a North American writer, Derezotes (2000: 77-81), identifies the following as important features of the helping relationship:

- integrity
- use of self
- reciprocity
- mutuality and
- multidimensionality.

Although Lee (2001) claims relationship as basic to social work practice, she gives greater priority to 'relatedness'. By this, she means connection:

- between interpersonal experiences and political issues and solutions (2001: 52-3); and
- between human beings (2001: 143, 152) so that the quality of their interpersonal attachments facilitate empowerment through mutual support.

For her, these two aspects of social work are linked: being empowered through relatedness with others enables people to exercise political power.

This account of communication in a relationship has shown how historically relationship and communication have affected social work through therapeutic ideas, sometimes presented with a social order perspective. Transformational views have sought to emphasise equality and connectedness between worker and the people they relate to. As with intervention, this is an attempt to reconstruct the historic therapeutic view. Theory and research into social work, and the knowledge and skill base of social work, discussed below, often focus on how communication might be effective to achieve which results.

## Process

A process is a series of actions and the factors affecting them that go towards making or achieving something (Payne, 2005b: 23). Seeing social work as a process is another crucial element in therapeutic narratives about social work. The idea of process usefully distinguishes how things are done – the process – in social work from what is achieved – the outcome (Trevithick, 2005: 134). Social work, in this view, is not a series of discrete events. Instead, each interaction between client, worker and others is part of a social order. The idea of process integrates the people involved, their social contexts and their actions in relation to one another. It emphasises the connectedness of everything involved in a social work action, and in this way contributes to the claim to integrate the social and the personal. Unlike counselling, for example, which focuses on influencing the client's personal reactions to the world, social work claims also to seek to improve services or change the impact of external factors on the client; its process is therefore different, because it integrates the social with the purely personal. It also differs from other professions like medicine or nursing, which focus on particular aspects of the person and their treatment or care, without needing to engage with the person as a whole, their social context or to invoke the relationship with the professional.

Each communication in a process affects all the others to produce a flow and sequence of events. We saw earlier that intervention also assumes a continuing flow of life in a social order. By virtue of being in a continuing relationship with the participants, the social worker has the means to influence the sequence. Sheppard et al's (2000; Sheppard and Ryan, 2003) research into the process of thinking in social work sees process differently. It identifies how social workers engage in a critical appraisal of the situation they are presented with, and go through a process of hypothesis formation, which then directs their practice. They create 'causal accounts' (Bull and Shaw, 1992), which contain social workers' explanations from the information. While this research is about thinking processes, it illustrates the characteristic of process ideas, that they examine how many different elements are connected. This particular work usefully draws attention to how they are connected by thinking processes, which use language, knowledge and theoretical and practical understanding as a way of making connections.

In group and community work, process gains another important aspect, as an objective in its own right, of bringing people and activities together, and dealing with the differences that arise from the increased connectedness. Mondros and Wilson (1994), for example, discuss empowerment through social action work with community and self-help groups. They describe '[p]rocess goals [as] desired ends that focus on the process by which the organization becomes more and more able to effect its outcome goals. Long-term process goals go to strengthening the organization....' (Mondros and Wilson, 1994: 137).

Professional work with such organisations, however, has among its aims strengthening the capacity of the group or organisation to function to achieve its own objectives. One aspect of that capacity is the ability to create useful interactions within it. So strengthening process becomes a group or community work objective, and not, as in casework, a means to a therapeutic objective. As Brown and Smith (1992: 100) put it in relation to groupwork: 'One of the most profound characteristics of group process is the way in which the whole mood and functioning of a group, the roles, behaviour, communication patterns and interaction of the members can and do change dramatically over a period of time'. Clearly, here, process has a therapeutic aim, rather than to transform the group to achieve desired social change.

As with relationship, this therapeutic narrative of process has two dissenting positions:

- the social order position argues that social work activities are separate events given coherence by their relevance to an assessment of need, as in care management (managed care);
- the transformational position gives coherence to social work activity by reference to identified social objectives of the work.

The social order conception of process describes it as a sequence. However, consistent with the historical focus of social work on assessment, many formulations emphasise the early stages of the sequence, and in particular do not develop material about monitoring and evaluation of work as part of practice. Wood and Middleman (1989: 69) distinguish understanding social work from doing it:

> [O]ne must do it one step at a time. Therefore a second, complementary model is needed, a process model that indicates what to do first and what to do next, a process model that tells workers every step of the way what to ask themselves and what to do contingent upon the answers ... a process model that translates principles and procedures ... into sequential practice behaviour.

Similarly, Dominelli (2004: 81) argues that '[t]he processes of intervention are those elements of practice which focus on *how* social workers engage their clients'. In her conception, they 'involve a number of phases:

- Referral;
- Data gathering;
- Assessment of the problem;
- Planning and agreeing a plan of action;
- Implementing the action plan;
- Evaluating the action process;
- Evaluating the outcomes;
- Evaluating client performance;
- Evaluating practitioner performance; and
- Reflection for/on future action' (Dominelli, 2004: 82).

Transformation perspectives on process bring together phase or sequence ideas about process with work such as Sheppard et al (2000; Sheppard and Ryan, 2003) on thinking processes. Healy (2000: 95), for example, sees an emphasis on the connections between power and knowledge as a way '... to highlight the processes through which the truth claims of critical practices are established and what and whom these critical truths include or exclude'. For Fook (2002: 91), this involves four stages of thinking:

- critical deconstruction
- resistance
- challenge and
- critical reconstruction.

Both writers place a strong emphasis on examining the social context within which truth seeking through critical thinking takes place. I have emphasised, elsewhere, that social context itself is in constant change, and cannot be regarded as an unchanging basis for what takes place within social work (Payne, 2005b). However, as Archer (1995) makes clear, each social construction forms a historical context for the next social construction, in the same way that, as we saw in Chapter Two, identity derives from both differentiation and identification within social relationships. Fook (2002) argues that her four-phase process allows for the analysis of situations by workers and service users to identify power relations, and then for their reconstruction to make use of and incorporate different power relations. Deconstruction involves looking for themes and shared experiences in the present situation, which point to oppressive power relations; Mullaly (1997, 2002) emphasises the importance of oppression as a focus of analysis and action. This work involves exploring and accepting the client's conceptions of their lived experience (Healy, 2000: 131-2). The worker and client would look for ways of resisting the effects of these relationships, of challenging oppression and through doing this recreate new power relations. Healy (2000) emphasises consciousness raising and working to identify collective and shared interests as important strategies for action.

## Knowledge and skills

Social workers use knowledge and skills in their work. We often regard the knowledge and skill characteristic of an occupational group as marking it as a profession, because, as we saw in Chapter One, power over the social territory of an occupation often comes from control of knowledge. Bartlett (1970: 63) reports that a North American committee on the nature of social work practice '... recognized that mature professions rest upon strong bodies of knowledge and values from which scientific and ethical principles that guide the operation of the practitioner are derived'. Knowledge has been valued from the earliest days of social work, when the attempt was being made to distinguish a defined activity that was different from mere beneficence. Loch's (1883[1977]: 10) guide to 'charitable work', for example, says:

> Two kinds of knowledge are required ...: a knowledge of the social life of the class of which the person in distress is a member ..., and a general knowledge of character – a discernment of the value of evidence, combined with a knowledge of the modes and possibilities of charitable assistance.

Here, again, there is a recognition of the role of social and psychological knowledge, as in the current IFSW international definition of social work (see Table 2.3), and an early instance of the claim of the connection between the social and interpersonal in the mention of 'social life' and of 'character'. In this view, knowledge is about understanding a situation, whereas skill is about capacity for doing something about it. The connection between the two arises because social workers must have the capacity to use knowledge in practice, applying and adapting it to the particular situation that they face. The skill with which they can do so defines the validity of knowledge in a practical activity such as social work. The capacity to reason using knowledge is a crucial element of social work (Lewis, 1982). Knowledge that cannot be applied at best merely contributes to attitudes and contexts. At worst, it may not be useful at all. Skill that cannot use knowledge is less skilled than it might be. Judgements about how knowledge and skill should and should not be used are the province of values, considered in the next chapter.

However, Healy (2005) draws attention to a postmodern view that questions this certainty about knowledge. Instead, knowledges to her are discourses about particular aspects of situations, from particular points of view. Dominant discourses in social work are biomedical, economics and legal, and propose that professional knowledge should be derived from sources validated by social groups that possess power to define our understanding of the world. However, the validation of knowledge in these discourses creates social orders that disadvantage and oppress others, in particular relatively powerless groups from which social work service users are drawn (Askeland and Payne, 2001a). Therapeutic approaches to knowledge draw on the same discourses, but seek to apply them in accordance with personal growth and fulfilment objectives, particularly those drawn from professional knowledges such as psychology and sociology. However, in doing so, they may support the social orders created by the knowledge discourses that they use. Transformational perspectives propose giving priority to knowledge discourses from consumer rights sources and from people's spirituality. Healy (2005: 82–91) also proposes religious discourses, because these are important to people and derive from a powerful social institution, which can provide support for people's own free perceptions of their world. However, religious social institutions can also be oppressive, whereas referring only to spirituality allows us to focus on people's own interpretations of the meaning and importance of different aspects of their personal experience.

## *What is knowledge?*

Knowledge is awareness of or understanding about an external reality; thus, we can know *of* something (that it exists) and know *about* it (its features or character). This statement assumes that there is an external reality, and that it is capable of being known. Moreover, it assumes that the connection between the knowledge and the external reality is uncomplicated. Much of the debate about knowledge in social work is around these assumptions about knowledge. Social work mostly deals with insubstantial things.

Pawson et al (2003) identify five potential knowledge sources in social work:

- organisational knowledge, from social care service management and governance;
- practitioner knowledge, from practice in social care;
- policy community knowledge, from the wider policy community;
- research knowledge, gathered systematically with pre-determined design; and
- user and carer knowledge, gained from experience of using services and reflecting on it.

Mattaini (2002: 97–126) identifies a number of types of knowledge that social workers need to integrate together to use in practice:

- practice wisdom, including rules and guidance explicitly formulated by experienced practitioners and agencies, and less explicitly formulated patterns of practice about how to do things: the tacit knowledge of social work;
- biological, behavioural and cultural sciences, which often provide knowledge about the external reality that social workers interact with;
- practice-relevant research, which provides knowledge about what practice actions have proved effective to achieve particular objectives;
- knowledge from the case, provided by service users and agencies;
- personal experience, which often helps in forming the relationship and process;
- history and current events, which may inform workers about why something is an issue at present for this particular service user;
- cultural perspectives, which provide knowledge about different interpretations of the situation that might be affected by cultural difference;
- art and literature, which often provide insights, metaphors and interpretations to help participants in social work to understand emotionally and intellectually the situation they are involved in; and
- theoretical and conceptual frameworks, which help to order knowledge.

Mattaini's account usefully points out that to act practically involves interacting with a variety of external factors. Therefore you need a variety of ways of knowing from multiple sources. The debate about whether 'evidence-based practice' provides better guidance for action than more qualitative knowledge derived from naturalistic research which focuses on how human beings interpret their surroundings, only refers to a small part of an integrated whole (Gomm and Davies, 2000; Payne, 2005a: ch 3). A related debate refers to social work as a practice, which is therefore artistic rather than scientific (England, 1986; Munro, 1998: ch 3). These debates emphasise different ways of knowing that create different knowledges.

Pawson et al (2003) propose a framework of standards to assess knowledge – TAPUPA, as set out in Table 3.2. This emphasises that the value and veracity of all these different types of knowledge can be assessed critically. So, we do not have to accept without thinking a 'pattern of practice', as Mattaini puts it; we can see where it has come from, how sensibly it is formulated, whether it fits other knowledge about the external reality that we are dealing with and so on.

Most accounts of social work knowledge take a social order perspective on social work; they assume an external reality that can be known and affected by rational decision making based on evidence. This leads to certainty in action, and gives authority to act. Therapeutic

**Table 3.2:** TAPUPA framework standard for assessing knowledge

| Standard | Explanation | Question |
|---|---|---|
| **T**ransparency | The process of generating knowledge should be open to outside scrutiny | Is it open to scrutiny? |
| **A**ccuracy | Knowledge claims should be supported by and be faithful to the events, experiences, informants and sources used in producing it | Is it well grounded? |
| **P**urposivity | The methods used to gain knowledge should be relevant to the stated objectives of the exercise | Is it fit for purpose? |
| **U**tility | Knowledge should be appropriate to the decision setting in which it will be used and the information need that the knowledge seeker expressed | Is it fit for use? |
| **P**ropriety | Knowledge should be created and managed legally, ethically and with care to relevant stakeholders, including their informed consent | Is it legal and ethical? |
| **A**ccessibility | Knowledge should be presented in ways that meet the need of the knowledge seeker | Is it intelligible? |

*Source:* Adapted from Pawson et al (2003)

accounts focus on the ambiguity of knowledge and give priority to the personal knowledges of the participants, in this case authority to act derives from the client's personal choices. Transformational perspectives take authority to act not from expert knowledge but from collective support, particularly from shared personal interpretations of the world, and from consumer movements (Healy, 2005).

## Skills

In the same way that knowledges are seen in different ways, there are also different conceptions of social work skills. There are three ways in which social work skills are seen: as activities undertaken by workers; as personal capacities of social workers; and as competences involved in carrying out social work tasks.

*Activities undertaken by workers:* Compton and Galaway (1999), for example, distinguish between 'tools for deciding what to do', which include engaging with potential clients, communicating, data collection and assessment, and tools for doing the decided, which include interventive methods, case management, mobilising informal support, teamwork and evaluation. Morales and Sheafor (2001: 153) refer to 'two universal social work competencies': 'interpersonal helping and professional competence development' representing '... the most clear indication of a common set of work activities that help to bind social workers into a single profession'. They refer to abilities to understand different aspects of situations, and ability to reflect critically. Coulshed and Orme (1998) refer to practice skills in assessment, care management, community work, counselling, interpersonal and entrepreneurial skills, negotiation and probation work.

*Personal capacities of social workers:* The UK Barclay Report (1982: 151) on the role and tasks of social workers distinguishes three groups of skills: in human relationships, in analysis (assessing people, analysing situations and evaluating outcomes), and in effectiveness (doing what was planned). The National Occupational Standards for Social Work (TOPSS UK Partnership, 2002), which sets what UK social workers need to know in order to practice, does not specify skills, but its 15 mentions of the word include reference to communication, interpersonal, leadership and coordinating skills. The Benchmark Statement, which defines the skills that should be taught in UK social work degrees (QAA, 2000), identifies a range of skills that might be useful in many different situations: analytical thinking, building relationships, working as a member of an organisation, intervention, evaluation and reflection. These vary in their application to social work because they are applied in different contexts, by being given different weights, with problem solving being particularly important. Another example of variation is how different purposes may be achieved by the same skill development, with research skills used in academic development also being focused on investigation of clients' social situations, for example. Another characteristic of social work is the need to integrate a wide range of skills. The Benchmark Statement then identifies five sets of skills that social work students must develop and integrate: communication and information technology and numerical skills, problem-solving skills (including managing problem solving, gathering information, analysis and synthesis, intervention and evaluation), communication skills, skills in working with others and skills in personal and professional development.

*Competences involved in carrying out social work tasks:* These are derived from functional analyses such as the work of Teare and McPheeters (1970), Baker (1976), and BASW (1977). Such analyses break down social work into descriptions of specific activities with which a definable and testable skill can be associated. These can then be integrated into different roles, according to the way an agency wants to organise its work. They can transfer skills more readily from one activity to another, because they have not been learnt as part of a large, complex activity. For example, a role such as social worker for a child in care might involve many of Teare and McPheeters' tasks including advocate, teacher, behaviour changer, care giver, mobiliser of resources, administrator, evaluator and outreach worker from the agency into the community. BASW (1977) would also recognise roles like being an agent of social control, being an adviser, enabler and protector. The worker might see these as childcare skills. If they were learnt separately, however, they could more easily be applied to the role of helping the family of a man with mental ill health support him. The same skills might be applied, using different knowledge, to deal with the problems faced by people with mental ill health in this situation. Skill analyses may therefore be regarded as more generic than client group specialisms.

Trevithick's (2005) handbook is a recent publication using this approach. She divides skills into four groups: communication, listening and assessment skills; basic interviewing skills; providing help, direction and guidance skills; and empowerment, negotiation and partnership skills.

Adams (2002) criticises this competency-based approach because:

- it focuses on areas of expertise most appropriate to stable bureaucratic work settings, rather than developing creativity for future job requirements;
- it encourages fragmentation rather than integration;
- it thinks in convergent ways, so narrowing ideas and focusing on outcomes, rather than being creative about process;
- it focuses on measurable aspects of performance, rather than the incommensurable;
- by focusing on techniques and skills it gives a lower priority to values, critical evaluation and complex knowledge;
- it emphasises acquiring specified techniques rather than developing capacities for critical reflection.

Rosenfeld (1984) presents two broad areas of expertise, in assigning priorities and in inventing interventions. In his (therapeutic) view, the skill of social work lies in the capacity to be creative, rather than in explicit lists of competencies. Even when we examine the more detailed examples of what comes under each heading, such analyses do not help us to clarify or analyse the ability required to take action in social work situations. Ife's (1997: 150) transformational view is that skills are held by both service user and worker, to be shared and used together, rather than reflecting professionally educated abilities reserved to the worker.

Examining some of the commentary and authoritative documents on knowledge and skills over the years suggests, therefore, that these apparently concrete aspects of practice raise issues about the interaction of the three perspectives on social work, just as other aspects of social work practice do.

## Use of self

The interpersonal practice narrative claims that social workers use their own personality and self-understanding as part of what they do, even in structured forms of practice. 'Task-centred practice, like any other social work method, cannot be applied on its own and is dependent on the worker's use of self in the development of a relationship with the person with whom they are working' (Ford and Postle, 2000: 59). Since social work is interpersonal, the personalities of workers and clients must both be involved in the relationship, reflecting, as we saw in Chapter Two, their identities. The relationship must, as we have seen, be genuine and warm, so the worker must feel and convey these feelings. However, the relationship gives workers possibly covert power over the client through having a purpose. As Goldstein (1995: 202) says:

> The crucial issues [in the use of self] are whether the worker is disciplined (consciously purposeful) in using him- or herself in the relationship and bases his or her actions on an assessment of the client.

Therefore, the fact that it is not a friendly and loving relationship must also, for the sake of genuineness, be conveyed.

What is meant by a 'self'? It relates to the notion of identity, since self means having a continuing character that we or others can identify. It means more than a name and more than a body, since it also implies established and characteristic ways of thinking and acting. Shaw (1974: 19-20) summarises the idea of 'self' as follows:

> ... as a result of socialisation, an individual comes to take a partly conscious, partly unconscious view of his own totality. This structure consists of a set of attitudes towards, or beliefs about, one's own needs, goals, abilities, feelings, values, prejudices, self-characteristics and methods of relating to other people.... This structure, or self-view, operates at a number of levels; it acts as a filter through which experience is mediated; it acts as a framework by means of which meaning can be given to experience; it also acts as a guide to decisions, choices and selections of possible alternatives. Once the self-concept is formed it is very resistant to change and comes to constitute the basis on which future psychological development is likely to take place.

The use of self within social work is often associated with the following:

*The aim of personal growth and self-actualisation for clients:* For example, Howe's account of social work theories says (1987: 113-4):

> To help her clients, the social worker must be able to make imaginative use of her own experience, particularly as it occurs in the immediate relationship. The 'use of self' defines both the social worker's practice knowledge and her practice behaviour. The worker must be aware of her own thoughts

> and emotions: if she feels hostile or protective towards the client, she must know this, note it and be prepared to use it.... This intuitive feel of the other person and the effect on oneself produces an understanding that becomes an integral of the worker's self. Thus, the worker gains her understanding, not by a struggle to explore external issues but by articulating her own consciousness. The worker having self-awareness, including understanding and being able to accept and value what is found out about oneself.

*Individuality and creativity in social work:* Davies (1994: 178) argues:

> Each social worker is a unique being, and, since the use of self is one crucial part of her function, it follows that the development of self-confidence is an appropriate ambition in its own right. Social work is a creative job and artistry of the practitioner is a vital component once the other qualities have been mastered.

*Intuition:* England (1986: 32) treats the two concepts as almost identical:

> ... this use of self extends far beyond the worker's emotional involvement and in fact determines the character of his professional knowledge and behaviour. Competence in social work therefore will be found not by seeking to avoid intuition, but by its recognition and development, by the creation of uncommon common sense. Social work is a matter of intuitive understanding, but it must be intuition which is unusually sound, unusually fluent and accessible and subject to unusually careful evaluation.

*Worker style:* Worker style is a characteristic way of acting that develops through workers' training and experience. It may include the acquisition of a theoretical perspective, or with an eclectic self-developed amalgam of perspectives (Brown, 1977). This connects worker style with arguments for the professionalisation of social work. Borel (1997), for example, argues that creating a synthesis of appropriate styles of work permits professional social workers to defend themselves against inappropriate political and managerial incursions, which circumscribe flexible practice.

The idea of use of self presents problems. First, it implies that the workers' approaches to clients will be stable and unchanging. They will have a style, use their stable and continuing personality and respond consistently. This contributes to congruency, but detracts from the possibility of flexibility. Second, it might imply that workers do not take on new ideas and theories once their self has become established. Third, the eclectic and intuitive character that many associate with the idea of worker style raises all the problems of eclecticism: how are ideas selected and integrated? If this is only on personal preference, what is the justification for the selective judgements made? What actions and observations in the relationship and more widely lead to the particular intuitions that the worker feels? The conscious use of self in social work relationships implies that workers are constantly trying to bring intuitions into conscious thought to explore openly the evidence and justification for them.

All these ideas are directly associated with therapeutic conceptions of social work. However, rather than concentrating on the worker's use of self, transformational practice, for example, focuses on how people construct and renew self and identity (Healy, 2000, ch 5; Fook, 2002, ch 6), often in reaction to their difference from others. Therefore, the self may be ambivalent, may incorporate aspects of ourselves that we dislike and resist as well as aspects that we incorporate happily and develop. Dominelli (2002: ch 2) suggests that many social groups that social workers help develop their identities as oppressed people, rather than as susceptible to workers as selves, whereas therapeutic accounts of the use of self assume the possibility of creative relationships between the worker's and client's self. Therapeutic accounts of the use of self focus more on creating a working alliance between worker and client, rather than therapeutic use of self (Cooper and Lesser, 2002: 6).

## Conclusion: interpersonal practice in social work

The narrative of interpersonal practice in social work involves intervention in the lives of clients, using human communication within a relationship, in a process, using specific knowledge and skills and the worker's own self. Practice is also based on values, which are dealt with in Chapter Four. Practice may be seen as a flexible performance of roles in interaction with clients. Alternative conceptions of these elements of practice from each of the three views of social work identified in Chapter One can be seen in the social work literature. While the interpersonal practice narrative is primarily a therapeutic one, practice often takes on social order objectives and may also be reinterpreted in transformational ways. Therefore, the discourse of interpersonal practice, while apparently overwhelmingly therapeutic, is capable of reinterpretation to represent alternative perspectives, or often incorporates elements of the alternatives in a complex whole.

Personal and interpersonal activity of social work with clients often seems to be a coherent account of interpersonal social work in which many features of its nature interlock. However, narratives treating social work only as personal and interpersonal activity are inadequate as a characterisation of the whole. The existence of social order and transformation positions identifies the political nature of accounts of personal/interpersonal social work. Accounts of the use of self, knowledge and skill, relationship and process can be recast to different purposes other than the caring, congruent, interpersonal help model of the therapeutic narrative. Therefore, the balance of the three views that a social worker, agency and welfare regime implements in interpersonal practice incorporates into interpersonal acts the social objectives and context in order to achieve social work's claim to incorporate the interpersonal with the social. Accounts of social work as a personal activity, while apparently simple and understandable, and possibly socially acceptable, are inadequate as full accounts of social work. They convey only part of the truth. Social, political and moral authority for this personal activity is needed before it can be carried out, or before it can achieve useful outcomes. Therefore, the social worker embodies not only personal professional skills and practice in their work, but they also embody particular political and social objectives. The next three chapters focus on how this is also incorporated into interpersonal practice through values, agency management and the use of power.

FOUR

# Social work values: social justice and social care

A doctor telephoned to ask for Mr Cawson's compulsory admission to mental hospital, and was prepared to sign the medical recommendation. Mr Cawson had just made a serious attempt at suicide. A colleague visited his home and discovered that Mrs Cawson was away from work. She was prepared to stay with her husband all the time for a few days. The hospital would offer a psychiatric clinic appointment three days later for assessment and treatment. Mr Cawson would accept that, but he refused to be admitted. He would attend a day centre, but none was available in the area. It was unfortunate, my colleague thought, that Mrs Cawson should have to stay at home because we had no day centre. However, since she could stay with her husband at least until he was seen at the clinic, respecting his human right to freedom of decision making did not justify a compulsory admission. The doctor complained about the social worker questioning his judgement about his patient and that we might have put the patient's life and effective health and social care at risk. We identified several points that potentially raised value issues:

- The conflict between the value of reducing or eliminating a serious risk of death and the value of not restricting the liberty and human rights by compulsorily admitting Mr Cawson to hospital.
- Disagreement that reflected adversely on the judgement of the doctor, a professional colleague and might lead patients to trust him less.
- Compulsion was only considered, and professional activity interfering in the Cawsons' quiet enjoyment of life occurred, because we did not have adequate resources. A day centre would have prevented the issue arising.
- We relied on and applied extra personal pressure to Mrs Cawson as a carer to compensate for our inadequate services. This was another example of exploitation of conventional caring roles of women in place of providing adequate services.
- We were considering compulsion to prevent Mr Cawson committing a legal act that he was free to commit. The mandate for

> our action comes from an assumption that those concerned for general welfare, and perhaps the state, have a duty 'to do the right thing' even when the object of our help does not want it.

Conflicts of view among people involved brought these issues to prominence. Disagreement raises the possibility of alternative views. If most of the time we are not questioned, many actions are informed by unconsidered value judgements. As a result, we often do not deal adequately with the conflicts within clients' own minds. A wider public sanctions social work but is not aware of many doubtful decisions. We would also not have dealt with issues that might concern them. For example, Mr Cawson had to wrestle with the moral issue of committing suicide. Many members of the public would not accept the right to commit suicide as readily as we did. Following professional principles of openness might lead social workers to accept behaviour too readily which the general public or political elites would reject. They pay for and sanction social work powers and responsibilities. Horner and Whitbeck (1991) in the US showed that social workers' personal values differed from those in the general population because they assigned more importance to interpersonal relationships, service to others, open-mindedness and the self-concept. They perceived professional value as differing because social work gave more importance to equality, working for the welfare of others and open-mindedness. This study offers some evidence to support the narrative offered in Chapters Three and Four of the nature of interpersonal social work and its values. Should public views be given priority, since they provide resources and support legislation that social workers implement? If so, how might we know their views? Value issues, then, are important to understanding social work in three different ways:

- the fact that values are an important issue says something about the nature of social work;
- they illuminate social work practice because they are distillations of hard cases, which show how in practice social workers deal with difficult situations;
- they illuminate social work as a profession, by showing us how the institutions of social work have tried to formulate conventions about appropriate actions.

On the first of these points: why is the narrative of interpersonal social work discussed in Chapter Three so concerned to identify social work as a values-based profession? One reason might be that, as we saw in

Chapter Two, having a code of ethics and a practice that derives from altruistic service is an important part of achieving a profession. Second, social work helps with personal problem solving that, as we saw in Chapter Three, involves intrusion into people's private lives, and this needs to be governed appropriately. Third, social work implements particular political and social philosophies in public services, and a values-based practice is one way of identifying conflicts of philosophy and accountability.

However, a crucial complicating factor is social work's claim. Social work claims to incorporate social objectives in personal work; therefore, its actions involve potential conflicts in accountability both with agency, social and political discourses and in the interaction of those discourses with the worker's practice and the discourses taking place in the service user's mind and those of the service user's family and surrounding communities. An accountant worries about behaving ethically between accountability to their client and the public interest. The social worker also has to worry about difficult-to-define factors in the client's family and community, broader social and community philosophies, and how these interact with agency and professional judgements.

Since the three perspectives on social work are ways of responding to the difficulties in making this claim, they represent different approaches to the values base of social work. Therapeutic views focus on the client and their fulfilment, in relation to the family, and see the major conflicts as being conflicts of interest for the user. Social order views focus on the interaction between the state, as represented in the agency, and the needs of the client. Transformational views argue that there are always conflicts and tensions, and the task is to work transparently to allow the interplay to work itself out, compensating for the inequalities and injustices of oppressions in society.

The aim of this chapter is to see how these views are worked out in values debates in social work. First, we look at various attempts to express social work values, then at attempts to resolve some of the difficulties that social workers face in dealing with value conflicts. This leads us to identify the complexities generated by resolution of values difficulties in social work. Finally, we look at the politics of values within social work as a profession: that is, how discourse about the nature of social work is represented in the discourse about values.

## Statements of social work values

The two values present in the IFSW definition of social work (see Table 2.3) concern human rights and social justice. This represents the tension in social work's claim to achieve social improvement between individuals, who have personal rights because of their humanity, and society, whereas the social work profession defines itself as valuing social justice. If these are important, we might ask how social work has tried to implement them. Timms (1983) tried to evaluate a number of attempts:

- to make lists of and try to define relevant values;
- to explore and expand on particular values and see what advantages and problems they present;
- to identify 'disvalues' and their connection with values.

Most effort in considering values in social work has focused on list making and analysis, and some of the outcomes and difficulties of this work are considered in this chapter. The next three sections look at the two main approaches: lists of rules represented in codes of ethics, and then rights-based approaches. I then examine some additional possibilities.

Timms (1983: 66–106) explored three historic conflicts within social work, to identify the value issues that they revealed. The dispute between the Fabian socialists and the Charity Organisation Society (COS) in the early 20th century was about the extent to which social work should accept the civic responsibility to make and act on moral judgements about its clients. The principles of the COS were to see clients and workers as part of the same society, whereas the socialists pointed to social divisions and the distance between worker and client, which suggested that their interests were not the same, and their moral interests might be different. The socialists identified the individualistic method of the COS as a social order perspective focusing on individual failings; they promoted, instead, a transformational approach seeking general political change in social welfare. The debate between functionalist and diagnostic social work counterposed a non-directive therapeutic approach to casework practice to one that was more concerned to take into account social order responsibilities of the agency and more structured practice. The debate about radical social work in the 1970s focused on whether transformational perspectives should displace social order and therapeutic perspectives, which are elided in the radical view. All of these debates are concerned with resolving difficulties in integrating the personal and social elements of social work's claim.

Timms (1983: 61–5) interestingly identifies disvalues in social work, that is, things that it is said social workers should not do, the negatives of positive values. An example is the ethic that a worker should not manipulate people, whereas it is a valued skill to manipulate the environment on behalf of a client. Partly this arises because of a difference in meaning attached to manipulate: manipulation of people is considered to be devious and secretive, while manipulation of the environment is a personally neutral skill. However, this distinction falls apart if we personalise the meaning of 'environment'. Is manipulation of all human beings outlawed, if it is done on behalf of clients? Is it permissible for a worker to manipulate a mother for the benefit of the child, which is environmental manipulation on behalf of the child? Another example: last year I spent some time trying to persuade my local funder of continuing healthcare to be more generous to my hospice's clients. Is it permissible to advocate a change in social policy for the benefit of a client, if the manipulation is not devious, because I tell another agency what I am doing? I am trying to gain this benefit for my client and the principle will benefit other clients. But what if I put up arguments for a change in the legislation, arguing for the point of view of my clients, while realising that spending resources on my clients may disadvantage other groups of people: is that unacceptable?

This example of disvalues illustrates that, because of the claim, not all social work actions are about direct benefit to a particular individual. If they are collective actions, they may involve ambiguous or conflicting values. Therefore, systems of values that focus on individuals, which may work adequately for doctors or counsellors, may be insufficient for social work, but collective actions may involve very complex issues between the interests of different groups.

Another approach to ethics and values is to identify concepts that stimulate workers' imaginations in considering their ethical responsibilities, while focusing on practice. For example, Derezotes (2000) describes love, connection, awareness, non-abusiveness and justice as ethical elements of practice. We often say that a particular worker is caring or sensitive in their approach to clients. This is an example of an agent-based or virtue-based view of ethics: it seems impossible to set rules for behaviour, so instead we look at human attributes that we would like to encourage that represent our view of what our services should be like. This approach acknowledges the way in which, as we saw in Chapter Three, social workers in many senses embody the nature of social work and its conflicts within themselves. However, the main approaches to values in social work have focused on rules expressed in codes of ethics and rights, embodied in lists of principles, and it is to these that we now turn.

## Rules-based approaches: codes of ethics and practice

From the preceding section, we can see that there are complexities in looking at some very simply stated overall principles, like social justice or human rights. However, one answer to this is for the social work profession to gain from experience a more detailed set of statements that indicate the ethical rules we should follow. We may see social work value conventions most extensively set out in formal statements of social work ethics contained in codes of ethics and practice. IFSW has expanded on the definition by creating international guidance on principles of practice (IFSW, 2004). In addition to these, many national organisations of social workers have produced their own codes of ethics (accessible from IFSW, 2005). The US has a range of specialist social work bodies, many producing their own statements of ethical or practice principles. Regulatory bodies also produce standards of practice; the Care Councils for the UK nations, for example, have agreed a code of practice for social care workers and their employers (see Table 4.1). These all, in effect, produce what Timms (1983) called 'lists' of values that we should pay attention to. However, the problem with a list is that it is often not complex enough to deal with actual situations that we might face.

Banks (2001: ch 5) compares 20 social work codes of ethics from around the world. She notes that in general they:

- are based on implementing principles, such as self-determination and confidentiality, rather than on identifying 'virtues', such as integrity or honesty, that social workers should embody;
- establish rights and duties, rather than promoting utilitarian approaches to ethical decisions, which establish principles for making decisions according to their benefits for stakeholders.

Important aspects of many codes are:

- the principle of respect for persons (Downie and Telfer, 1969); and
- user self-determination;
- concerns for social justice; and
- professional integrity;
- identification of a range of duties to different interests, such as users, colleagues, and employers;
- identification of practice issues such as advertising, fees, use of video recording, and confidentiality.

**Table 4.1:** UK Social Care Councils: codes of practice

**Code for employers**

Social care employers must:

- make sure people are suitable to enter the workforce and understand their robs and responsibilities;
- have written policies and procedures in place to enable social care workers to meet the General Social Care Council (GSCC) code of practice for social care workers;
- provide training and development opportunities to enable social care workers to strengthen and develop their skills and knowledge;
- put in place and implement written policies and procedures to deal with dangerous, discriminatory or exploitative behaviour and practice; and
- promote the GSCC's codes of practice to social care workers, service users and carers and cooperate with the GSCC's proceedings.

**Code for social care workers**

Social care workers must:

- protect the rights and promote the Interests of service users and carers;
- strive to establish and maintain the trust and confidence of service users and carers;
- promote the independence of service users while protecting them as far as possible from danger or harm;
- respect the rights of service users while seeking to enure that their behaviour does not harm themselves or other people;
- uphold public trust and confidence in social care services; and
- be accountable for the quality of their work and take responsibility for maintaining and improving their knowledge and skills.

*Source:* GSCC (2005); also available from Northern Ireland,Wales and Scottish Councils

A number of difficulties arise with codes of ethics and practice, summarised in Table 4.2.

A further difficulty of codes of ethics, identified by Banks (2001: 102-6), is that they assume professional autonomy, whereas social workers are often mainly directed by the organisational rules of their agencies. Indeed, this has sometimes led commentators to doubt the professional standing of social work (see Chapter Five). Consequently, Banks argues that it might be better to explore how and by whom professionals' practice is controlled, and to evaluate the claims advanced to give reasons for the control; this is the approach I take in Chapters Five and Six.

The conventions of codes of ethics and practice, therefore, do not offer absolute standards of what is right or wrong in social work practice. They represent the view arrived at for now of a suitable approach to

**Table 4.2:** Difficulties with codes of ethics and practice

| Assumption | Alternative perspectives |
|---|---|
| Codes come from the profession | ... but ethics may equally come from the worker's own values |
| Much social work cannot be expressed as rules and duties | ... they may come from cultivating attitudes such as compassion and respect |
| Codes are connected with one profession | ... but work is increasingly multiprofessional; other professionals may not be concerned about the same issues, or their codes may have priority |
| Codes assume accountability to the user | ... but professionals also have to exert social control, may also be responsible for other family or community members, and may have to manage resources or priorities |
| Codes assume consensus on values within the profession, and with other professions and the public | ... but users, other professionals and public opinion interpreted by the media and politicians may assert other values as more important |

*Source:* Adapted from Banks (2001: 107)

practice. Moreover, if they are only views that have become the professional convention for the present, they might change or be renewed. If so, what appears to be a clear standard hides the fundamental uncertainty of the discourse that it, for the moment, represents. This is made clear by the IFSW statement of problem areas in the implementation of social work values (see Table 4.3). They identify the existence of many complexities in implementing widely accepted statements of social work values.

## Rights-based approaches – human rights and social work

An alternative to rules-based approaches to resolving values issues is considering human rights. There are a number of international conventions on human rights: Table 4.4 sets out some of those thought relevant to social work by IFSW (2005). The political importance of rights, the fact that they are built into many legal systems and the clarity and complexity with which they are set out in the various conventions has given them a wide currency. For example, a European

**Table 4.3:** IFSW ethical problem areas

**2.3 Problem areas**

2.3.1. The problem areas raising ethical issues directly are not necessarily universal due to cultural and governmental differences.... The following problem areas are, however, widely recognized:

1. when the loyalty of the social worker is in the middle of conflicting interests
   - between those of the social worker[']s own and the clients
   - between conflicting interests of individual clients and other individuals
   - between the conflicting interests of groups of clients
   - between groups of clients and the rest of the population
   - between systems/institution and groups of clients
   - between system/institution/employer and social workers
   - between different groups of professionals
2. the fact that the social worker functions both as a helper and controller The relation between these two opposite aspects of social work demands a clarification based on an explicit choice of values in order to avoid a mixing-up of motives or the lack of clarity in motives, actions and consequences of actions. When social workers are expected to play a role in the state control of citizens they are obliged to clarify the ethical implications of this role and to what extent this role is acceptable in relation to the basic ethical principles of social work.
3. the duty of the social worker to protect the interests of the client will easily come into conflict with demands for efficiency and utility This problem is becoming important with the introduction and use of information technology within the fields of social work.

*Source:* www.ifsw.org/home (accessed 19 March 2005)

**Table 4.4:** International conventions

International human rights declarations and conventions form common standards of achievement, and recognise rights that are accepted by the global community. Documents particularly relevant to social work practice and action are:

- Universal Declaration of Human Rights
- The International Covenant on Civil and Political Rights
- The International Covenant on Economic Social and Cultural Rights
- The Convention on the Elimination of all Forms of Racial Discrimination
- The Convention on the Elimination of All Forms of Discrimination against Women
- The Convention on the Rights of the Child
- Indigenous and Tribal Peoples Convention (ILO convention 169)

*Source:* IFSW (2005)

analysis (EASSW, 1995) examines concepts of legal rights, citizenship, rights to participation, service, cultural sensitivity, children's rights. Giving value to aesthetic and expressive work all comes out of consideration of how being human is relevant to rights.

Ife (2001) discusses human rights as a moral basis for social work. He identifies three generations of human rights. The approach and practice within the first generation is procedural or distributive justice. This means that procedures treat everyone equally, and that resources are distributed by fair processes (Weale, 1978). The advantage of this approach is that human rights under it can be clearly defined and enforced, whereas rights in the other two generations are more subject to debate and complexity. Techniques such as advocacy, user participation and feedback, promoting values such as self-determination, and effective complaints systems and regulation are all social work responses. Most of these responses are social order responses: they focus on maintaining a just social order, within the social systems as they are at present.

Second generation human rights issues focus more clearly on inequalities between groups in a divided society, and the way in which we discriminate against particular groups. This refers to substantive equality (Weale, 1978), that is, equality in the outcomes or benefits that people receive should be our objective, rather than equity in how we treat people. The response might be to change practice and organisations so that they recognise and try to deal with inequalities. For example, the numbers of people from minority ethnic groups referred to my hospice are not proportionate to the population we serve. Therefore, we have instituted diversity policies in staffing and service provision, for example making available more culturally appropriate food in our menus, and we have increased the range of religions regularly represented in our building and our work. We have also encouraged expression from cultural minorities in our therapeutic programmes, surveyed and interviewed people who refer patients to us and run programmes to persuade them that we do provide culturally appropriate services. We have also trained staff to be aware of possible discrimination and to avoid unconscious racism and sexism. In this way, we hope to move away from assumptions that Western behaviour and environments will always be appropriate for our patients, and gender-oriented assumptions about our services. For example, we have started to provide more complementary therapies, which women who are in the majority like, but have also offered artistic activities, which men do not see as masculine, using computer and digital technology, so that men are able to take advantage of art therapies within their own preferences. The point about such approaches is that we recognise that social divisions exist and lead to particular reactions of our service, and it is important to respond to the consequences of those divisions in providing more equal services.

The third generation focuses on underlying assumptions in societies that prevent equality which often seem a long way from social work. An example is the way older people are prevented from taking advantage of the cheap food available in out-of-town supermarkets, because they do not have cars to transport heavy shopping. Internationally inequalities in food subsidies advantage Western countries, so that cheap food in Western societies impoverishes resource-poor nations. In the hospice where I work, we have allocated resources to educate palliative care professionals in resource-poor countries, to even up some of the inequalities between developing/ non-industrialised and industrialised countries. This also has second generation consequences, because we learn techniques for provision of services with very few resources, which we can use to make our own provision more effective, and our staff gain cultural experience of countries where minority ethnic groups in our area come from. Recognising that we will never have the resources to provide full-scale palliative care to everyone in our locality, we have developed education programmes to help local communities and schools respond more effectively to the emotional and practical difficulties of people dying and bereaved in their communities.

## Alternative approaches to ethics

Banks (2004) identifies a number of other ways in which ethics have been considered in the social professions. She divides them into approaches that seek to be impartial (the first four), and those that are situated (the last four), that is, they argue the value of a particular point of view.

- Principle-based values, which take the position that values can be reduced down to a number of core ethical principles, for example:
    - Kant's principle of 'respect for persons';
    - Mill's utilitarianism: 'the greatest good of the greatest number';
    - the contractarian view of 'principles to which everyone would agree' of which the best known is Rawls' principle 'to seek the greatest liberty for individuals compatible with the liberty of others, with inequalities arranged to benefit the least advantaged'.

- Rights-based values, which involve protecting important rights including the rights to life and liberty, or freedom of speech or faith, from being encroached on by others.
- Discourse-based ethics, in which principles for formulating values positions are established, such as wide, rational and uncoerced involvement in creating value principles.
- Case-based ethics, or casuistry, which involves examining the principles arrived at in major cases and using these as broader principles, as in the law of precedent.
- Agent-focused ethics, which focus on the virtues of the person making the moral decision, for example whether it is made with good intentions, and respecting the cultural preferences of those involved. More broadly, Wilkes (1985) argues that a historical conception of the professional is one who has been trained in thoughtful and critical habits of mind and is therefore better able to deal with complexity and difficulty.
- Community-based ethics, for example, communitarianism (Etzioni, 1995), which focus on the need for a good communal life as an important basis for human beings flourishing, and therefore examine whether behaviour promotes cooperation and solidarity.
- Relationship-based ethics focus on the importance of human relationships, particularly, in the case of feminist views (Gilligan, 1982), the duty of caring for others, rather than seeking rights and justice.
- Other-based ethics, which focus on responsibility for those around us, particularly those in close proximity to us.

A number of these approaches are relevant to social work. Case-based ethics are useful when working with user groups; for example, we look at intentions in judging whether a child in care has behaved appropriately in residential care and at cultural appropriateness in judging a social worker's intervention. We look at whether someone has made a good contribution to their community, or is caring beyond the call of duty, or responds to help with problems around them. Many of these ideas get mixed up together in thinking about people.

Beckett and Maynard (2005: ch 3) point to religion as a source of ethics. While social work codes have often excluded workers' personal values, and in particular emphasise the humanistic (and therefore secular) origins of social work, Christianity is an important historic origin of social concern and social services. Christianity motivates many individual workers. Increasingly, other religions such as Buddhism, Hinduism, Islam and Sikhism, are important in societies where they did not originate, or where other religions are dominant. Therefore, there may be differences in ethical approach between religions, and differences in the importance given to religions as a source of ethical behaviour in social work practice. This means that looking at potential religious differences in ethics becomes more important in practice, as services in all societies have to represent and respond to values that are not from the dominant culture or religion.

Another important source of values is political philosophy (Clark, 2000), since different approaches to the role of the state assume different principles for dealing with people. Different views taken of the people that social work serves according to different political philosophies are summarised in Table 4.5. This draws attention to the way in which some of the ideas of practical values in social work already discussed also connect with social and political ideas. They relate to difficult distinctions. For example, people may feel that they have rights as human beings, as consumers, as citizens, as community members and in caring relationships; others might define those rights differently.

Moreover, conflicts over religious belief and political ideologies often symbolise feelings of breakdown and conflict in the coherence and strength of communities and societies (Hough and Briskman, 2003). Concerns about terrorism, conflict over asylum seekers and similar broad political debates, with an ethical dimension often concerning human rights, seem to be overwhelmingly complex, requiring people to confront social movements and change in ways that ethical debates about issues that affect individuals do not. Different views about people's rights to commit suicide or to help a disabled relative die can seem

**Table 4.5:** Views of welfare and views of service users

| View of welfare | View of user | Explanation |
|---|---|---|
| Social democratic | Client | State has a duty to care for people in need |
| Consumerist | Consumer/user | State provides services according to individual choice |
| Communitarian | Member | Welfare is an exchange for community contributions |
| Feminist | Partners in care | Caring derives from ongoing relationships with people |
| Citizenship sharing | Citizen | Rights to welfare arise from increases in prosperity |

*Source:* Clark (2000, 2002)

impossibly difficult, but do not face societies with the need for resolving broad religious and political conflict as well. Thus, current ethical issues seem to present us with concerns about whether and how we can maintain present social and community strengths, and this leads to widespread fear and uncertainty, which heightens the sense of conflict and difficulty of these new social issues. This may particularly affect professionals where trust in services breaks down, either because oppression and inequality has affected the attitudes of particular service users, or because in general there is lower trust in professionals and public services and greater demands for choice and freedom (Banks, 2004: ch 6).

## Values complexities: maps of the minefield of practice

Value statements always represent complexities in relationships and imply debates between value statements and their alternatives. A code of ethics is a map of the minefield of practice. Each of its simple prescriptions identifies a complexity. Apparently clear value statements guiding practice conceal wide variability and the availability of alternatives. Taking a complexities approach (Adams et al, 2005), however, sees guidance and prescription as presenting an agenda for action, rather than a final formulation. Rather, guidance draws attention to where social workers have found that there are often issues to be addressed. Table 4.6 takes some social work principles and identifies some of the complexities that lead to discourses within social work value debates.

Thus, for example, the rule of confidentiality presumes a duality: that we must also know about and understand openness, its opposite. To explore this through complexity thinking requires us to examine how those opposites may be relevant to each other and incorporated together; it is more than a duality of confidentiality-openness. Many situations require confidentiality, but many require openness. Social workers must consider the degree to which each is appropriate and provide protection for people when confidentiality may lead to risk for individuals or when openness may lead to distress. It is a widely accepted convention that workers should keep secret matters imparted to them in confidence during their work. However, there are widely accepted exceptions to this convention. We can breach confidentiality when life is at risk or perhaps where it benefits the client. Usually, though, we would not do so without consulting them, unless the matter is urgent. We might not bother consulting them if an

**Table 4.6:** Value complexities

| Value | Duality | Complexity |
|---|---|---|
| Individualisation | Collectivisation | When do we individualise clients' needs, or deal collectively with shared interests? Eg people on a housing estate who want to change their environment and how repairs to their houses are carried out |
| Acceptance | Anti-dependency | How do we balance acceptance of need for help with the process of helping people to become independent? Eg parents who make their child with learning disabilities too dependent on their care |
| Being non-judgemental | Critical evaluation, confrontation | How do we balance being non-judgemental, with the need to critically evaluate behaviour, and confront unsatisfactory behaviour and social realities? Eg when protecting children from abuse |
| Anti-discriminatory approach | Avoid labelling and victimising | How do we balance breaking down barriers caused by inappropriate discrimination, but also avoid people in minority or oppressed groups from feeling picked out, avoid pressing them to take on battles that they cannot afford or cope with and avoid treating them as always the victims instead of having influence and freedom of action? Taking an anti-discriminatory approach sometimes involves focusing on aspects of life that label and victimise. Clients and workers often differ about the value of expressing or avoiding difference as part of anti-discriminatory practice |
| Self-determination | Rule-following or interdependent | How do we help people to be more autonomous, when often they should be interdependent? Everyone follows rules and conventions of behaviour: to be self-determining implies partly that one can choose whether or not or how to be rule-following |
| Respect for people | Respect for community | How do we respect individuals' needs, but also heed the value of community support and involvement? At times, wider social networks take priority over individuals |
| Confidentiality | Openness | How do we promote confidentiality and openness at the same time? Confidentiality is a decision to limit openness; openness is a decision to forego confidentiality in favour of openness for some reason |

unimportant breach was to another professional whom we are sure would keep confidentiality. Exceptions to an apparently clear rule involve complex judgements in real life. In different settings, different levels of importance might be given to injunctions and exceptions. For example, I was involved with a child advocacy service, which represents the views of young people to agencies who are responsible for caring for them. The service had a principle of not telling the agencies anything without the permission of the young person, unless a life was at risk. This was because it is the service's job to represent, and therefore to be on the side of, the young person, and only the young person, and their views. The agencies were accustomed, being usually concerned with the child's 'best interests', to being told matters of concern by other professionals, without the young person being consulted. This example underlines the actual variability of the application of the confidentiality convention in everyday practice. To go further, the confidentiality convention is a cultural assumption, based on the individualism characteristic of most Western societies. In many societies, the accepted approach to dealing with an individual's problems is to involve friends, neighbours and community in the resolution. Silavwe (1995) gives an example of this while discussing social work in Zambia. Helping with a family problem there would involve relying on the extended family, the tribe and elders. This places the authority for intervention clearly with the people around the person or people affected. Sometimes, it places the worker in a position of, in effect, giving consultation to others who are working to resolve issues in their community – genuine community care. Western social workers also involve family members or neighbours in therapy or care for someone in need, but usually they negotiate the degree of openness required. Once others are involved, however, we move into an open rather than a closed situation. This might have gains, in strength of support and understanding, authority to act and in commitment. We must balance these against losses in privacy, unpressurised self-motivation and freedom of thought and action for worker and client.

Many other complexities have been identified within particular social work principles. Campbell (1978) suggested that welfare services are often seen as provided 'as of right', but this is limited by:

- the discretion of the people who make decisions within the system;
- the capacity of people or the knowledge available to do the work; for example, if not enough trained workers are available who are competent to do the job, it may be better not to seek your right to

provision; equally, we cannot have the right to a medical or social work treatment that has not been created or researched yet;
- the availability of resources; and
- the idea that it would be unethical to offer a service, or start to provide it, if the resources available will not permit you to complete its provision.

Stalley (1978) similarly argues that social workers do not have just one aim, in relation to a clear focus on a single client, but deal with families, and broader social objectives represented in social work and in their agencies. Leighton (1985) points out how personal values of the worker, a client, members of the client's family, and professional values of workers and colleagues may all interact in a case.

Social workers play a moral role in society, deciding in complex social situations who and what is right and wrong (Payne, 1999). For example, in childcare assessments in the UK, they are often expected to make moral judgements about blame, and responsibility for parental failings (White, 2003). Political and social criticism of social work often arises because of a perception that social work is claiming moral neutrality in pursuit of professional impartiality, when 'society expects' a moral decision about who is a good parent, or child. In providing many welfare services, social work cannot be morally neutral since the services are created as social rewards, or restricted resources mean that services cannot be universally offered. In both cases, moral decisions are required rather than neutral ones. Anti-oppressive and anti-discriminatory practice ideas are at least in part an attempt to validate an alternative morality.

Making value judgements in social work, therefore, often means making complex judgements in ambiguous situations. This suggests that the rules or rights often set out firmly in official statements of codes of ethics cannot be sustained. Conventions or guidelines may allow more flexibility about suitable approaches to that practice, in a way that arises from the political situation within the occupational group. Gill (1992) argues that there are 'moral communities' which have arrived at an agreed position about the approach that they will take to issues that involve ethical decisions. These positions derive from tradition and shared experience in that group. Thus, while we cannot arrive at a particular view about a situation that all people would agree with, it may be possible to recognise an 'occupational ethic' with which many social workers would agree. We noted some evidence, above, that social workers at least in one country do view the world differently from the general public and therefore from such a moral community. Also, values cannot be represented unless workers have faced and appreciated the relevant issues. For example, greater priority was given to anti-discriminatory principles in the 1980s. Such principles are consistent with ideas of respect for people and acting in an unprejudiced way, which might come from the sort of principles we have been discussing. They came to prominence in the 1980s because of larger numbers of minority ethnic groups in some important Western societies. There was also rising social conflict around gender and especially minority ethnic groups in countries formerly assumed to be ethnically homogeneous. Thus, an implied and assumed value becomes explicit, and then is refined and debated. It therefore becomes an important element in social work debate. Until it became an issue, however, it had no chance to develop as a value. Who knows what other important professional values are lurking, unthought of, awaiting their period of topical relevance? Who knows what groups of people are being oppressed and ignored because the profession has not yet faced an issue about them?

Reamer (1999) has tried to deal with this issue by devising rules for organising thinking where value complexities arise (see Table 4.7). However, he does not claim that they may resolve all complexities. What such guidelines do is help to identify issues and allow people to begin thinking.

IFSW's 'problem areas' of practice that often raise issues for social workers in practice (see Table 4.3) is another useful basis for complexity thinking. The first of these is where different interests are in conflict: individual interests, such as conflicts between clients, family members, and members of the community and institutional interests, such as conflicts between clients, the agency, other agencies and professions. Such conflicts are another example of the tension in social work's 'claim' to connect the personal with the social. Social workers face these problem areas because, unlike many healthcare, counselling and other professionals, they cannot say 'the patient' or 'the client' must be the most important. The reason for this is that they claim to make connections between the individual and the social.

The second and third areas are special examples of this difficulty for social work. Being a helper and controller focuses on situations where the social worker faces conflicts between client and agency, or between general social expectations and the expectations of clients to receive help, or the social worker to be primarily a helper.

The third problem area focuses on conflicting interests between general pressures for efficient organisation, and the right and need of people to be less than efficient. At first sight, this is a special example

**Table 4.7:** Reamer's guidelines for thinking through value complexities

| Guideline | Complexity | Example |
|---|---|---|
| Rules against basic harms take precedence over rules against harms caused by human lapses and over additive goods | Not all values have the same degree of importance | Life, health, food, shelter (basic harms) are more important than lying or confidentiality and recreation, education or wealth |
| Individuals' rights to well-being take precedence over another's right to self-determination | Different people's rights conflict | Protecting a child from abuse is more important than a relative's freedom to pursue their religious belief eg, in the need to free the child by violence from possession by spirits |
| Individuals' rights to self-determination take precedence over their rights to well-being | People experience conflict over their different rights | An elderly person can return home, even though we fear that they will not be able to care for themselves properly |
| Obligations to obey laws that we have consented to override our freedom to pursue our desires and interests | Law and formal policy conflicts with our freedoms | A worker should implement the law even though it adversely affects a client, seeking to change it afterwards or leaving that work |
| Individuals' rights to well-being may override laws and regulations | Laws and formal policy conflict with our well-being | A worker might refuse to visit a client, if it places their safety at risk |
| The obligation to prevent basic harms and promote public goods overrides the right to control over property | Personal interests conflict with public services | A worker may insist on gaining entrance to a building to assess the situation where there is a credible allegation of abuse of a vulnerable child or adult |

*Source:* Adapted and expanded from Reamer (1999: 72-5)

of the first problem area: agencies have to be efficiently organised, and this conflicts with people's needs for time and trouble. For example, it may be efficient to arrange for a hospital bed to be vacated quickly when Joan's condition has improved so that she may be discharged, because this makes the hospital's resources available to someone else who needs them more. However, arrangements need to be made for Joan's care at home after discharge. At some point, Joan might have to give up her home and move to a nursing home; this is a decision to change her whole life to such an extent that anyone would need to think through the ramifications of it before agreeing to it. Giving time to allow for this 'thinking through' does not get the hospital beds efficiently used.

## Politics of values and social work professionalisation

This chapter has been concerned to identify social work's discourse about values. Values and ethics have been important to social work for many of the reasons that they are to other professions, as a representation of their altruism and social mission, and as guidance in dealing with difficult issues. However, I argued at the outset that they are more important to social work than that, because of the difficulty of social work's claim to incorporate the social in the personal, and to achieve social improvement through personal intervention. This means that the social and the personal have particularly complex interactions for social workers thinking what to do in daily situations.

To deal with these issues, extensive debate about social work values has created a variety of ways of considering values issues, but this has had little impact on everyday practice. This is because ethical codes, values debate and literature:

- are used for socialising and educational purposes; most workers do not refer to values regularly, and are only introduced to them specifically when in training;
- are political documents in the public domain used to present or represent social work in the ways that it would like to be understood in public.

Often this means that codes of ethics are presented as conventional, acceptable guidelines, and represent a social order view of social work, rather than representing the possible complexities. As Watson (1985) argues, they offer an opportunity to the public to test out social work actions. They also alert workers and clients to areas where they might make complaints, or where adjudication about issues is needed. These last two reasons refer to the effect of value documents being in the public domain. Both their educational and political purposes lead to simplifications, since complexities are unsuitable both for people who are used to social work decision making and public debate.

The therapeutic view of priority to the client is also unsustainable in a social work that claims incorporation of social objectives into, and achievement of social improvement from, interpersonal practice. Thus, ethical codes and values debate in social work maintains the claim in the face of potential oversimplification in therapeutic objectives. Both therapeutic and social order views of social work would probably see transformational views as revelling in the complexities that value debate reveals, because the complexities show up unsustainable conflicts in the present social system, leaving it ripe for change. But transformation is confronted, in value debate, by the complexity of its objective, and this fact leads to a retreat for many social workers into social order and therapy.

## Conclusion

This chapter, and Chapter Three, have focused on interpersonal social work, the starting point and the centre of many perceptions of what social work is about. Interpersonal social work emerged from a therapeutic discourse, but is also capable of interpretation within social order and transformational perspectives. Values discourses attempt to create a moral social order for social work, but the complexities of doing so in the face of social work's claim keep on breaking through the attempt at order. The next two chapters examine other attempts to provide an order for social work. But, a warning: these prove complex as well, so if there are no easy answers to the social ordering of social work to be found in the values discourse, neither are they to be found in management or power.

FIVE

# Social work, management and the agency

I work in a hospice, a charitable voluntary organisation providing care for people who are dying and bereaved and their families and carers. One of my jobs is to organise volunteers. Mr and Mrs Evans came to see me about becoming volunteers in our social care day centre; they seemed pleasant, committed and competent, and had got over the death of Mrs Evans' father at the hospice more than two years previously. They were checked to see if health problems or criminal records prevented their involvement with vulnerable people. Everything was satisfactory and they began work. At the same time, they involved their teenage children in fundraising, as a practical way of teaching them social responsibility. After a while, Mrs Evans applied to become a volunteer bereavement counsellor. She did the training and started work, but there were concerns about her practice, and the social worker who supervised her decided she should no longer do this work. She was offended by this decision, and felt that her contribution to the hospice in the past had been devalued. The fundraising director came to see me, to ask if the decision could be changed, because their contribution at the hospice was valuable, and as the Evans were directors of a successful business, they could potentially be large donors through a legacy when they died. I tried to get them reinvolved in the day centre, but Mrs Evans' husband supported her in withdrawing from the hospice, and they all withdrew from involvement in the hospice. We then found that several other people who were friends of theirs also began to criticise the hospice.

## Social work is agency-based

Social work is usually carried out in agencies. Even if it is a piece of individual private practice, the organisation of the practice is like a simple agency. It requires clarity about the kind of work that will be undertaken, for example, enough to advertise the service, and arrangements for dealing with inquiries, payments and facilities for clients. More commonly, social work is part of an official organisation, where social workers act on behalf of the state, and therefore their work is conditioned by political and social policies expressed through the law. Sometimes, it is done within a private or voluntary sector agency, and they must accord with the business plans and objectives of the organisation.

This chapter deals with two related issues for social work that arise from its agency base.

- Does the fact that social work is always practised in agencies mean that it is not a professional activity? Some views of professionalisation in social work (see Chapter Seven) claim that it cannot be a profession, because social workers do not usually have an important characteristic of full professions – independent discretion in taking their professional decisions. Instead, they are subject to the legal mandate and managerial control of the agency that employs them. Doctors, lawyers and ministers of religion are not employed in the same way and can therefore have more direct control over their practice.
- Is the management of agencies damaging to social work practice? The fact that social work, rather than being controlled independently by the profession itself, is subject to agency management makes it subject to trends in management and political thinking. In particular, management has become a much more powerful aspect of political responsibility and more controlling in the last quarter of the 20th century.

We understand the relationship between social work and the agency in three different ways:

- as a professional–organisation relationship
- as a managed relationship
- as a complex structure of accountabilities.

The professional–organisation approach sees the organisation as a context, which facilitates effective professional practice and enables the organisation's services to be delivered using professional practice. Social workers are seen as 'bureau-professionals', who are slotted into a hierarchical pyramid of responsibilities. Each level in the hierarchy is accountable for their work to a higher level, and delegated with authority to act from the higher level. Within this, the professional receives a wide discretion, within defined limits, for carrying out the work. This is necessary, because, as we saw in Chapter Three, social work is a 'performance', that varies widely, depends on the skills, knowledge and values that the worker embodies, and cannot be observed or checked from records. It is also useful to the organisation because social care services deal with complex issues in people's lives rather than matters that can be resolved by systematic rules.

The managed relationship approach gives priority to the agency's political and social mandate, as expressed through the organisation. In public organisations, responsibility and resources descend from a body whose power comes from the fact that it is democratically elected. In private and voluntary organisations, it descends from a board appointed by those who have set the objectives (in British company law, which also applies to most voluntary organisations, a memorandum and articles of association) and financed the organisation.

The complex structure view expresses some of the unstated complexities in the previous two models. Organisations balance various forms of accountability, often in an informal way. We may see the case of Mr and Mrs Evans in this way. The bereavement service is accountable for its professional standards of service through the organisation, and also to the bereaved people who are being helped. The organisation is also accountable to its community. One way of getting redress for their dissatisfaction is for Mr and Mrs Evans to complain about their treatment to the trustees of the organisation. Another way is for them and their friends to reduce their financial commitment to the hospice. If this becomes widespread, the future of the hospice's finance is endangered. Exactly the same thing happens by a less direct route with public bodies. If people perceive social work as unhelpful or wrong, by not helping people who want to adopt children to do so, or by being too authoritarian in taking children into care, public criticism can lead to loss of political support and finance from government, or to the reorganisation of services to exclude social work, or reduce its importance. Maintaining accountability to public and community support has to be balanced with standards as seen by professionals. Agencies provide a structure to maintain that balance, and management is the activity that makes that structure work. In achieving these balances, both must at times conflict with pure adherence to the sort of professional values we examined in Chapter Four.

In this way, agencies inject social order requirements into social work practice, because they require acknowledgement of political and social influences on the nature of social work. A purely therapeutic view of social work might reject that influence, in favour of accountability solely to the client. However, as we saw in Chapters Three and Four, therapeutic work involves a relationship in which the worker embodies social work's broader social objectives and values. Therefore, political and social objectives are incorporated into therapeutic work, but in a less transparent way than where a care manager openly carries out an assessment for provision of a public service, according to politically derived criteria and priorities.

Including a social order perspective into the therapeutic perspective on social work requires us to recognise the political and social pressures within it, in a way that many professions find it less easy to analyse. In social work, the analysis is easier, although this does not make it any easier to do something about social and agency pressures as we work. It is possible to identify and analyse the processes by which the agency operates to control and intervene in social work practice. I also argue that because the social order perspective is not inimical to the therapeutic core of social work, both become entwined in the agency. In this way, social work tames the agency and learns to live with it. The agency becomes adapted to the needs of semi-autonomous social work, as social work adapts to the power of the agency.

The question to ask about this symbiosis is whether, in accepting the agency's power, and taming it a little, therapeutic social work becomes so allied with social order it denies social work's transformational objectives. The transformational view would say that, in being seduced by and seducing the agency's power, social work abandons its potential alliance with the oppressed people who are the clientele and the justification for social work's claim of the incorporation of the interpersonal with the social.

## Social work agencies and management

Social work grew up in three important management settings:

- state provision for the poorest people, most recently Poor Law workhouses;
- rescue and reform movements, particularly in charities;
- hospitals and municipal services provided through agencies whose main purpose, for example, education, healthcare and housing, was not social provision.

Many welfare developments developed to respond to the increasing complexity of industrialised societies in the 19th century (Payne, 2005c). They often involved large residential institutions. Management in the Poor Law was of large municipal bureaucracies, locally administered, following central government policies. Rescue and reform movements, like Dr Barnardo's children's homes and many other charities dealing with a myriad of practical social problems, were more individualistic social enterprises, often managed locally. However, coordination became an important objective in the early 20th century. Hospitals and schools increasingly became the responsibility of the state as the 20th century progressed, and social work found a place in them to deal with various personal and emotional complexities that emerged and obstructed their main purposes. However, their main focus was, for example, medical or educational, so social work was a secondary provision.

As all these systems of social provision came together in the mid-20th century to form the social services, several features of their management developed into a socially planned bureaucratic system:

- political and social objectives were formed by a socially concerned elite, who influenced cultural assumptions about appropriate social responses and as magistrates, local authority councillors and members of charity management committees took part in organising and setting policy for social welfare organisations;
- social workers became mainly state-sponsored bureau-professionals, working in fairly small local authority departments;
- voluntary organisations and healthcare organisations provided alternative settings for practice that offered greater freedom for alternative forms of practice, because they allowed independence from state responsibilities and medical assumptions supported independent discretionary professional practice.

These settings provided a protected environment for the development of independent professional practice in the UK. A similar pattern of development was experienced in many other Western countries, under the international influence of the primarily therapeutic perspective of North American social casework (see Chapter Two), which could be used in many social order forms of social work.

The social services reorganisation of 1971 in England and Wales, implementing the Seebohm Report of 1968, and the linked local government and health services reorganisations of 1974, created a new environment. The main social work organisation became a large and locally politically important and more visible agency. At the same time, charities and voluntary organisations developed community work roles of critic and change agent for local communities, and a consumer movement developed, in which eventually service user participation in, and rights to influence and choice over, services became important.

Later still, a carers movement sought the same influence and rights for carers of people receiving health and social care services. A policy of corporate management, in which the services of local authorities were to be managed together, and the creation of much larger public bodies in local government and the health service seemed to require more effective management. In particular, 'consensus management' in the health service, in which different professional groups negotiated from their different areas of expertise, came to be seen as ineffective, even though a degree of recognition of different perspectives and interaction between them is essential, and now promoted through multiprofessional work (see Chapter Seven).

Harris (2003: 17) identifies four levels of management in this system:

- central government, setting policy and overall guidelines and developing legal and administrative systems;
- local government, in which corporate management by local politicians and senior managers coordinated a strategy to achieve overall provision to meet the needs of its area;
- middle management, which implemented policy, managed resources and set standards;
- front-line management, which supported and directed professional practice, often through professional supervision of work in particular cases.

Professional practice was at the bottom of this heap, and led to the criticism of heavy bureaucracy stifling independent professional discretion, derived from the medical model of independent professional judgement (Glastonbury et al, 1980). There was equally a criticism from a community, consumerist and carer perspective of lack of responsiveness to users' preferences. There seemed to be a pincer movement: no one would argue against user choice and effective management, but professional judgement and discretion was being squeezed out and seemed to need defending.

From social work's point of view, the change of management approach introduced in the 1980s, and continuing, reinforced greater management rather than professional development. However, it must be seen in a wider political and social context as the development of managerialism.

## Managerialism

Two aspects of managerialism are important for social work. The first is the *generalist view of management*. This claims that management is itself a discipline and practice, separable from the activities that are managed and capable of general application to many different kinds of organisation. The second is the application of techniques derived from generalist management in the public services, particularly in the context of new Right policies that transformed the perception and organisation of the state in the 1980s in the US and UK. Clarke (1998) identifies three aspects of this:

- the ideology of *expanding managerial authority and discretion*, the 'right to manage' over the work of an organisation, to achieve more effectively its objectives;
- a *calculative framework*, which comes from the ideas of Taylorist 'rational management', discussed below. Work is defined by mathematically established targets, and often financial targets, assessing inputs of work and outputs of achievement, and through comparing the organisation's position in league tables in achieving those targets;
- a focus on *discourses* about how to manage, such as quality, excellence and human resource management. These discourses seek to restructure organisations to make management visible, so that consciousness of 'effectiveness' and 'managing' is widely dispersed. The power of managers is enhanced and professional work becomes less valued. Stratification grows so that levels of professional work develop, in which management becomes an increasing component in the upper strata (Causer and Exworthy, 1999), with professionals becoming 'hybrids'.

The generalist view has direct impact on the daily experience of social work. For the first three-quarters of the 20th century, social work in Britain developed on a professional model derived from comparison with other better-established professions, in particular medicine and psychiatry. Thus, university-level education based within the social sciences was developed by middle-class practitioners to justify a degree of autonomy in individualistic practice, as we saw in Chapters Two and Three. This was supported by a professional ethos of moral and ethical responsibility to clients of social work services, as we saw in Chapter Four. Managers of social work, in this model, are promoted professionals, who exercise a form of supervision, derived from medicine, which respects the autonomy and commitment of the individual practitioner. The generalist view claims that management may be divorced from experience of and capacity to practise. Supervision in this model pursues organisational objectives, such as financial and organisational effectiveness, rather than professional objectives.

The second aspect, *policy managerialism*, has indirect impact on social work because it was allied with efforts by new Right governments in the 1980s and 1990s to transform the role of the state in the US, the UK and in Western societies more generally. This policy imperative has had an impact on locally delivered government services, within which many social work services are situated. Managerialist policies in local and central government provide a context that facilitates the growth of the generalist model of management. In turn, Pollitt (1993) considers that policy managerialism is a form of Taylorist rational management within the generalist model of management. Taylorism sees the essential purpose of management as *control*, best achieved by defining quantitatively levels of effort required to achieve desired organisational outcomes, through techniques such as performance indicators.

The policy context for management was transformed in the 1980s and 1990s by the major political impetus from the new Right of what Australians such as Rees (1991) and Ife (1997) call 'economic rationalism'. In Britain and North America this has become attached to personalities as 'Thatcherism' and 'Reaganomics'. There are two factors in this transformation of managerialism: a particular view of the role of the state derived from an economic philosophy and, building on that view, a political approach to the management of state services.

Pollitt (1993) argues that managerialism arose in response to social trends following the end of the Second World War (1939–45). European countries established welfare states, relying on economic growth to maintain and develop social policies that supported the welfare of individuals and communities. Most government expenditure went on social issues soon after the War. Thus, social expenditure was rising. However, frequent swings in economic growth and recession led to increasing concern about whether growth could continue to provide for this expenditure. Increases in the population of elderly people and in single-parent families, mainly headed by women, led to pressure on social expenditure. The general child population dropped, leading to less need for schools expenditure.

Governments of the 'new Right' in the 1980s argued that economic development must have priority, to deal with these economic problems.

To achieve this, they argued for curbing state social expenditure. Otherwise, the economy would not sustain it (pensions), or social change was needed to avoid dependency and (possibly) immorality (single parents), or there was scope for reduction (education). However, politically, the public were committed to maintaining state involvement in these services. Therefore, the new Right approach was to manage these services more economically, and managerialist ideas provide an approach sympathetic to this political philosophy to doing so.

Clarke and Newman (1997: ix) argue that managerialism from the 1980s onwards represents a new 'settlement' of relationships between the citizen and the state and between management and politics. They see three aspects of this settlement. One is a *political-economic* settlement between, first, capitalism and the free market, and second, socialism and public provision of services through the state. The argument is that an accepted balance between market-driven inequality and equality was guaranteed by citizenship. Thatcherism in the 1980s threw it off balance, and the 'new Labour' or 'Third Way' policies of the Blair government in power from 1997 represent efforts towards a new balance. Another aspect of the settlement is *social*. A welfare state supports national unity and citizenship within it, because rights to welfare support are universal, provided that a society maintains the conditions of full male employment and the familial division of labour (Williams, 1992). The 'familial' division of labour is where men work and women mainly manage the home and do domestic tasks and childcare. Finally, there is an *organisational* settlement, which coordinates state provision through a balance between bureaucratic administration and professionalism. Bureaucracy supports social, political and personal certainty, clarity and neutrality, through administration by a system of formal rules. Professionalism, on the other hand, offers flexibility achieved through the acceptance of some interventions based on expert judgement. This is how social workers became bureau-professionals. They operate within the state bureaucracy, but their professional autonomy and discretion allows the potential inflexibility of administration by formal rules to be humanised.

These settlements were destroyed during the 1970s and 1980s in Britain and in many other, mainly English-speaking, countries. First, economic weakness destroyed the political-economic settlement. This produced a political movement, the new Right, arguing for change that removed the possibility of economic equality, and was even opposed in principle to equality. On the other hand, social movements questioned the division of labour within families and supported diversity of family relationships. These social and economic changes affected public services, which were challenged to respond to these changes.

One response to these challenges, from the new Right, was to reaffirm the economic and family values through the way state services were organised. Thus, social security and social welfare services were reorganised to emphasise economic and family responsibility. Against this, social pressures built up to recognise diversity and change. However, recognising diversity and change requires recognising new economic and family behaviour. Most obviously, these pressures came through movements for equality between ethnic groups, gender equality and broader anti-discrimination. This implied a different approach to provision of services. In this way, public services became the battleground for the colliding forces of these movements (Payne, 2000). Social workers were a particular focus of this battleground, because of the relatively flexible and liberalising role they followed in public services. The new Right sought to transform public services and attain a different culture of service. In particular, it sought to displace the power of 'bureau-professional' relations.

## Privatisation and marketisation

One of the ways in which this was achieved in the social services was a process of privatisation and marketisation of public services, including social services. Privatisation is various processes that reduce public ownership and control of organisations. Marketisation organises services so that different providers of services compete to provide them. There are different ways of achieving both.

The claim that markets are the most effective way of providing goods and services is connected to conservative or neoliberal political philosophies and the economic philosophies and values that underlie them. These assume that individuals know best what they want, and therefore, the most effective way of providing for those wants is for individuals to be free to choose between a range of providers – the image is of a line of market stall-holders, all more or less providing the same thing. The alternative socialist view is that it is more effective to plan a system of provision, so that there is no waste in having several competing providers of the same thing, and so that enough is provided. There is no guarantee in a market that what is required will be available, particularly if people cannot afford to pay for it, as is the case with many social services. Both systems need regulation, because markets may lead to unfair competition, for example by slanted advertising, and planned provision may lead to people having no alternatives if the quality of provision or the resources available are inadequate.

The idea of social work as a business or enterprise is also connected to privatisation from the public sector. Privatisation is a social policy that emerged from government attempts to deal with the financial crisis of state ownership during the 1980s. Privatisation was a way of reducing the expense of public services and, in consequence, made reductions in taxation more possible. It did this by divesting the state of services that it managed. Some services, such as telecommunications, which previously had been thought to have strategic importance in wartime and incurred heavy infrastructure costs to develop, now seemed capable of wider development, They were turned into businesses and operated as private organisations. In the social services, it was uncommon for agencies to be turned into private companies. Instead, various forms of market mechanism were introduced to encourage cost reduction by competition in markets or quasi-markets. Quasi-markets are ways of organising public services so that different elements within them compete against one another. Also, arrangements were built up for public agencies to contract with and regulate private agencies to provide concrete services such as residential and home care.

According to Drakeford (2000), privatisation has several elements:

- treating people as *customers not clients*, so that they had greater choice in the services they received and the way they were provided, similar to the choice they would have had if they were customers of a business;
- public authorities as *purchasers not providers*, so that they did not always provide the service through their own staff, but paid other organisations to do so, creating competition and cost reduction and pressure to be more efficient among providing agencies;
- getting public servants to be *managers not administrators*, so that they were made more responsible for containing costs and controlling the practice of staff in public organisations;
- encouraging *competition not allocation* as a way of dividing up resources that paid for services;
- public organisations become *regulators not planners*;
- services provide *equality of opportunity not equality of outcome*, because markets produce results that depend on the deserts and abilities of people, rather than some public view of entitlement.

Drakeford (2000) argues that privatisation policies gained support because they pragmatically resolved the problems of state finances by allowing governments to claim that social rights were not being lost by placing responsibility for them on private sector organisations, which would increase financial inputs and manage things more efficiently. Privatisation also responded to disillusion with the idea of trying to achieve equality and social integration. Universal services led to bureaucratic rigidity in service provision and a concern for impartiality between groups or 'political correctness', which created uniformity rather than flexibility in responding to a diverse society. New Right political philosophies also preferred private over public ownership and individual enterprise rather than public management through hierarchies.

The consequences for social work of privatisation policies were:

- to create opportunities for alternative patterns of working:
  - through employment agencies providing substitutes for permanently employed staff
  - through social workers setting up residential and home care services as private businesses
  - through social workers working independently as counsellors, or in child protection roles, such as guardians ad litem in the adoption system;
- to incorporate social workers into roles within the system of contracting for services, so that they assess people's needs on behalf of the public commissioner for services;
- social work services needed to become more clearly definable and marketable as a service that can chosen by a service user or commissioner and be contracted for, rather than being part of, a seamless professional provision, which incorporates therapeutic, social order or transformational objectives.

## Social work as enterprise

The idea of enterprise has been an important aspect of the development of managerialism. This is not new to social work, since its creation partly came from social entrepreneurs such as the Dr Barnardo and similar reformers in the 19th century, who created organisations to achieve their social objectives. However, late-20th-century neoliberal thought gave enterprise a particular flavour.

Entrepreneurs create and implement new ideas through setting up and expanding new organisations. 'Entrepreneur' is the French word for 'enterprise'. An enterprise is another word for a business, or an activity, but most people understand it to mean more, especially when the French word is used in English. Being entrepreneurial implies wanting to build up your job, organisation and influence, an imaginative 'go-getting' style of working. It can apply to any job or activity. Entrepreneurship is another word for creating and running a business. The two are connected because it is often assumed that a successful business will achieve more if its employees are entrepreneurial. This is contrasted with businesses and people who do not seek development and expansion, and in particular with large businesses, government employees and civil servants who are bureaucrats. Bureaucracy is often assumed to be non-entrepreneurial because it relies on rational dispersal of authority – meaning rights to use power given by accepted mandates for action – through an organisation. The obvious implication of seeing entrepreneurialism as the opposite is that it must be the seizure of power without rights mandated by law or organisational authority, with the advantage that this leads to creativity and development for the benefit of the organisation and the people it serves. The question is: who judges, and by what right and what benefits the organisation and its service users? The answer is: those who have seized the power through their entrepreneurialism.

During the 1980s and 1990s, public organisations were encouraged to become more enterprising. Pinker (1990) represents this trend. He argued that societies needed enterprise, to ensure economic success, and that being enterprising was becoming more generally valued. Social work, therefore, needed to incorporate greater elements of enterprise, not only in being more imaginative and innovative, but in taking on organisational structures and policies that reflected business and managerial practices.

Harris (2003) points out that social services did indeed take on some of the practices and language of business; sections of agencies were called 'business units' or were required to produce 'business plans' for development. Rather than publicising the availability of services, public sector workers were encouraged to 'market' their work. One of the benefits of this approach is to point up similarities between public services and private sector services and use some of the same techniques in making public services more responsive to the needs of its 'customers'; 'customer care' became an important idea. However, in achieving this, political and social trends have changed the concept and role of a social service agency. This has come about through the development of managerialism and through processes of privatisation and marketisation of social services and the social work that they provide. That is, they have become less 'of the state' and less monolithic, but rather do their work within a mixed economy of state, profit distributing and not-for-profit organisations operating in networks of provision, in which there is a degree of competition between organisations for work.

## New management challenges

The consequences of these changes are that traditional concerns about management's relationship with social work have been heightened by new challenges. Table 5.1 lists the main subject headings from one book about social care management from the early 1990s and three recent texts on social work and health and social care management. Adams et al (2002) is an introductory social work book with a section on management. All include managerialist topics: quality assurance, a focus on finance, budgets and contracting, effectiveness and control, and aims, targets and results. Martin and Henderson (2001) and Seden and Reynolds (2003) are longer works, and cover more content. However, the new topics in the more recent works include risk, protection and decision making, work and information flow and information technology, and evidence-based practice. These latter topics show a more 21st-century managerial concern about more structured practice, but do not altogether focus on the managerialist assumption of management by quantitative and target-based data and economic effectiveness. Some of the continuing foci on professional development and supervision and workload management reflect long-standing concerns for management of professional work, and the continuing focus on the management of change and reorganisation points to a continuing concern for professional responses to the pressures exerted by organisational demands.

There are signs of a move away from the focus on quantitative management of organisational processes, towards a stronger focus on structured responses to professional practice. These developments suggest a complex picture of management challenges to professional control of work. If social work can find ways of managing effectively and demonstrate outcomes through measurement of its work and success, the tide of managerialism may be more balanced by professional influences in the future.

**Table 5.1:** Management challenges: four formulations

| **Taylor and Vigars (1993)** | **Martin and Henderson (2001)** | **Adams et al (2002)** | **Seden and Reynolds (2003)** |
|---|---|---|---|
| The new world of social work | Your job as a manager | Management | Becoming a manager: acting or reacting |
| Aims, targets and getting results | Managing outcomes for service users<br>Working with standards | | |
| Assessment of need and marketing | Customers and service users<br>Managing processes | Assessment and planning | |
| Costs, budgets and contracts | Planning and managing projects<br>Working with a budget | Managing finances | Managing budgets and giving best value |
| Quality assurance | Quality in services | Quality assurance | |
| Achieving results through people | Improving your effectiveness as a manager<br>Values and vision<br>Management control | Managing the workload | Managing the team<br>Managing mistakes and challenges |
| Networking and joint working | Management and leadership | Coordination and teamwork | Leadership and vision<br>Managing across professional and agency boundaries |

continued.../

**Table 5.1:** contd.../

| Taylor and Vigars (1993) | Martin and Henderson (2001) | Adams et al (2002) | Seden and Reynolds (2003) |
|---|---|---|---|
| Training and development | Developing effective performance | Supervision | Managing significant life events<br>Managing professional development |
| The management of change | Managing change | Reorganisation | Managing change |
| | Service planning accountability and risk | Risk and decision making | Managing to protect |
| | The flow of work and information | | Managing information and using new technology |
| | Evidence and investigation | | Supporting evidence-based practice and research mindedness |

## Conclusion: assessing management changes

How may we assess the implications of management changes for social work?

The first point is that managerialism, privatisation, marketisation and enterprise create a cultural environment in which social work, and other professions, must exist; what Hough (1999) calls the 'culture of the market'. Creating a social culture in which the market is seen as the best way of providing goods and services implements a particular political philosophy, conservative or neoliberal, and assumes that many individuals making personal decisions based on their own economic interests is appropriate for an activity like social work. It suits best a social order view of social work, which says that the main priority is to provide services and solve problems, according to users' preferences. It provides less well for a therapeutic view of social work because it denies the value of spending resources and planning for freeing up people's perceptions, which would allow them to develop greater personal and social fulfilment than they are currently aware of. Thus, community work and personal development are potentially excluded. It permits transformational work, but limits it to that which the market and management can understand and incorporate into existing cultural assumptions. The crucial limitation is not what is done and how it is managed but the way in which managerialism and the market create its particular culture in which competition is preferred to cooperation. We can see this in Foster and Wilding's (2000) analysis of the practical consequences of managerialism. They suggest that closer managerial control may:

- reduce the quality of work, through 'proceduralism' and 'bureaucratisation';
- adversely affect professionals' morale, motivation and commitment;
- reduce the impact of a potential (professional) challenge to state power;
- create, by empowering consumers, adversarial relationships between professionals and consumers;
- create defensive and cautious practice;
- fail to build on the strengths of professionalisation, such as a service ethic, colleagues' responsibilities for controlling each other and commitment to high-quality work.

Some of these problems might equally well affect a bureau-professional organisation of social work as a market. However, the striking thing that we have learned through the management changes of the past quarter of a century is that there are benefits of professional organisation, and managerialism creates a culture that fails to take advantage of it.

Consequently, some have argued that these changes contribute to a deprofessionalisation of social work (Charles and Butler, 2004: 58-61). However, Dominelli (1997b) argues that it is more accurate to depict this as a change in the nature of the professionalisation of social work. This issue arises again in Chapter Seven, after a consideration of issues of power and social work in Chapter Six. However, throughout this chapter we can see that there is a continuing debate in various different ways about how agency management has always had an impact on social work as a professional activity. They are entwined in a complex relationship, rather than in opposition, and to do social work requires understanding analysis of the complexity.

SIX

# Social work, power and society

## Using power in practice

I first met Sylvia when I was a probation officer, standing in for the colleague who supervised her because of a series of theft offences, and doing work that would nowadays be the remit of a youth offending team. She was a lively teenage woman who had just started in employment. She had failed to turn up for work for several days and had been sacked. On behalf of my colleague and her distraught mother, a lone parent, I summoned her to the office to remonstrate about her lack of commitment. She giggled through the interview and probably ignored everything I said. Sometime later, I took over a new caseload in the social services department, and Sylvia's was a name on it. She was not present, having absconded from a residential school for young people with emotional and behavioural disorders, after throwing a senior member of staff across the room – Sylvia was physically powerful. I renewed my acquaintance with her mother, and waited until she reappeared. This happened in due course, when a police officer saw her shopping near her home. I talked to her in the police cells. She had been living at home for about six months, had found a new boyfriend and had not got into trouble.

I wondered what to do. The conventional course was to arrange for her to return to her school to finish her programme. I thought this was inappropriate. For one thing, I knew that she had already been out at work, and I thought putting her in a school was a backward step in her personal development. Unfortunately, we did not have any facilities for providing her with employment or workshop experience. Anyway, relationships had broken down at the school and sending her back was likely to lead to another outburst. Also, although she had a history of committing thefts, she had remained at home for six months without being picked up by the police at all. Another factor in my mind was the positive relationship with the boyfriend. On the other hand, I (representing the public through the social services) could not condone the violence, the absconsion and the record of offending. So I struck a deal with her. I said I would have to place her in a residential school: she understood this and why it was necessary. But, I said, I would send her to a different one. If she behaved impeccably, just as she had done all those months while she was 'on the run' at home, I would do my best to persuade senior officials to allow her home after two weeks. So she would get her punishment, she would have to prove she could contain herself, but there was a realistic target, she would soon be back with the boyfriend, and she would not have to face the place from which she had run away.

I kept my side of the bargain. She was a totally acceptable resident in the school. After dire warnings and threats of blame from my superiors if anything went wrong, I was allowed to follow this course of action. A year later, I was able to discharge her supervision, since she had settled down very successfully. Later still, Sylvia's mother died, leaving her youngest child an orphan. I knew nothing of this until Sylvia arrived at the office to see a colleague, with her husband, the former boyfriend. Could we do anything to help her look after her sister, since their income as teenagers was not enough to maintain her? We arranged a guardianship allowance and other support, and found that Sylvia acted as a very competent substitute parent. Her preparedness to come to the agency at all was, she told my colleague, a result of respect I had shown her in her own difficulties a few years previously. One of the advantages of the original conception of social services departments as multipurpose agencies is that this sort of link between different social experiences was possible.

With Sylvia, I used official powers on several occasions. As a probation officer, I carried out the form of the responsibilities that came from those powers, by berating her for her behaviour. This was an oppressive use of power, without any worthwhile outcome, because it did not involve her participation or commitment. The best that could be said for it was that justice was done, because deviations from the rules were picked up on. When probation orders are made, the courts and the public expect probation officers to be clear about the requirements set by the order and to ensure that people on probation are picked up on their responsibilities. We saw in Chapter Five that agencies represent a negotiation between various interests in society. Going through the form of the use of official powers when their use is in itself pointless is one compromise that arises from that negotiation. It allows at another point useful social work to go on, and allows others in society to feel that justice is done. Form is very important in matters of justice: it must be seen to be done.

As a social worker, I used the powers given to me by the court to incarcerate Sylvia in residential school. This also made clear to Sylvia her responsibilities, as the courts and the public required that I did. Therefore, it had the same worth in meeting that public responsibility as berating her for not being committed to her work. But it was a much more valuable use of professional power, although it was potentially even more oppressive. Power was properly used here because it was used with understanding and participation, if not consent, and used with a purpose that might (and in the event did) achieve valuable results for Sylvia and for the general public. I also used my professional powers in a different way: to work out and argue for a beneficial course of action within the agency. Here I used my thinking and analytical powers and powers of persuasion in getting managers to go along with my ideas. So personal power can be used against clients and not for their benefit, with them, perhaps to their benefit, and with others, to their benefit or perhaps not. In gaining a guardianship allowance, we used our knowledge and skills to obtain Sylvia's and her sister's rights to the allowance.

In social work, then, we can identify different powers, which also derive from different social orders:

- legal powers, from the legal order;
- the capacity for personal influence which, we saw in Chapter Three, is so important in social work as it is seen as a personal activity, and derives from the social order of interpersonal relationships;
- professional knowledge and skills, deriving from orders of knowledge and power;
- used with clients, to their benefit or disadvantage, assessed by their own class, gender and other social orders;
- used with others, for clients' benefit or disadvantage, assessed by their official or organisational social order.

In another case, I was called to see Mrs Forbes, who had residual problems from very severe schizophrenia. She now managed a relatively normal life, with only occasional relapses. However, her life was chaotic, and her small flat was stacked with years of accumulated newspapers and magazines. I found more than twenty layers of dirty plates and half-eaten food interleaved with sheets of newspaper used as tablecloths on her table. Her bed was covered with various items obtained from dustbins. Some of her symptoms probably came from tiredness, since she was unable to sleep properly because her bed was unavailable for this purpose. I persuaded her to accept, somewhat reluctantly, help in tidying and cleaning the flat. A team of home helps sorted the place out. Unfortunately, when I returned a week later nearly all the property had returned, retrieved from the dustbins as soon as the home helps had left.

In this case, I used no statutory powers, but she would have known that I had these in reserve, since many social workers in the past had been responsible for her compulsory admission to mental hospital. This factor may have persuaded her to accept my pressure to tidy up her life, although obviously, with hindsight, the removal of her unhealthy accumulations was distressing and uncomfortable for her. More likely, Mrs Forbes accepted the arguments of this bright young man, knowing that if it all went too far she could get her own way in the end. The power of my speech and mental strength, my enthusiasm to help, and perhaps my middle-class assumptions and official role just bowled her along. She agreed to something that she did not really want and she frustrated my aims because I did not take the trouble to get real consent from her. On the other hand, she retained her own power and control over the situation.

These case examples make the point that we can have all kinds of formal and informal powers. We often use them legally to ensure compliance or informally to achieve results. But these cases also re-emphasise the point made in Chapter Two that in some respects what we do interpersonally is a performance. There are positive and negative aspects of performance: in these cases, going through the form of things without addressing a person's insecurities and complexities is just playacting. Our efforts can be frustrated unless we genuinely achieve agreement and participation. This is something that senior politicians in democracies learn at the highest levels of political activity: that you cannot in the end govern without consent or oppression. In the sense that social work is about social governance, this is also true of social work.

However, that 'consent' may be achieved in all sorts of ways, many of which are overtly or covertly oppressive. Concern about these issues has surfaced at two different levels in social work debate:

- The role of the occupational group and social services agencies within the system of social governance or control. This level concerns social work as a profession. Thompson (2005: 19) analyses professional power in relation to social stability and social change, arguing that power and authority is required both to achieve social change and to maintain social stability.
- The use of various powers during the practice of social work to achieve clients' compliance with social or agency policies or the

worker's wishes. This level concerns personal and interpersonal social work.

Chapter Three drew attention to the way in which different understandings of practice and knowledge gave different sources of authority to act: social order perspectives from 'certain' biomedical, economic and legal sources, therapeutic perspectives from clients' personal objectives interpreted through psychology and sociology and transformational objectives from alternative spiritualities (conceptions of and meanings applied to the world) and collective movements. Fleet (2000: 8) suggests that '[i]n statutory social work, even the most carefully negotiated mandates take place in a context of constraint and unequal balance of power, which call into question the degree of consent that is possible, or the reality of the client's capacity to terminate the counselling or limit its boundaries....'.

## Social work debate on power

The history of debate about these issues has occurred in three phases; this section looks at each in turn:

- *The authority problem:* how to practise therapeutic social work when agencies are concerned with social governance and control and practitioners have various forms of legal, professional and agency authority.
- *The power problem:* how the practice resolution of the authority problem fails to deal with the complex ways in which power is used in our societies, particularly to oppress others.
- *The empowerment problem:* the extent to which it is possible to practise social work so as to empower or at least avoid oppressing service users.

### *The authority problem*

The authority problem arose in the 1950s as social casework achieved influence for a therapeutic, voluntary model of social work. A crucial point about therapeutic social work is that its authority derived from the client and relied on a client's right to be self-determining, that is, to decide for themselves what and how the social worker should act on their behalf, even if this was sometimes limited by the social worker's responsibilities to other sources of authority. As two influential texts put it:

> Today one of the firmest convictions of the profession of social work is that the person has an innate ability for self-determination and that a conscious, wilful [sic] violation of the client's freedom by a caseworker is an unprofessional act which transgresses the client's natural rights and impairs casework treatment or makes it impossible.... (Biestek, 1961: 101)

> ... [the client's] decision to go forward together with the agency should be self-determined and chosen as freely and understandingly as is possible for him. This action, the result of joint consideration and discussion, constitutes the difference between making up one's own mind and having it made up by another person or a pushing circumstance.... (Perlman, 1957: 135)

The first quotation suggests that practice is impossible unless the client determines its direction; the second that clients need also to accept the agency's role. However, sometimes social workers suggested, pushed and directed their clients, and some agencies enforced social expectations, implemented legal requirements and provided public services according to public policy and law.

Moreover, analysis of the relationship between worker and agency (see Chapter Five) suggested that through its formation and, in a public agency, legal backing, it provided a social mandate, legitimating the right to intervene in people's lives through social work practice. This was a way of understanding how social work's claim could be achieved: social objectives were incorporated into social work through the authority of the agency, derived from legal and administrative authority.

So, exercising social control was seen as a recognised and socially useful role, but the fact that it was debated recognised the tension:

> Social work treatment, whether casework or group work, is one of society's alternative ways of exercising social control of persons who manifest deviant behavior.... Society uses other control methods.... These forms of control are clearly recognizable, which is not true of control through treatment. A treatment service, the purpose of which is to enhance an individual's social functioning, nevertheless contains an element of control. (Weisman and Chwast, [1960]1962: 252)

Yelaja (1971: 170) raised some of the questions that arose for social workers at the time. Does the use of authority in social work practice conflict with basic values and principles of social work? What conflicts and limitations arise when social workers carrying some form of authority are called on to help their clients? This debate was also allied to concern about professionalisation. Unless social workers were autonomous and therefore independent of the need to carry out agency and other social requirements, they could not, it was argued, be or become 'professional'. One concern about the use of power and authority within practice was that it might take away from the possibility of becoming a recognised profession (see, for example, Ohlin et al, 1956, on probation and related work). Analysis of the ways social work used authority led texts of the 1970s, building on the previous work to contain the tension between helping and authority as follows:

- Clients needing non-directive, therapeutic casework are distinguished from those for whom '[a]ssertive methods, more controlling techniques, may be more effective in helping....' (Foren and Bailey, 1968: 24), and '... which enforces and controls *in the interests of the client*' (1968: 29; emphasis original). This is particularly so in probation, prison welfare and parole work (Ohlin et al, 1956; Fink, 1961; Hunt, 1964).
- Using controlling techniques occurs in many different settings, even those where the agency is voluntary or not-for-profit (that is, authority is not only associated with statutory functions), or even where the purpose is not particularly controlling, such as in social work in hospitals (Foren and Bailey, 1968: 114–32, 196–225).
- Controlling is related in many instances to caring activities. Parents (or workers dealing with childcare and welfare) set boundaries of acceptable behaviour as part of the educative and socialising role that adults undertake. Depressed people might commit suicide, and control might prevent loss of life, and allow them the opportunity to build a more satisfactory life afterwards. Satyamurti (1979: 95) argued that, in Britain, the 'repressive and consensual functions' became merged as the Poor Law disappeared, and the traditions of social work which came from the pre-Second World War voluntary sector began to interact more closely with the Poor Law tradition in the new local authority welfare and children's departments of the 1950s.
- Control is justified by public policy. We all have an interest in preventing people from assaulting their spouses, or abusing their children, and a general social duty to act to prevent such things

happening (de Schweinitz and de Schweinitz, 1964; Yelaja, 1965). We also provide social services and other agencies to take on these responsibilities more widely.
- Other professions, such as medicine and the priesthood, have powers because of their occupation and social status. Sometimes they also have legal powers (for example, to make medical recommendations for compulsory admission of people with mental ill health to hospitals or to marry people). These factors do not prevent them from having recognised status as a profession.
- Authority and power could enhance the activity and make the social worker more effective '... to support and educate his client' (Studt, 1954: 122).

The problem is that these approaches to the use of power and authority in social work assume a consensual society (Day, 1981), that we all have an interest in an ordered society. Therefore, those who are coerced are helped and those who use authority and power can benefit society by what they do. Using power to achieve compliance is valued because it leads to effective organisations and a well-ordered society. However, a well-ordered society is of benefit mainly to those who are advantaged by present arrangements. The use of power continues to disadvantage those who do not have it, since they might achieve more from society if they were not so compliant. These views also focus on personal and interpersonal aspects of social work. They ignore the problems caused by the social work profession's position using power on behalf of the already powerful. These issues all came to the fore as the radical critique of the social order elements of therapeutic social work began to develop in the 1970s.

### The power problem

Radical views took up new sociological analysis of power to point to complacency in the casework resolution of the authority problem. This starts from the assumption in political science that power is a capacity to influence, and achieve others' compliance with our wishes, which comes from a variety of sources, including personal qualities and the resources to apply coercion in various ways (Lukes, 1974). Seeing this in a more complex way, Lukes (1974) noted that power is distributed among groups and organisations in patterns that reflect people's ability to control agendas and expectations – so its exercise may be hidden. People and groups exercise power in pursuit of their interests. Patterns of power within societies and organisations persist, even when the ability to apply coercion is not exercised regularly. Among the origins of radical critique were consumer research showing that clients were confused by neutral, non-directive approaches, disliked the lack of advice and opinion in traditional non-directive casework and expected a degree of direction (Mayer and Timms, 1970; Rees, 1975). This pointed up the extent to which submission to authority was an accepted part of welfare practice. Another factor was the experience of larger state agencies set up in many countries from the 1970s (see Chapter Five), which drew attention to social workers' exercise of power. For example, Garrett's (1980) account of the experience of the use of authority starts from various experiences of workers who, in responding to their clients' needs and wishes, aroused the opposition of managers in the organisation. Satyamurti (1979: 97) reported from an interview study of local authority social workers that they all disliked exercising authority. Handler's (1974) study of the use of discretion showed that while apparently making professional decisions, childcare social workers imposed conventional social assumptions. There were also connections to radical critique of other professions, such as radical psychiatry (Steiner, 1975).

An activist expressed the professional issue thus:

> If social workers' professional discipline is, as they claim, to consider the needs, strains and problems of their clients, then their actions and recommendations should be motivated solely by those considerations. Thus, when a social worker, knowing that resources are scarce, puts pressure downwards onto the clients then s/he is not only acting as, at best, the pawn of the system, and at worst, the bailiff or policeman/woman of the system, but also unprofessionally. (Bailey, 1980: 224)

Radical social work relies on a Marxist class analysis of power held primarily by a class of capitalists who own the means of production, with society organised so that working-class people mainly fulfil the needs of industrial production. The state, including social workers, is part of the system that maintains capitalist power, and in some cases there is a considerable commitment to the status quo, emphasised by statutory responsibilities and professional power. This leads to a separation between social workers, whose professional and agency position gives them access to power and coercion, and clients, who are generally in a less powerful position and also have few ways of resisting professional and agency coercion. The welfare state is a result of struggle by working-class people to achieve collective benefits within this system, and is accepted by capitalists because it maintains the system that strengthens their wealth. Social workers are thus put in a contradictory position. They help working-class people but while doing so maintain the power of the owners of capital. The radical critique of the use of power by social workers asks: 'whose side are you on?' and presumes the answer is 'clients'. If you are not, then you must be against them. Mullender and Ward (1991) argue that social workers' professional power and oppression of clients is inextricably linked.

The idea of 'hierarchy' is crucial to this analysis. People with power can get others in lower-status positions in society to comply with their wishes. This is also true in families. There is a hierarchy of power with, usually, a male 'head of household' figure, and female 'mother' and children in lower positions in the hierarchy. Hierarchy is also important in many organisations and in the development of professional careers, from learner to junior to senior positions (Hugman, 1991: 53-81). An important aspect of many radical views of social work is to reject hierarchical functioning in agencies and families and to seek a more participative style.

As Hearn described radical practice:

> Radical social work is characterised by two major and sometimes contradictory thrusts – a positive strand, the advance of socialist collectivism that propounds social change and even social revolution; and a more negative strand, the avoidance of ritualised, inauthentic relationships with clients, that seeks client preeminency and even client control. (Hearn, 1982: 23)

The latter practice could gain wide humanitarian and professional support, as we saw in Chapter Two, discussing radical therapeutic work, and is the source of radical social work's continuing influence. However, in the context of providing a state social service, social revolution was unlikely to engage many social workers. Criticisms of radical ideas (Payne, 2005a) include the conflict in social work between treating people as individuals and seeking collective social change, weaknesses in dealing with psychological problems and in offering practice prescriptions, conflicts between the different interests of oppressed social groups and a discouraging, always critical, approach to social issues.

A crucial issue was its conflation of power with control. Thus, radical social work always saw exercising social control as oppression on behalf of capitalism. However, social workers must always be powerful in relationship with their clients, because of the professional nature of that relationship and the duties attached to the role. We saw in Chapter Three that professionals are not in a relationship merely for mutual interest, as in a friendship. Workers are always in the situation for particular purposes. If they have the capacity and are disposed to use power, the fact of having professional purposes will construct many of their acts as powerful. People will see them as powerful and they will in fact use power a great deal. The corollary of this analysis is that if social workers are not disposed to use their power, or if they are pursuing the relationship for confused or uncertain objectives, they will dissipate their power and make it less influential were they to use it. Power may be helpful and its presence in social relationships is inevitable. Its problems must be set against the advantages of making available to disadvantaged people the role of social work.

Therefore, broader analysis of oppression grew up, that drew on the idea of social divisions other than class. Two important social movements dominated the oppression thesis:

- Feminist analysis argues that a system of 'patriarchal' relationships exists in which men as a class dominate and have power over women. This has consequences for social work as a mainly female profession and for assessing people and their social problems:

  > Returning to the first of the main activities comprising social work: the definition of welfare problems for intervention, feminist action through the contemporary women's movement has put gender oppression on the map of social problems, exposing its detrimental effect on women's welfare. In doing so, it has unearthed the innumerable ways in which patriarchal social relation undermine the whole of women's well-being. These include women's right to emotional and physical health, access to material resources, political power, freedom from fear, and enjoyment and definition of their own sexuality and talents. (Dominelli and McCleod, 1989: 11)

- Anti-racism and anti-discriminatory practice perspectives argue that inequalities deriving from 'race' or assumed ethnic differences cannot be understood as deriving from individual prejudice against minorities (Husband, 1991: 50). Instead, they derive from a system of social relations that depend on prejudice and discrimination against ethnic minorities. So Dominelli argues in relation to anti-racism:

> ... social work, in common with other elements of the welfare state, is being dismantled and restructured to exclude more and more people from receiving its provision. This trend is a residualising one which will target public services on the most needy.... In a climate of public expenditure cuts which ration social services resources, the state becomes a force intensifying social workers' responsibilities as agents of social control whose tasks encompass that of reducing demands for scarce public provisions. (Dominelli, 1997a: 31)

Thompson draws attention to the importance of power in anti-discriminatory practice:

> Social work is a *political* activity; that is, it operates within the context of sets of power relations – the power of law and the state, the power inherent in social divisions such as class, race and gender, and the micro-level power of personal interactions. Indeed, power can be seen to operate at all three levels, personal cultural and structural.... Also, many of the problems social workers tackle have their roots in the abuse of power. (Thompson, 2001: 163 [emphasis original])

### *The empowerment problem*

The response to this broader view of sources of oppression has been the development of an empowerment practice in social work, drawing mainly on concerns about social divisions arising from ethnicity and gender, but also other divisions of concern to social workers, around ageing, disability and sexuality. Two elements of empowerment practice are as follows:

- Advocacy includes cause advocacy on behalf of interest groups and case advocacy on behalf of individuals. Case advocacy also has two different elements: workers arguing within existing agency or cross-agency structures on behalf of clients, and advocacy services organised by or on behalf of particular groups within social care (Brandon et al, 1995; Schneider and Lester, 2001), such as children in care (Dalrymple and Hough, 1995) and people with learning disabilities (Brandon et al, 1995).

- Empowerment practice also divides into two elements. Anti-discriminatory, anti-oppressive and anti-racist practices highlight where discrimination, oppression and racism occur and combat them (Dalrymple and Burke, 1995; Dominelli, 1997a, 2002; Thompson, 2001). A broader and more positive empowerment practice aims at facilitating individual clients to learn confidence and skills to act independently to deal with their own problems, and both individually and collectively. Practice aims to identify, understand and overcome barriers to achieving personal, group and community objectives (Solomon, 1976; Braye and Preston-Shoot, 1995; Gutiérrez et al, 1998; Lee, 2001), particularly through self-help groups (Wilson, 1995).

Ideas have also developed that seek to shape the perceptions that social workers and others have of social services. For example, normalisation requires workers to seek socially valued environments and methods of practice to develop patterns of life for people receiving care services which are as close as possible to the lives of ordinary people (Brown and Smith, 1992; Race, 2003). Disabled living approaches to care focus on enabling people with disabilities to manage and control services to develop patterns of life that they value (Morris, 1993). Social models of disability (Oliver, 1990, 1991) and political economy models of ageing (Laczko and Phillipson, 1991) and ageism (Bytheway, 1994) seek to show that these are not conditions which result in inferior or disadvantaged lives for those affected. Rather it is the way we organise society to exclude people affected by disability and ageing which leads to their social isolation and many of their 'problems'. These ideas seek practice where workers actively approach people and services organise their activities in ways that do not fall in with social assumptions that exclude people from good-quality lives. While many of these approaches focus particularly on service users, their carers are also the focus of similar ideas, and their needs are increasingly seen as separate from the interests of users.

Important service user movements also developed, which derived from the experience of oppression in health and social care and other social services. Survivors of abuse, particularly sexual abuse of children (Bass and Davis, 1988), or domestic abuse of women, drew attention to the difficulty of escaping from abusive relationships, of being heard by official services and the long-term effects of the oppressive experiences. Prisoners' rights, protest movements and riots in prisons

(Adams, 1992) and mental health survivors' movements (Campbell, 1999) were all influential in questioning the use of power and lack of protection afforded by public agencies, including social care agencies.

An important concept in the early 21st century is exclusion, drawn from European and particularly French policy debate. Byrne (1999) argues that the advantage of this term is that it conjoins societies and some of the people within them in a continuing process, rather than seeing individuals as part of a deprived, delinquent or destructive group outside society. It suggests that social processes happen over time in particular societies that exclude some individuals and groups from some social relations, determining aspects of their lives, and also of the lives of people who are not excluded. However, different views of this process arise: a neoliberal view is that excluded groups are alienated, redundant underclasses, focusing on their responsibility for their condition, while Marxists focus on how exploitation of excluded groups leads to their condition. One of the approaches to social inclusion is increasing the possibility of inclusion in major social processes, such as voting, work and community facilities and resources (Askonas and Stewart, 2000; Percy-Smith, 2000). An important way of doing this is by enhancing social capital (Baron et al, 2000; Putnam, 2000), the mechanisms, such as voluntary organisations, volunteering and social participation that enhance cohesion and reduce alienation. Thus, community work approaches and regeneration are important aspects of social inclusion policies. Positive attempts to involve users of social work services in improved social relations, increasing their social networks, and developing their participation as citizens in policy and service development may provide a useful protected experience of successful social participation that may be empowering (Barry and Hallett, 1998). While this approach emphasises the reciprocity between excluded people and the society that contains them, it does not consider the social justice and rights aspects of a practice that seeks to involve people from a relatively powerless position.

Empowerment practice has been criticised, often by writers who consider that it fails to consider more complex forms of oppression. Blakemore and Boneham (1994), for example, explore the interaction of age, 'race' and ethnicity. Humphries (1996) suggests that many apparently empowering practices, such as equal opportunities policies, contain rather than confront inequalities and divisions and collude with unequal resources and undemocratic policies, and with competition between oppressed groups for resources, rather than seeking increased resources for all oppressed groups. Also, she argues that socially powerful groups, such as Christian fundamentalists or pro-life, anti-abortion groups, often construct ideas of empowerment, claiming that their ideas are oppressed, whereas groups oppressed by social divisions suffer from serious exclusion from decision making and power. Finally, Humphries (1996) argues that empowerment practices often lead to nihilism, in which groups feel themselves to be victims who are unable to extract themselves from social exclusion.

Healy (2000: ch 5), in the most extensive, practical but theoretically informed recent discussion of power and control in social work, argues that critical social work has adopted the more complex analysis of power, seeing it as a discourse. Mullaly (1997: 113) argues that:

> ... power is to be found in different localities, contexts and social situations. The prison, the school, the asylum, the hospital, and the social worker's office are all examples of places where power is dispersed and built up independently of any systematic strategy of class or gender or ethnicity.

Therefore, in the critical view, controlling and non-controlling social work cannot be distinguished; all social work includes both. This view accepts the arguments in the earlier authority debates that professional roles and organisational structures inevitably include the use of power, but sees this as problematic. However, it also does not see the worker as powerful and the client as powerless; they are all both powerful and powerless in different ways, and use various strategies to enhance those aspects of power that they can control. Taylor and White (2000), for example, show how clients establish credibility and moral and other entitlement to help in the hostile environment of a social agency, and have ways of resisting professional authority, by withholding or controlling information and participation. Healy (2000: 74-7) argues that social workers concerned with child protection need to identify which factors affecting the situation arise from local constraints on clients' behaviour, and which are wider oppressions, such as poverty and vulnerability to social pressures, because of poor parenting experiences, mental ill health, such as depression and anxiety, and poor-quality education and social facilities. She argues that critical social workers differentiate themselves from traditional social workers through their preparedness to use power to facilitate clients' capacity to gain power over at least some of their environment and resources, facilitating meetings, mutual help, additional resources and opportunities, while also accepting responsibility for constraining behaviour for the benefit of the child. The use of power should be overt and explicit rather than covert and unconsidered, so that it may be challenged and respond to clients' legal rights. Healy (2000: 82) suggests that communication skills are important in facilitating power by clients. Thus, for example, social workers should take control of the process of taking turns to speak, so that everyone gets the chance to make a contribution, and of making sure that people get enough time to say what they want to say and are encouraged to feel that the worker and others are interested in what they have to say and take it seriously. This has been an important point in protection work: listening to a child and vulnerable adult. Social workers should recognise that they feel vulnerable when they give up control of the situation, and find strategies for gained support and approval for risky strategies in their work. They should also take responsibility for identifying where differences between them and clients may lead to inappropriate use of power and responding appropriately.

## Law and risk as issues of power

Throughout the debates within social work about its involvement with power, three themes have run through the concerns – power derived from:

- professional role and personal influence, the therapeutic concern;
- social authority derived from agency, policy, class, division and exclusion, the transformational concern;
- law, the social order concern.

All activities are bound by legal constraints in any society, since agencies must be set up according to legal requirements and people must behave according to legal duties and constraints. However, in many societies, social work also enforces legal constraints on its clients, or the law establishes what social workers may and may not do. However, we must beware of understanding that involvement in the same way that our own system has been constructed. For example, Cooper et al (1995) undertook studies of legal action in child protection in different European countries and found that the British system was particularly inflexible and vested great authority in the courts by allowing them to remove children permanently from their parents' care. Flemish and French systems had a more negotiated, flexible system in which legal action was taken as part of a process of involving the law to reinforce family and social expectations (Hetherington and Cooper, 2001). In the same way, in discussing values (Chapter Four), we found that some African cultures required the involvement of families and communities in decisions that in Britain would be a private matter between social and legal professionals and individuals or at most, families. Gilmore (2001) argues that social work decision making is indeterminate, predictive and value-laden, while legal decision making strives to be value-free, clear and refers to past events rather than possible futures. Thus, legal decision making in welfare matters often seeks consensus, or relies on resolutions of past events, rather than planning for the future. On the other hand, as Dutt (2001) argues, both social work and the law seek to deal with social issues such as racism, by partnerships coming from different points of view.

Thus, we may see social work's relationship with the law as being one in which social work is used to enforce legal requirements in relatively diffuse situations, aimed at improving social relations in the future, which are not very susceptible to legal clarity about behaviour in the past. On the other hand, when social work decisions come into contact with the law, for example where action is taken in child protection matters, the requirements of evidence can be inappropriate to the information and approach of social workers. This is because the adversarial approach to resolution of cases pits one side against another, instead of permitting an investigation of a situation that needs resolving in partnership, which is more the inquisitorial approach in European and Scottish systems. Both in their different ways seek to get at truth; inquisition may be more appropriate in complex personal cases, although it runs the risk of appearing authoritarian, with the judge's powers being more flexible and therefore sometimes apparently more arbitrary.

Legal frameworks also affect service provision and policy in different ways. The British law of *ultra vires* requires public authorities to have a legal mandate from Parliament before they can provide a service, whereas in most European countries public authorities are free to pursue actions that are reasonable to meet their objectives. Moreover, the British political system is much more centralised than in mainland Europe, and this has been enhanced by managerialist control, in pursuit of economic management, as we saw in Chapter Five (Payne, 2000). Hence, British social work is much more conscious of the use of the law to secure public service accountability, and the legal justification for actions or the allocation of resources. In the community care system, for example, service users have gone to law to enforce their view of social work assessments for the allocation of services, and this seems constraining for workers (Braye and Preston-Shoot, 2001).

A further impact on social work has been the use of public inquiries structured as though they were legal processes designed to allocate blame for something that went wrong in health and social care scandals (Reith, 1998; Corby et al, 2001; Butler and Drakeford, 2005). In this way, social services have been affected by broader social trends in which increasingly complex societies seem alienating and frightening. Consequently, people try to use modern technology, which in this case would include services such as social work, to avoid risk (Beck, 1992; Cvetkovich and Löfstedt, 1999; Adam et al, 2000). In the same way, public authorities are expected to protect citizens against contaminated food, irresponsible corporate behaviour or practical risks in the environment; public authorities are blamed if things go wrong, and individual responsibility is allocated to public servants, including social workers.

This means that being prepared to take risks, or to be flexible for clients' benefit is more circumscribed by legalistic administrative constraints on social workers' actions, and that this pressure adds to the managerialist pressures of quality management discussed in Chapter Five. Social workers both enforce the law, and implement the legal right to services in a context where legal pressures are towards social order approaches to social work, rather than the therapeutic and transformational concerns that were the focus of professional debate in the 20th century.

## Conclusion: the continuing discourse on social work power

This chapter has explored the continuing debate within social work about power. This debate is connected with the professional debates about values, since the therapeutic perspective on social work sought professionalisation, protected by professional values, on the assumption that greater expertise and influence would be for the benefit of disadvantaged clients. Moreover, the social order perspective on social work accepted the value of social workers being implicated in imposing social and legal authority. The current transformational perspective is to acknowledge that this occurs, and to try to understand and work with the complexity in a way that is empowering for clients. However, complex analyses and understanding of the interaction of professional, legal, and users' and carers' power are necessary to be able to act in this complex field.

We cannot say that social work is not a profession because its clients do not have freedom of action within the legal requirements on social work agencies and the social pressures on professional relationships. A more complex understanding has displaced this view, if anyone ever held it so crudely. We can now see that all professions exercise different aspects of power and authority, and that professional workers must understand and implement their professional values using, avoiding and constraining that power and authority. What they do and why derives from the value of freedom and empowerment in a complex society; and also from the value of cooperation and self-control.

Power, of various kinds, exercised and available in different ways, is one of the factors in understanding how social work meets its claim. To use social power with people is to achieve social change. To do so under constraints is to move social change towards a social objective. Using power has an impact on individuals. So the struggle within social work about power and authority, as we have seen it in the texts discussed in this chapter, is an indication of the importance of these social forces in the achievement of social work's claim.

SEVEN

# Social work: profession among professions

At one time, British passports required you to state your occupation. One of my friends looked at mine, which said: 'social worker'. She said: 'You don't do social work, you're an academic or perhaps a manager or a writer'. My view of my identity at one time or another, and mostly at the same time, is all of these things. But my work colleagues are clear. The medical director and nursing director know that I was trained as a social worker, and have written books and articles about various aspects of social work. When registration of social workers was introduced, they know, because the personnel manager checked, that the GSCC, the English registration body for social workers, has registered me. That registration entitles me in English law to call myself a social worker. I manage an area of provision called 'psycho-social and spiritual care', which includes various departments. One is called 'social work', led by a 'director of social work'. This is different from the spiritual care department, which has a 'spiritual care lead' (an ordained minister of religion). The day care unit is different again. It is managed by a music therapist, and includes complementary therapists, nurses, various other kinds of art therapists and a horticultural therapist. The mental health team comprises part-time psychiatrists at various levels of training, led by a consultant psychiatrist and professor of psychiatry. All these different departments provide recognisably different elements of our overall palliative care service for the slice of south London that we cover. They are themselves recognisably different from each other. Everyone working there accepts that the various professions involved in 'psycho-social and spiritual care', including social workers, are different from doctors, managed, except for the psychiatrists, by the medical director, and nurses, managed, except for those in the day unit and complementary therapies, by the nursing director. Those exceptions, managed by me, make for a complicated pattern of professional and organisational responsibility.

Even in this fairly small-scale voluntary organisation, there are people within a complex system of occupational labels, many of which are widely regarded as professions. Chapters Five and Six pointed to ideas about accountability in organisations and how this is connected with the distribution of power in society. In our organisation, as it happens, people called 'social workers' are not employed outside the social work department – except for the chief executive and myself, senior managers who are also as it happens social workers, but could be from any professional group. A separate project helping children with bereavement employs some registered social workers, but not called by that title. How does it work, then, that I and the music therapist manage nurses and 'allied health professionals' (AHPs), and I manage doctors (the psychiatrists)? We do it in a variety of ways. The hospice has a contract, which I manage, with a psychiatric healthcare NHS trust, and psychiatrists are professionally responsible only to psychiatrists for their professional work. If anything goes wrong, my job is to require the consultant psychiatrist to comply with the hospice's requirements, but his job is to judge what is appropriate in psychiatric decision making. We negotiate; well, actually we have lunch together every so often and talk over how things are going and what we could each do to improve things, but we would negotiate within our responsibilities if there were a problem. The music therapist manages the organisation of the day unit, and the AHP (he is registered as an AHP), does music therapy and gets advice from the nursing director on things to do with nursing. All the nurses have separate professional group supervision, unconnected with the management structure. The hospice pays independent consultants to provide independent professional supervision for the spiritual care lead and the music therapist in their professional work, because they are managed by a social worker, me.

Many complexities occur in any organisational structure. In many services, there are complicated relationships between people with different professional identities and knowledge and skill bases. What does this mean for social work? Is it one of those professions? How does it, with its particular identity, interact with other professions?

This chapter therefore asks two questions:

- In what ways is social work professional?
- How does the multiprofessional element of much social work affect its position as a profession?

The next section explores various meanings of 'profession'; the following two sections explore how social work fits with those meanings through looking at how it has sought to become a profession, and the critique of this. I then examine how multiprofessional work affects its position as a profession.

## Occupations, jobs and professions

These questions bear on the nature of social work as an occupation, rather than as an activity. Is social work, or in what ways is it, a profession, or is it 'just' a job? There are some commonsense understandings of 'profession' to consider:

- *As paid rather than unpaid activity.* We sometimes say that someone is a professional because they are paid and employed to do a job, rather than being unpaid and an amateur. A professional footballer is paid, while the participant in a Sunday league is unpaid. Social work is such a job, but some people also do voluntary work, or work at social services tasks without being a social worker. What distinguishes paid social workers from them? Is it only the pay?
- *As implying a recognised type of job.* We sometimes use 'profession' as a polite way of asking what someone's job is, at parties or on forms. Sometimes other occupational groups such as police officers or teachers complain that they have to do social work as part of their tasks. Thus, they simultaneously recognise it as something different from their occupation, but also imply that doing it would be possible for them if they did not have other important priorities in their work.
- *As implying high quality.* We sometimes say that someone did 'a very professional job' or that she is a 'real professional'.
- *As a description of a special category of occupation.* We talk about the medical and legal professions, but we would not generally refer to the 'plumbing' or bricklaying' profession: these are crafts or trades. The ticket collector at the station has a job, but not a craft, trade or profession.

These distinctions are not clear. The cook in a high-street café might have a job, their colleague in the restaurant next door might have a craft, their colleague in the restaurant with 3 Michelin stars for cooking might have a profession. What distinguishes them is public recognition, effort and training, and an approach and attitude to what they do. These distinctions are partly, in many people's minds, about quality. In a job, you try to provide a good service that people find acceptable, or turn out a good product. A craftsperson achieves satisfaction from a product that represents a special quality. A professional does both of these, but seeks to achieve high quality because of altruism, a wish to benefit others rather than themselves. People think that this disavowal of self-interest is important because the expertise involved in professions means that the people using professional services often cannot control the quality of what the professional does, and the work often exposes them to risk, or an uncertain outcome. Evident altruism is a mechanism to reassure service users that professionals will act in their best interests. However, this does not assure successful outcomes, since what is judged successful is different from what might be in your best interests or what you might want. A craftsperson, on the other hand, might simply want to achieve a result to meet their own standards, whatever the customer thinks, and somebody 'just' doing a job might be careless if the pay is not enough or the manager is not keeping them up to standard.

## Professionalisation and social work's development

The four meanings of profession are related, however. Being paid rather than unpaid, being in a recognised job, and carrying out a task well are related to the idea of a special occupation. Professionals profess: that is, they claim that expertise makes their occupation special. They seek to define an area of specialisation that is theirs alone (Wilensky and Lebeaux, 1965: 285).

Social work during the 20th century took this path of professionalisation, as a voluntary occupation for middle-class women became a job, around the time of the expansion of social work during the First World War (Payne, 2005c). An important early influence was a famous speech at that time in 1915, by a North American educationalist, Abraham Flexner. He argued that social work did not have important characteristics of a profession. This led social workers into a quest to achieve Flexner's markers of a profession. A progress report by Greenwood (1957), after the formation of the unified American NASW, still claimed that social work in the US had not achieved these markers of professional standing. British social workers at this time, in divided specialist groups, similarly sought recognition of social work as a professional entity partly as a way of achieving unity.

Success came through a unified local government department responsible for social services through the implementation in 1971 of the recommendations of the Seebohm Committee (1968); the Scottish social work departments in local government were formed the year before. At much the same time, the North American sociologist Nina Toren (1969) described social work as a semi-profession. She argued that it would always be impossible for professions like social work to achieve full professional status. Among the reasons was that social workers were employed by agencies that could limit their capacity to use discretion based on expertise and knowledge. The professionalisation debate in 1970s Britain reflected the concern that bureaucratisation and poor responsiveness to community and client needs meant that the achievement of unity had not necessarily achieved a profession (Glastonbury et al, 1980).

Knowledge development was also a factor. Nokes (1967) argued that welfare professions should not be based on an exclusively scientific basis with a technocratic, rational approach to knowledge. He argued that welfare professions expressed and communicated ideals of caring and concern in society. By promoting social relationships and interactions, welfare professions facilitated solidarity in societies. He also usefully distinguished an idea of 'treatment' in welfare professions from medical treatment. He argued that welfare 'treatments' are only partially in the control of the professionals, who provide space, time and environment to facilitate personal and social change. The control that professionals provide lie in the planning and operation of the environments in which service users may have opportunities to grow spontaneously. Similarly, Sainsbury (1980) reported research on family work from which he argued that an important skill was to orchestrate a social work team's work effectively, matching and developing skills in the team to changing need.

At the same time, Halmos (1965) argued that 'counselling' has to some extent replaced the traditional advice-giving professions of the law, medicine and the Church with a more secularised and accessible form of response to the more complex social difficulties of industrialised societies. These counselling occupations have shared views of human nature and of appropriate social responses, that have come to influence the organisation of many social institutions, including business organisations (Halmos, 1970). Halmos' analysis draws a parallel between the group of 'counselling' occupations, of which social work is one, and more general historical and social trends. Social work developed alongside the same professionalising social trends and, at least at some times and in some quarters, its ideals have had recognition and even influence. Such views connect with the debate about what kinds of knowledge are acceptable for professional status. A long-standing opposition between interpretivist and positivist views of knowledge (Brechin and Sidell, 2000) has affected social work in the late 20th and early 21st centuries. Interpretivists argue that all knowledge is interpreted by human thought and therefore responds to the social and historical contexts in which it originates; positivists that there is an unchanging objective reality that can be observed and defined.

Social work developed and codified knowledge as a basis for claiming a distinctive professional group. The 19th-century charity organisation societies from which social work practice methods emerged were committed to 'scientific charity': '... these pioneers of practice considered scientific inquiry to be the systematic study of causation through gathering thorough and helpful facts' (Orcutt, 1990: 126). Germain (1970: 26) argued: 'The scientific commitment had seemed to promise social casework a secure position in the profession'. When, in the 1970s, it seemed that science showed that social work was ineffective (Fischer, 1976), it seemed that one of the arguments for social work as a profession was gone.

Questions therefore were asked about the process of professionalisation, and whether social work should follow this route for development. There are three approaches to professionalisation; this account is based on Brint (1994); Freidson (1970, 1994); Turner (1987); and Hugman (1991).

- The *naturalistic* approach (for example, Perkin, 1989) sees professionalisation as a natural part of the increasing complexity of society and changes in the structure of society towards more middle-class occupations, rather than routine factory work. What needs to be done is more complex and needs broader knowledge that is hard for people to hold in their heads. Consequently, jobs become more specialised and people become more expert in smaller areas of understanding. Routine and manual work becomes less important, and is done by machines. Bell (1974) argues that these developments are integral to a post-industrial society where knowledge-based service occupations are more important than labour in manufacturing.
- A *social order* approach suggests that occupations of a kind that develop altruistic services are important in maintaining the social system. They develop a privileged position in society because their services are socially valued. Their high valuation arises because they accumulate characteristics including theoretical knowledge and skill, specialised training and education, usually in universities, the testing of members' competence, the development of professional associations and the emergence of a professional code.
- The *occupational control* approach suggests that professionalisation is a way of structuring the relationship between experts, patrons and clients. Professionals gain prestige and social distance from their clients through their expertise, which excludes clients. External regulation and social control of the professionals is then required,

because the average client cannot hold professionals to account. Regulation of the use of the expert knowledge is undertaken by the profession.

## Professionals, the public interest and the critique of expertise

More recently, it has become clear that occupational groups are increasingly subject to external influence, through complaints systems, consumer movements and other systems of accountability. People are much less deferential in the 1990s than they were in the 1950s. Governments and public bodies have taken greater responsibility for regulation of professions, often in search of financial controls, than they did in the 1950s. They claim to do this on behalf of their constituents, in particular non-expert consumers.

This raises the issue of the public interest (Saks, 1995). If the state or the public has an interest in the provision of a service and how a profession is organised, how may that interest be represented? There might also be differences in view. Saks (1995), for example, looks at alternative medicine, where there are major disagreements about whether it is worthwhile, in which powerful medical profession interests are often critical of practices that they disagree with. This means that politics arises around professionalisation, because power is used in institutional relationships to resolve disagreements, by professions, both professional organisations and individual professionals, and by others. This politics arises between organisations and individuals around who should have the authority to decide what actions may properly be taken as part of a professional activity. This then leads into questions of knowledge and, further, into education, since deciding what knowledge is 'true' and what education effectively conveys 'accurate' knowledge also raises matters of disagreement, in which groups representing particular interests disagree, and engage in power relations to achieve ascendancy for their point of view. This politics is a separate issue from whether knowledge is 'true' in that it represents what all the evidence, when collected and assessed rationally and without bias, shows to be the case. The extent to which it is possible to say that something is true varies, depending on the type of thing we are looking at and the care and clarity with which the evidence has been accumulated. When it is not absolutely clear that something is true, a politics will often arise around the debate about whether it is true, with people trying to use political power to have their position accepted as true.

The 1970s and 1980s saw a further debate, in general and in social work, about whether professionalisation was desirable. This focused on the conflicts of interest between professions, the public interest and the interests of service users. Wilding (1982) summarises the critique of professional power, arguing that seeking power through such claims disadvantages people whom professionals seek to help. There are seven points of criticism, and I give some examples that might apply to social work:

*Excessive claims and limited achievements:* Examples of this are criticism of claims that casework in the 1950s could deal with a wide range of human problems, evidence in the 1960s that it was ineffective and the evidence-based practice movement's argument that much social work is based on faulty assumptions rather than available evidence. Not all such claims are created from within the profession itself. Unrealistic expectations are laid on the profession from outside. Government and the public, for example, have laid upon social work in many countries the expectation that social workers can protect children at risk of being abused in their own homes, while being able to avoid excessively punitive action against parents. Evidence of effectiveness of social work is at the small scale, rather than presenting achievements of wide social significance.

*Failures of responsibility:* Scandals about failure to act have affected social work. There have also been problems with heavy-handedness where social workers have official or bureaucratic roles, the frequently poor quality of residential care, and the inadequacy of services. Social workers say that these are exceptions rather than the rule, and that many failures stem from poor resources for services rather than professional inadequacy. Organisations and professions often make such points when protecting themselves from criticism. While much social work may be helpful, it is still often experienced as oppressive or failing. Attempts to professionalise social work have been frustrated by such issues. For example, Malherbe (1982) argued that managerial control was the most important way of ensuring clients' needs were met and that accreditation had not worked well in the interests of clients in other countries. Parker (1990), reviewing this debate, emphasised how, in the 1990s, changes in the organisation of social services by fragmentation due to privatisation of services, made managerial control less possible. Instead, greater inspection and regulation of non-state services had grown up, but this did not provide for the supervision of standards of work. However, most countries have increased the level of regulation of social workers, by accrediting their qualifications or standing as practitioners, and the UK followed suit by establishing under the Care Standards Act 2000 councils in each of its constituent countries to register social care workers. This led in April 2005 to 'protection of title', so that only registered people could call themselves 'social workers'.

*The claim for neutrality:* Expertise and a 'scientific' knowledge base are claimed to give professionals independence from political pressures, because they are more knowledgeable than others about what is true in that area of knowledge. Therefore, they should be able to make decisions altruistically in the best interests of the people they serve, rather than pursuing their own or other sectional interests, because otherwise knowledge comes from political power rather than a rational assessment of the evidence.

The knowledge base of social work is criticised as inadequate to support claims for effectiveness. Social work decisions often reflect fashionable or organisational, political or social objectives rather than concern for the individual needs of clients. The second criticism of neutrality is that social work is always on the side of those governing, those with power, against the governed, those without power. It might be argued that social work is more aware of this issue than many professions, and thus less liable to be unconditionally oppressive. It is also, as we saw in Chapter Six, more inclined to do something positive about it. A third criticism is that professions are inherently about enhancing their own power, and oppression of clients inevitably derives from that objective.

*Neglect of rights:* This criticism is also about the powers that social workers exercise on behalf of society in pursuit of social governance. There are systems for complaint and occasionally appeal, but much decision making goes unobserved, is practised on shaky evidence and a poor knowledge base. Frequent scandals about particular cases have led to concern about social work's tendency to ignore rights in its everyday work, contrary to the rhetoric of its value system.

*The service ideal:* Professions are supposed to give priority to their clients' needs, and act from altruism in their work. However, use of industrial action to pursue salary payments, influence and conditions of service and evidence of incompetence or failures of service raise questions about the service ideal. Altruism is a controversial issue. It might be seen as natural (most human beings will help others) and as exceptional (most humans are egoistical). Seeing altruism as natural connects with social order views, which accept that, in orderly societies, one individual helps another and societies organise to provide such help in order to contribute to the social order. However, Schwartz (1993) argues that market societies that assume individualism and autonomy for individuals are the least likely to encourage altruism among their citizens. Altruism may bring social work into conflict with some aspects of justice and equality, because it involves responding to people's needs whether this is fair to others or not. A strict points system for allocating a service does not sit easily with a more complex interpersonal assessment using discretion. Wakefield (1993) argues that one of social work's roles in society is to form the altruistic side of a range of services with alternative objectives, such as justice and equality. The collective interest in altruistic services being available becomes apparent only when a market-based society evades the social responsibility to offer them.

Transformational views argue, in opposition to this, that societies need to be planned and organised to combat this. Rather than altruism workers should primarily respond to the interests and wishes of service users, working with transparent, participative methods that involve users in dialogue and decision making. They should also use methods that are explicitly on the side of clients, such as advocacy. Services should be planned participatively. Workers should empower self-help and self-advocacy groups so that users are more able to take action themselves.

Therapeutic views of altruism treat knowledge development in a different, interpretivist, way. Following the work of Schön (1983), rather acting on principles of 'technical rationality', effective professionals in occupations that work with people have common techniques for improvising according to informally learned guidelines. They react to a variety of situations using these guidelines in a spontaneous, intuitive way. However, the variety and complexity of the situations that they deal with often present 'surprises' which their guidelines do not help them to deal with. They then reflect on the situation and adjust their ways of working to deal with it. In turn, this alters their guidelines for intuitive action. Reflective practice has become an important way for social work to be flexible, but still use knowledge when it is available. This approach fits the idea of social work as a practice (Chapter Three) since it is centred on the interpersonal interaction between client and worker. Practitioners adjust their practice in response to the stimuli coming from the people they serve. This respects service users and makes a role for them in the developing of social work, rather than seeing it as constructed in theory or research by the profession and in higher education. As with other professions (Eddy, 1984), social work is inherently about the use of discretion, since it is often used in social service systems to deal with complex problems that are not amenable to merely administrative actions, and reflection is a therapeutic model validating discretion as part of knowledgeable practice.

*Disabling effects:* The argument here is a personal and social one. At the personal level, individualists argue that professions actively take away responsibility and impose control on people so that they are forced to act in ways that are alien to their culture and preferences. This might have been so in the Pakistani family with childcare problems, for instance. At the social level, people come or are sent to social workers for help, but eventually become dependent on that help. Then, personal and social capacities to deal with problems are gradually reduced. These criticisms come from transformational views, concerned for the empowerment of oppressed groups, and from social order views, concerned for the way in which dependence on the welfare state is created.

*Lack of accountability:* If professionals are independent, who are they are accountable to? Clients may not have power or knowledge to make them accountable, and professional associations may be more interested in mutual protection rather than abuses of power or incompetence. It is impossible to turn to complaints systems, courts or tribunals for rulings on every occasion. Many discretionary decisions are made in private and are not observable. It is difficult to explain to outsiders the complexity of social work decisions and issues.

Professionalisation has ceased to be an important objective for social workers for two reasons. One is that the complexity of the issues renders the debate unending. The critique of professional power and discretion, the questions about knowledge and expertise, and distinguishing between professions and other occupational groups are now accepted as matters of social processes and relationships between occupational groups, rather than problems of definition that can finally be resolved. The second reason follows from this. Social work is for practical purposes a profession. It is an accepted paid middle-class occupation, in many countries is regulated as such by governments or other processes, requires an advanced education, is widely recognised as a distinguishable activity, and is regarded as having a moral value.

This does not mean that occupations are equal in status, or equally approved of, or on the other hand, that there are no professions. Rather, it accepts that the influence, knowledge base and boundaries of occupations will change over time, and that this will be influenced by social changes in the environments in which it exists. There is no point at which we can agree that social work is a profession, and that its knowledge and value base is distinguishable from that of other professions. Instead, we might say that in some places it is in some ways a profession; in other places it is in other ways not a profession.

## Social work among professions

Various approaches to understanding and working on the relationship between professions are:

- organisational strategy and structure
- partnership working
- multiprofessional practice and teamwork.

## Organisational strategy and structure

Organisational strategy and structure approaches seek to design organisations so that cooperation is enhanced. Early in the development of UK social services departments, for example, a great deal of research and consultancy work (for example, Rowbottom et al, 1974; Billis et al, 1980) sought to identify organisational designs that would help to bring different services together and manage them effectively. Part of this work was also to find ways of managing practice so that it met the overall objectives of government and departmental policy. These studies reflect a belief that structure and organisation were the main factors in understanding, changing and developing social work organisations.

At the time of local government reorganisation in 1974, for example, there was a belief in the benefits of corporate management, in which local authorities would plan and manage their activities jointly, instead of as separate specialised departments. Coterminosity, to ensure that the borders of local and health authorities were the same, was sought to promote better coordination, but was not achieved everywhere, and was later lost in many areas. Joint and then partnership working developed from that time: this account is based on Payne (1995); Hudson (2000); Lewis (2002); Charlesworth (2003); and Glasby and Littlechild (2004).

Lewis (2002) usefully identifies three aspects of the boundary between health and social care: financial, administrative and professional. The NHS Act 1973 required health and local authorities to set up joint consultative committees. Joint care planning, a structural way of encouraging cooperation on health, housing, transport and education (DHSS, 1976, 1977; Wistow, 1982, 1990), mainly focused on joint finance, an arrangement to transfer funds from healthcare to social services. From 1973, because of difficulties between Catholic and Protestant communities in Northern Ireland, an integrated structure of health and social services boards has worked successfully, similar to arrangements in the Republic of Ireland.

Under the Conservative government in power during the 1980s and early 1990s a stronger involvement of the private sector developed, and arrangements for regulation and cooperation developed. The NHS and Community Care Act 1990 introduced a marketised approach to health and social care (see Chapter Five), which led to a separation between the providers and commissioners of services, although in some cases these remained in the same organisation. This then led to joint commissioning of services, in which health and social care organisations jointly agreed the pattern of services in their areas. The different ways of funding health and social services authorities and the cumbersome joint arrangements limited the effectiveness of this.

## Partnership working

The New Labour government elected in 1997 produced a discussion document, *Partnership in Action* (DH, 1998), promoting more extensive joint working between health and social services. The reasoning behind the proposals is set out in Table 7.1. This demonstrates the thinking that health and social services agencies and carers were to be formally involved in partnership; users are not mentioned. The three levels of joint working refer to planning and commissioning and then to the importance of working together to provide services; these relate to Lewis' boundary areas, referred to above. The focus on broader policy objectives, and in particular combating social exclusion and inequality, is an important sign that these health and social care policies are connected to the government's more general policy thrusts. This moves beyond the attempt to promote cooperation mainly by structural and organisational means. The Health Act 1999 permitted health trusts and social services authorities to delegate functions to each other and pool funds. The Health and Social Care Act 2001 made it possible to set up joint trusts for specific groups of service users, but, in many areas, the partnership arrangements organised under the previous Act were the preferred way of working. The Children Act 2004 requires movement towards complex joint arrangements for cooperation in

**Table 7.1:** Partnership working: New Labour policy

The Government's strategic agenda is to work across boundaries to combat social exclusion, encourage welfare to work, tackle inequalities between men and women and other groups and improve health in local communities. Both the White Paper "The new NHS: modern, dependable", and the Green Paper "Our healthier nation – a contract for health" emphasised the need for effective working between the NHS and local authorities (both in their social services functions and more widely), underpinned by the new duty of partnership, and set in the strategic context of a local Health Improvement Programme. The Social Services White Paper, due later this year, will emphasise the importance of the social services in this partnership. The National Carers' Strategy will look at the role of carers in this wider context. (DH, 1998: para 1.2)

**Joint working is needed at three levels:**

- Strategic planning: agencies need to plan jointly for the medium term, and share information about how they intend to use their resources towards the achievement of common goals;
- Service commissioning: when securing services for their local populations, agencies need to have a common understanding of the needs they are jointly meeting, and the kind of provision likely to be most effective;
- Service provision: regardless of how services are purchased or funded, the key objective is that the user receives a coherent integrated package of care and that they, and their families, do not face the anxiety of having to navigate a labyrinthine bureaucracy. (DH, 1998: para 1.6)

the interests of children, and at the time of writing arrangements are not fully formed.

## Multiprofessional work

So far, then, we have seen that thinking about organisation and strategy as a way of achieving cooperation across health and social care boundaries has been developed towards promoting partnership, as a form of greater integration of organisation. The logical development of this was to promote the integration of practice. In this case, since the major division was seen to be between professions, the professional groups promoted a long-standing ideal of multiprofessional and interdisciplinary work as the answer. However, we can see from Table 7.1 that multiprofessional work is not a major priority for government action. Multiprofessional working has often been the local managerial or professional response to structural cooperation, rather than a government prescription. In other services, such as the local Connexions organisations to coordinate a response to young people in the move from school to work, in community mental health and community learning disability teams, in youth offender and drug action teams, services have been brought together in a similar way. These structures put representatives of different local authority departments often from different professions together in local or specialised teams to tackle a specific group of people or issue. Rather than being a coherent strategy for multiprofessional work, although this is welcomed, the aim is a focus on the issue dealt with, rather than on professional reorganisation. Moreover, the New Labour government has formalised the regulation of social work and other professions, such as AHPs and teachers.

Different professions are in flux in relation to one another, have closer interactions and are based outside a non-specialist unit. They are expected as individuals to maintain their professional practice, rather than its identity being generated within a professionally led department. If all professions are in flux in relation to each other, with their boundaries altering, how can we see social work's relationship with other professions and occupational groups? Social work is part of a network of services and agencies. It has an interface with users of those services and the complex environment that surrounds us. Trying to understand social work as part of those networks seems useful, therefore.

A traditional approach has been to see agencies and professions as connected, so that one agency expresses organisationally the values and approach of a profession. Hospitals, clinics and healthcare agencies represent a medical model, schools and education services teaching, social services agencies social work, legal practices and law centres lawyers. This approach led social workers in Britain to value the foundation of local authority social services departments in 1971 as the culmination of the development of the standing of social work as a profession.

Figure 7.1 represents in the four squares four related services: criminal justice, education, healthcare and social care. Kamerman (2002), reviewing North American fields of practice, refers also to housing, employment and income transfers or social security, but the four areas in Figure 7.1 represent both at present and historically, sites where social work is strongly represented in the UK. The white-edged circles represent various professional groups. Psychological and social work straddle most of these services areas, while lawyers, the police, medicine and teaching are more involved with one specific service area. Nurses are mainly in healthcare but do extend into social care and education to some degree. All these are examples; many professional groups that

**Figure 7.1:** Networks of professions, knowledge and services

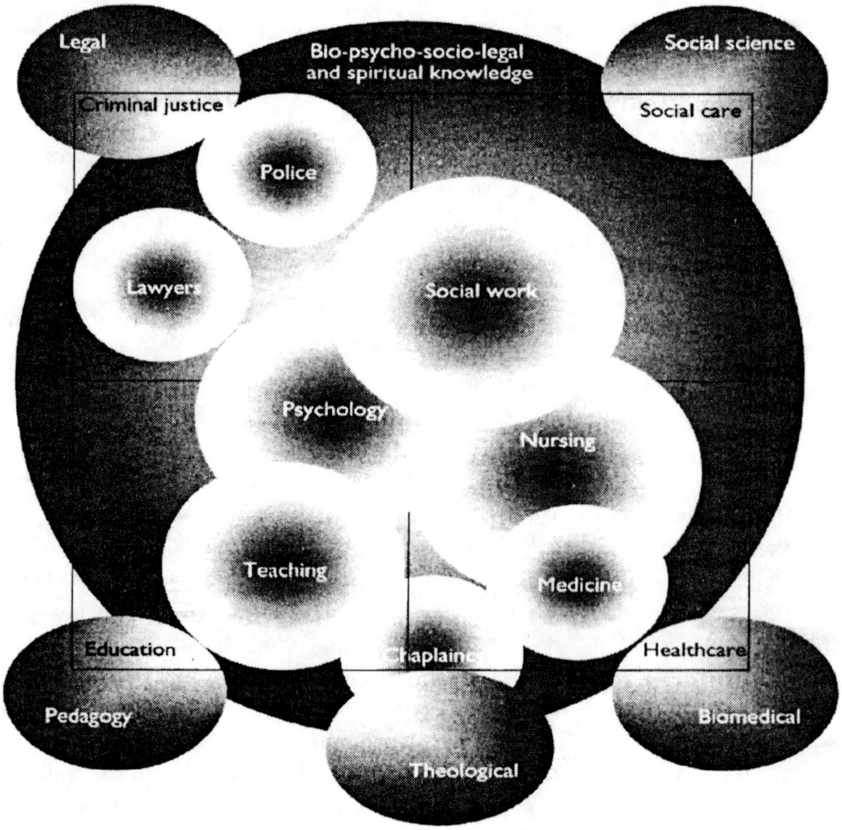


could be mentioned are excluded. All these services share a broad knowledge base, represented by the dark area lying behind most of the services and professions. Finally, specific areas of knowledge and skills inform particular services, social work being mainly based on the social sciences. Some professions, for example psychology, have a strong knowledge base and dominate the production and management of knowledge in that area, but do not have one service base; they operate as part of a wide range of agencies. Social work has both: identifiable social agencies in which social work is a strong element, a clear focus on broad social science knowledge and participation in a range of agencies where the primary profession and knowledge base is not social work.

So we can see these three aspects of connections between professions as sets of networks: a professional network, a service network and a knowledge network. We saw in Chapter One that social work's identity was formed in the professional network by people's paths into and away from the centre of social work. That centre can be regarded as where the knowledge network and the service network most strongly represent the profession. So a social worker is clearly identified with the social work profession if they work in a social care agency, using social work knowledge and skills, and is a member of a social work team and social work organisations. However, a social worker in a healthcare organisation, the lone social worker in a multiprofessional team, who is dual-qualified and also does a lot of family therapy, mainly working with psychologists and nurses, is much less clearly identified with social work.

Particular theories and knowledges are strengthened by some multiprofessional connections. For example, cognitive-behavioural work is little practised in social work, and not strong in social work education, but where there is a strong psychological representation in the team, it can be much stronger. I see the three networks as rather like plates in a pile, as each network, knowledge and skill, profession and service shifts, the strength of particular individuals' identity also shifts.

However, any such service is more complex than that. Hospitals, for example, contain a variety of professions as well as medicine, some of which are very powerful, but perhaps for different reasons. For example, nursing dominates many of the concerns of hospital managers because it is the largest workforce. Also, many large services contain different grades of practitioner. Schools have teaching assistants, laboratory technicians, playground supervisors and school meals staff. Some of these staff groups have a very high professional status, but are a minority group, such as liaison psychiatrists in a hospice – while liaison psychiatry is an infant specialism, other services find psychiatric expertise helps to deal with severe problems that are hard for other professionals to tackle. Others are present in large numbers, but have little status and influence, such as personal carers or home helps – there are many people in this role, but they lose influence because of low status, poor training, and the fact that their jobs are scattered and often part time. Some people appear to be marginal but have practical influence because of the centrality of their responsibilities, such as caretakers in schools – their influence comes from the reality that not a lot can be done in a school building without their help.

As we saw in Chapter Five, organisational approaches to

understanding relationships between professions and occupational groups focus on lines of responsibility. Legal responsibilities and power over resources are traced from the management body at the top, through lines of responsibility for work and accountability for resources. This approach looks at the interaction of networks of different professional groups, knowledge bases and services. Relationships between these groups are constantly changing. For example, nurse prescribers are developing to take up some of the less complex prescribing duties that were formally reserved for doctors.

Why is it, then, that if social work has a clear organisational, knowledge and professional base, it seems so insecure compared with other professions? Part of the reason is the importance of social issues for many other services; they cannot be so clearly set off from medicine, teaching and criminal justice, and social concerns seem of less importance than the main focus of each of these services. Healy (2000: 129) argues that the technical knowledge base is susceptible to contest by other professionals and users because it is perceived to be non-technical. Her answer to this is to develop knowledge together with others in relationships, so that they are part of the creation of understanding and accept the value of the process of social work rather than the content.

For example, a social worker was asked by a healthcare team to arrange a discharge; however, the patient's wife did not feel that she could manage her husband's illness at home, bearing in mind her own disabilities, which were unknown to the medical and nursing teams. The primary nurse argued that the husband actively wanted to return home, but his wife and stepdaughter thought that this was unrealistic. This seemed to have all the makings of a family conflict. The social worker first spent time with the wife exploring her ambivalence: the wife wanted to respond to her husband's wishes but also realised the limitations of their home and her capacity. She was helped by listing all the factors that made things difficult, and balancing these with the possibilities that might be offered by local services, which she was unaware of. She also feared the cost of a nursing home, and the worker explained how NHS continuing care funding could be made available, if a nursing assessment found that it was needed.

Then, the worker approached the husband and asked him to assess how he would want to be cared for at home, and list his own care needs. She then asked him to look at each item on his list and consider how his wife could provide for these, adding in her own knowledge of local services. It became clear that several needs could not possibly be met, and in the end he openly said he did not see how his wife could cope, but expressed his fears about going to a nursing home. The worker explained the process. After this preparation, she called a family meeting, including the primary nurse and a junior doctor. This examined the whole situation, drawing on the previous assessments done by the husband and wife. A nursing home was agreed on, and the assessment process set in motion. But, there were provisos. The family agreed that they would investigate and report on the nursing homes to the husband. The worker explained how each home would visit the hospital to do an assessment before the admission, so that the husband could get to know at least one person who worked there. The healthcare team also agreed to make a bed available, or find other care, if the placement did not work out, although privately they hoped that this would not be necessary, as they felt it would be a struggle. With all this preparation, many of the anxieties attached to discharge were removed.

Therefore, all professionals *are* their area of practice in any multiprofessional setting; they do not just bring a professional label that defines a sector of responsibilities, they do not just bring their well-honed knowledge, expertise and skill but their practice represents alternatives and balances to each other. They represent their profession by what they do.

## Deprofessionalisation

We noted in Chapter Five a concern that the development of managerialist ways of controlling social work practice was reducing the professional standing of social work. There are a number of points to make about this argument. First, Chapters Five and Six show that this has been a long-standing argument about the fact that social workers' discretion relies on organisational or legal authority; it is not newly created by managerial changes of the 1980s and 1990s. Second, we have seen in this chapter that the 'project' by which social workers sought to gain professional status has been displaced by more complex understandings of the nature of professions and, referring to Chapter Six, the power and authority of professionals. Third, as the next chapter shows, a variety of social professions within any one welfare regime is possible; a single social work is not a necessary requirement, as at one time social work professions in the US and the UK seeking unification may have thought. As our understanding of the processes by which power, professions and organisations work has become more sophisticated, arguing that professionalisation of social work should take place, or that it has declined, seems inappropriate.

Charles and Butler (2004) summarise the following points of the deprofessionalisation thesis:

- power of organisational efficiency over professional values;
- contested and fluctuating knowledge bases and competing professional approaches;
- stress arising from conflict between workloads and professional expectations;
- organisational demands for mechanistic and depersonalised services, alien to professional practice;
- lack of devolved discretion;
- quest for certainty and risk elimination;
- drive for technical rationality;
- patriarchal, heterosexist, disablist and racist control encouraged by market competition approaches to service provision;
- relentlessness of organisational and professional conflict.

This concern is partly connected to the development of an organisationally mandated, routinised 'social care' or organising community care packages of services, rather than being involved in providing social work help. The shift of childcare and family social work to education departments removed the focus of social services departments on seeing the family as a whole, introduced by the Seebohm reorganisation in 1971. The development of many private sector providers rather than an integrated social work provision, which includes services, means that social work practice is much more fragmented. Development of healthcare social work specialisms is another aspect of fragmentation. Because of this, social work does not seem organisationally strong, in the UK, even though it is legislated for, regulated and is clearly identifiable as a separate occupational group.

## Conclusion: social work, a profession among professions

In summary, then, we can see that social work is a profession, in the following senses:

- It is a widely recognised job, which people distinguish from related jobs.
- Its useful social functions include (among many others) social assessment, interventions to help people solve problems and achieve greater personal fulfilment, protection of people from risk, organising

services offering useful personal help, exercising discretion based on investigation and understanding of complex social situations.

- It is recognised to require training at a higher education level and a degree of expertise.
- It is part of a general movement in society to create occupational groupings with their own hierarchies. These have a degree of autonomy in defining tasks and standards, but are part of large-scale organisations, dominated by the state.
- It has a recognised position in many societies as part of public provision in competition with other related agencies and professions. In competing for resources as an occupational group and as the dominant profession in a set of definable social agencies, it also has an accepted social role.
- It receives a degree of moral approval and recognition of altruism among its practitioners. They are not generally regarded as doing it for their own benefit, even if they derive benefits from doing it as all people who work do. Its value system (see Chapter Five) shows acceptance of moral responsibilities.
- It meets social expectations and carries out recognised social functions.
- It avoids oppression, exploitation and other forms of social damage in its work.
- It is generally regarded as competent and effective.

Against this, social work does not feel strong. If we are to understand the social nature of social work, we cannot neglect the preceding discussion of its characteristics as it professionalised, and views about that process. We can 'know' that social work is a profession, in the ways outlined above. Also, we must reflect and criticise that knowledge constantly, balancing it with our perceptions of actuality. In our practice, we must recognise the problems, contradictions and criticisms that the social process of professionalisation brings for interpersonal and personal work.

In a recent case, one of my social work colleagues worked with a large chaotic family with severe debt and housing problems. The mother was dying and being cared for by her teenage son, a daughter was failing to attend school, another daughter was supported in a housing scheme for people with learning disabilities and the mother's own mother was frail and elderly. A wide range of practical and interpersonal problems, dealing with housing, social security, school and the social services learning disabilities team were involved. The complexity of the reports back to the multiprofessional team, the range of contacts and agencies involved and the emotional intensity of some of the interpersonal work impressed the medical and nursing team. They commented that they would not have known how to contact all these agencies, and would not have had the patience to sort out all these complex problems. Yet, they felt comfortable contacting healthcare agencies, and took endless time with caring tasks.

What Clausen et al (2005) call this 'jack-of-all-trades' role is clearly necessary, but hard to explain and justify, and the distinction between it and other professional tasks is hard to draw precisely. Yet, when Clausen at al (2005) explored the lives of people in difficulty because they were dying of cancer, they found that this kind of flexible practice would often have been useful, and when other professionals see it, they value it.

In multiprofessional medical settings, social workers embody the non-embodied elements of situations; in multiprofessional education settings, they represent the non-intellectual and social elements of educational development. In all settings, they respond to the borderline, non-standard elements of people's lives that cross organisational and professional boundaries and impinge on the main focus of the agency's work and the other professionals' interests.

EIGHT

# Social works: global and local

I sat in a hotel conference room in a bombed-out city on the Croatian coast. Around me were representatives of all the new countries that were part of the former Yugoslavia. We were there to begin to recreate social work education in those countries; social work had not been strong before, but in several of the most Westernised countries it had become active, and our meeting included professors willing to help from Italy, Sweden and the UK. Some people had been driven through the mountains, because their borders with Croatia were still closed. Some of the countries that these people represented still had armies fighting each other. Some people found it hard to speak in the presence of representatives of countries and ethnic groups who had devastated their cities and families. Yet, in the week that we spent there, they ate and talked together, eventually drank and sang together and agreed a programme of development of social work. I returned 18 months later to visit another proud new country in the Balkans as part of the project. This time, it was me that was driven across the border from a neighbouring country, past bullet-pocked houses, past the UN tanks, to stay in a hotel still mostly devastated, covered in plastic sheeting, to give a lecture at the end of the first year of the joint social work course, and to launch a textbook. It was a symbol of improving cooperation between the former enemies. Most of the same people had travelled with some difficulty to get there. Two different parts of the former Yugoslavia were still at war. Yet we all talked social work, I lectured on social work practice and got a laugh for a joke about Harry Potter.

At that time, I also visited Beijing, to join a conference of social work educators at the Ministry of Civil Affairs College. Administrators and educators talked social work, where universities and colleges that I had visited two years before had barely had it accepted that this was a subject that they could develop. There was immense enthusiasm for the possibilities of this new profession. But the debate was about whether the country should follow Western models of social work, or create its own model. I visited Russia to discuss their developing social work, and was particularly asked about social pedagogy; I mentioned this to a British social worker and she looked at me blankly: 'What's that?' (if you are asking that question, see Table 1.1, Chapter One).

I joined a party of German social work students visiting the UK, and they talked to some youth and community workers in Manchester about their work; the Germans referred to it as 'social work'. The British workers were aghast: 'We don't have anything to do with social work'. To the German workers, youth work is a natural part of their local authority children and youth department. Obviously (to them), if you are concerned about young people you protect them from abuse, provide children's homes if they need looking after and organise support for young people in the community through youth work. But the British youth workers saw social work as an authoritarian activity that involved social control of problem children, completely unconnected with their work, which they saw as contributing an informal element to a universal education service.

These experiences point to the fact that there is an international conception of social work, international connections in education and research and exchange of personnel. We can see this by the fact that there is an international organisational structure to create the definition of social work in Table 2.3 (Chapter Two), which is widely accepted; this demonstrates that there is such an international conception. On the other hand, there are wide differences in the way social work is organised, according to what I called in Chapter Two a country's 'welfare regime'. This chapter examines social work and the social professions as international phenomena, and how they interact with the local. Social work originated in the West and is a significant part of Western societies. If it is primarily Western, however, how does it fit with those other societies? Is it the same activity and profession everywhere? And if it is primarily Western, why has it had such a worldwide influence? These questions connect to our discussion of social work as a profession, because they raise the issue of whether social work is universal, in the same way that medicine, nursing and religion or bridge and road building are part of life everywhere.

However, we mostly see social work as being part of a very local service responding to local and individual problems, and we saw social work practice in Chapter Three and values in Chapter Four as primarily interpersonal. Sometimes that localisation is incorporated into government policy, as the policy of subsidiarity (that issues should be dealt with at the lowest level of government possible) is part of European policy and German social services. So the debate about internationalisation is also raising an important issue for social work's claim: awareness and responsiveness to international movements is another way in which social work incorporates the social into its interpersonal response, and its activity at an international level incorporates the interpersonal into international debate.

## International social work

Is there an 'international social work'? The activities described above suggest that there are: for example, social workers travelling internationally to learn about and develop social work. In this section, I examine a number of documents and resources that describe international connections to see how we may interpret international activity.

The UK and US social work education organisations require social work courses to contain recognition of the international context in which social workers will practice (see Table 8.1), although sometimes this is minimal, and is part of broad social policy understanding. Commonly, the requirement is to provide comparative information. The (British) *Blackwell Encyclopaedia of Social Work* (Davies, 2000) does not mention international social work, but lists five articles on

**Table 8.1:** Social work education bodies' requirements for international understanding

**UK:** Department of Health Requirements for Social Work Training refer to National Occupational Standards for Social Work, and the QAA Benchmark for Social Work Degrees (DH, 2002).

The National Occupational Standards refer to the international definition (Table 2.3, Chapter Two), then divide social work topics into detail. Each requires content as follows:

1. The legal, social, economic and ecological context of social work practice
a. Country, UK, EU legislation, statutory codes, standards, frameworks and guidance relevant to social work practice and related fields, including multidisciplinary and multiorganisational practice, data protection and confidentiality of information....
2. The context of social work practice for this area of work...
b. International law and social policy, in broad terms, for the purpose of comparison.

The QAA Benchmark includes several requirements for international understanding:

1.9 In addressing the content and standards of honours degrees, the statement takes account of European and international contexts of social work and the desirability of the mutual recognition of social work qualifications within the European sector of the International Federation of Social Workers....

continued.../

**Table 8.1:** contd.../

2.2.1 Social work is located within different social welfare contexts. Within the UK there are different traditions of social welfare (influenced by legislation, historical development and social attitudes) and these have shaped both social work education and practice in community-based settings including group-care. In an international context, distinctive national approaches to social welfare policy, provision and practice have greatly influenced the focus and content of social work degree programmes....

3.1.2 The service delivery context...

- The location of contemporary social work within both historical and comparative perspectives, including European and international contexts....

3.1.5 The nature of social work practice...

- The place of theoretical perspectives and evidence from international research in assessment and decision-making processes in social work practice.
- The integration of theoretical perspectives and evidence from international research into the design and implementation of effective social work intervention with a wide range of service users, carers and others....

**The US:** The Council on Social Work Education includes within its accreditation standards for social work courses:

4.4 Social Welfare Policy and Services

Programs provide content about the history of social work, the history and current structures of social welfare services, and the role of policy in service delivery, social work practice, and attainment of individual and social well-being. Course content provides students with knowledge and skills to understand major policies that form the foundation of social welfare; analyse organisational, local, state, national, and international issues in social welfare policy and social service delivery....

*Sources:* QAA (2000); DH (2(X)2); TOPSS UK Partnership (2002); CSWE (2004)

'transnational issues': European perspectives on social work, globalisation and social work, intercountry adoption, 'race' and racism in social work and social work with refugees. The (American) *Encyclopedia of Social Work* (Edwards, 1995) is a much bigger production and contains three articles with 'international' in the title. Midgley (1995) writes about comparative research on social welfare services and social policy research, Healy (1995) on organisations in international work, focusing successively on UN organisations, North American government agencies and international social welfare organisations and Hokenstad and Kendall (1995) write about international social work education activities.

A number of publishing activities indicate the presence of international connections in social work. Individual texts, for example

Midgley (1997), and several series comparing social welfare systems have been published. Examples are series published by Greenwood Press, edited by Elliott, Mayadas and Watts (Watts et al, 1995; Mayadas et al, 1997), IFSW by Tan and colleagues (Tan and Envall, nd; Tan and Dodds, 2002), Routledge edited by Dixon and associates, and various British texts edited by Shardlow and associates (Adams et al, 2000, Adams et al, 2001; Shardlow and Payne, 1998), focusing on Europe. Journals called *International Social Work, Community Development Journal, Social Development Issues* and *Global Social Development* publish a great deal of material about transnational projects and activities in social work, and descriptions of activities in single countries with commentary on their relevance and interest for international audiences. Regional journals are well established, such as the *Asia-Pacific Journal of Social Work*, the *European Journal of Social Work*, the *Journal of Social Development in Africa* and *Nordisk Social Arbied* (*Nordic Social Work*). Many other journals occasionally publish comparative articles, material based in countries other than that of the country of publication and the journal *Social Work Abstracts* recognises a number of core international journals, mostly published in the US, but including the *British Journal of Social Work* and the *Indian Journal of Social Work.*

International academic and professional structures exist. These fall into four types of organisation:

- *International social work organisations.* Three organisations have had a continuing existence since the 1920s. These are the International Association of Schools of Social Work (on social work education), the International Council on Social Welfare (representing agencies and primarily voluntary or non-governmental agencies) and the International Federation of Social Workers (a grouping of national professional associations of social workers). Although of varying strength and size, and having different purposes, these provide a means of communication through publications, conferences and joint projects of various kinds. More recently, specialised bodies have developed, for example the Inter-University Consortium on International Social Development.
- *International non-governmental organisations (INGOs).* Examples are international charities and welfare groups like the International Red Cross or Crescent, Save the Children, Caritas, and Médicin Sans Frontiéres. These provide welfare services for people who are crossing borders, such as refugees, and development activities or welfare services in emergencies. Although these are not conventional 'social

work' as it is known in Western countries, these organisations represent international commitments to welfare in various ways.

- *Governmental and intergovernmental activities.* Examples are the provision of aid and joint projects such as the many European programmes which encourage shared training, research and other transfer of expertise across the European Union and, more widely, with the eastern European countries and the states of the former USSR. Similar schemes exist more widely, for example between the US and Latin American and Pacific nations.
- *International organisations.* Examples are the various United Nations (UN) agencies. In this context, shared policies are represented in various UN conventions (see Table 4.4, Chapter Four), such as that on children. Many nations become signatories to these. They represent policy and ideological objectives and markers against which local policies are sometimes measured.

These different forms of organisations allow for international interchange of ideas and to some extent of personnel.

In many parts of the world, therefore, social work and welfare activities are well established, although in different ways. However, this has not always been so. In many formerly and present communist countries, there was an ideological resistance to social work activity. It was seen as inconsistent with the dominant ideology, although social work activities were undertaken in association with related occupations. For example, I once asked a worker running a large youth centre in St Petersburg, Russia, how he had started in the work. He explained that as a police officer he had had to deal with young drug addicts and alcoholics, whose problems had not been recognised by the state, so the police established the youth centre to have something to do with an otherwise intractable social problem. These countries have become interested in taking up social work professions and methodologies, and are interpreting them in ways relevant to their academic and professional traditions. For example, in several parts of Russia, I have met people introducing social work from the perspective of education and psychology, which are professions with a high status in the former USSR, and who lean towards the social pedagogy of central and Nordic Europe rather than Anglo-American therapeutic work.

Another aspect of international structures is evidence of the presence of people who have an international career. Billups (2002) published a book of interviews with people alive during the 1990s considered to be 'notable' in international social work (Table 8.2). All but three of these received an important part of their social work education in the

**Table 8.2:** International social work 'notables'

| Country of origin | Trained in the US | Worked in the US | Worked for UN | Worked/ trained in Europe |
|---|---|---|---|---|
| Australia | | | | ✓ |
| Brazil | | | | ✓ |
| Canada | | | | ✓ |
| Egypt | ✓ | | ✓ | |
| India | ✓ | ✓ | | |
| India | ✓ | | ✓ | |
| Iran | ✓ | ✓ | | |
| Israel | ✓ | | | ✓ |
| Peru/Ecuador | ✓ | | ✓ | ✓ |
| The Philippines | ✓ | | ✓ | |
| Sweden | ✓ | | ✓ | ✓ |
| UK | ✓ | | | |
| US | ✓ | ✓ | | ✓ |
| US | ✓ | | ✓ | |
| Zimbabwe | ✓ | | | |

US, many also received training in Europe; some worked for the UN, or its agencies. Part of the reason for this pattern may be that the book was published in the US and edited by an American. Nevertheless, it illustrates the influence of the US on social work in the mid-20th century.

The subject matter of the IFSW texts is listed in Table 8.3 as an example of practice of recent interest internationally. These are selected as examples because they cover many different countries and focus on particular projects and practice methods, while other comparative books mainly compare national systems of social work, and because the selected texts derive from an international organisation, which should have a broader access to an international authorship than national projects and individual editors have. These cover many of the same client groups, and related professional issues such as ethics, cultural understanding and management issues. Conway (2001), giving an Australian perspective on international social work, comments on the existence of international organisations, the international definition (Table 2.3, Chapter Two), international exchanges of knowledge and information since the 1920s, the concept of social development and its relationship with social work, various South East Asian transnational activities, and some international work, on women's development, HIV/AIDS and adoption.

**Table 8.3:** Fields and methods of international interest

| Field method of interest | Country |
|---|---|
| **Tan and Envall (nd, probably 2000)** | |
| Physical disability – assessment | South Africa |
| People with mental ill health – interdisciplinary service delivery | Zimbabwe |
| HIV/AIDS | South Africa |
| Family work – war zones | Uganda |
| Poverty | Australia |
| Culture and values | China |
| Volunteer activity | Japan |
| Small group work | Aotearoa/ New Zealand |
| Pedagogy, children's rights, parent education | Europe |
| Ethnicity – promoting coexistence | Israel |
| Homeless children | Russia |
| Informal care – new welfare mix | UK |
| Self-determination cultural pluralism | US |
| Child maltreatment – women abuse | US |
| Asian satellite children | Canada |
| Globalisation – postmodernity | US |
| **Tan and Dodds (2002)** | |
| Ageing – UN policy | US |
| Families and children | New Zealand |
| Death and dying | Australia |
| Assessment – potential for violence | US |
| Youth problems – mediation | Korea |
| Practice development | Malaysia |
| Community networks – capacity building | Hong Kong |
| Practice context | South Africa |
| Sustainable development – neoliberal policy | Brazil |
| Organisational audit | UK |
| Social security – social development | China |
| Ethics education – early social work practice | Canada |
| International social work curriculum | US |

To sum up this survey of internationalism in social work there are international organisations to permit interaction on the international stage between social workers, and international agencies and funding programmes to pursue agreed policy. Social work education requires understanding of international issues, but mainly at a contextual level. The main focus of research and understanding is comparative: to provide contextual understanding for a national perspective. There is slightly more activity at a regional level, in areas like the Asia-Pacific and European regions. The need for social work developments in

Eastern Europe, the countries of the former USSR and China, have stimulated international help.

Thus, it is not easy to see an international social work. Conway's (2001) Australian analysis, by giving a local description of international activity, confirms the picture presented by the documents offered here on international developments having a low priority, with a focus on the local and national. There is an increasing range of activity, represented in the chapters in the international texts, in working with people who have migrated, or who have other cross-border concerns such as child abduction and adoption.

The picture historically suggests that social work arose in Western Europe and the US in response to secularisation, industrialisation and municipalisation, and developments in different countries influenced each other (Payne, 2005c). Other industrialising countries used aspects of this way of dealing with social issues that were causing difficulty, adapting them to cultural needs; an example is Japan. Two major traditions emerged: social pedagogy (Table 1.1, Chapter One), a European educational approach, which contests with Anglo-American social work for conceptual dominance. However, although pedagogy and German social science contests the Anglo-American practice-oriented approach (Hämäläinen, 2003), which emerged from the influence of the charity organisation societies on early British and American social work, it has not been substantially interpreted in English, and so, therefore, its critique has little influence where it is aimed.

During the 20th century, the development of international organisation in social work education, influenced by a group of people around the International Association of Schools of Social Work, such as Alice Salomon (Germany), Dame Eileen Younghusband (UK) and Katherine Kendall (US), has generated an 'international view' (Payne, 2005c), which claims a steady development of international mutual influence. The influence of this view is represented in Hokenstad and Kendall's (1995) encyclopaedia entry on international social work education, and in Kendall's memoir (1978) and historical writing (2000), which claims an early European influence, North American development and then worldwide interaction.

However, in addition to the alternative European perspective, the field of social development has grown extensively as a way of connecting social progress towards economic development in resource-poor countries in Latin America, Africa and Asia. This field interacts with Western community development, particularly through mutual influences on community work theory and practice. Moreover, there is a considerable body of work from resource-poor countries commenting on the inappropriate application and North American casework in the mid-20th century (Midgley, 1981), and a commentary about the rich cultural opportunities available in non-Western ideas for application in many countries (Chan et al, 2001; Graham, 2002; Ng and Chan, 2005). Promoting broader links between nations through international projects has questionable benefits, unless planned as a process of development, and with ethical attention to the needs of resource-poor countries (Askeland and Payne, 2001b).

In spite of considerable doubt, however, the discourse reviewed in this book is an international one. I have used quotations mainly from the UK, with some comparative material from the US, but have also used materials published in English from around the world. The practice theory of social work reviewed in Payne (2005a) is written in many countries. The picture, therefore, is of an international discourse, about local variety. How may we understand this?

## Globalisation and post-colonialism

The ideas of globalisation and post-colonialism are interpretations of international trends, which offer useful ways of understanding these debates in social work. Globalisation argues that improvements in information and communication technology, such as worldwide satellite television, mobile (cell) telephones and the internet, together with increasing speed and flexibility of travel, brings different parts of the world and their different cultures and assumptions up against each other more extensively than in any other time in history. We respond to local difficulties and disasters, such as the tsunami that affected South East Asian countries in late 2004, on a global scale. Wars and other conflicts lead to migration and reaction is international, as in the discourse about terrorism, initiated after the terrorist attacks on the World Trade Centre in New York in 2001 and the subsequent wars of invasion in Afghanistan and Iraq. Even minor events, such as the death and mourning of Princess Diana, have an international impact.

These changes are not just cultural and technological. They also have an impact on economics. Speed and cheapness of transport mean cheap clothes from, and telephone call centres in, a low-wage economy on the other side of the world. Ecological consequences arise, such as doubts about whether an economy based on cheap fossil fuels is sustainable, whether other human impacts on the environment are too much for the planet to sustain its equilibrium. Low-skilled work is less available in high-wage economies. The world is divided between highly developed, high resource-using, information and knowledge economies in the West, and resource-poor economies, exploited by Western economic power but less able to resist it. Thus, globalisation is connected to the hypothesis that the world is experiencing deindustrialisation, fragmentation, alienation, mass consumerism and political disengagement (Midgley, 2000). However, it is a complex process, which also offers possibilities. For example, print, information and internet technology makes it cheaper and easier to communicate minority views, run small-scale publications and represent the interests of poorer people. Moreover, use of excessive power often stimulates resistance; for example, Welsh people used their minority language as the basis for a revival of independent political systems and social and cultural independence (Pittock, 1999).

The idea of post-colonialism draws attention to the fact that much of the exploitation of resource-poor countries is not only economic and political, but also cultural, in the same way as the English oppression of the Welsh language (Lynn and Muir, 1996). The European nations have withdrawn from their empires, but rule through economic dominance. The US exercises massive economic and commercial power over poorer countries, and sometimes uses political and military power pursuing interpretations of social movements that benefit its economic interests. Both retain dominance in economy, education and ideas, through the cultural influence of their publishing and media industries. So, colonialism has not disappeared; it has transmuted into a new kind of dominance.

However, Ferguson (2003), examining the British Empire, the largest in history, argues that there are periods of economic and cultural globalisation and that the 20th-century wars and their economic aftermath from 1914 to the 1970s were a period of economic disintegration between two periods of globalising tendencies. He suggests that there is evidence that globalisation occurs when a global power is in a position to enforce globalisation, and that economic openness generally has long-term benefits for both poor and rich countries. There is broad agreement that present globalising tendencies are not exceptional in history, while the benefits or disadvantages are complex and less clear.

## Diverse welfare regimes and social works

Another way of understanding debates about whether social work is global or local is to recognise that, in order to meet its claim to connect the social and the interpersonal, social work, the practice and the profession, needs cultural and social diversity. It has to be relevant to social needs, and these vary according to the social order in which it exists. It also needs to respond to interpersonal needs, and these vary according to the social expectations of the people that social work deals with. Social work, to be diverse in response to social orders and social expectations, needs to offer a range of possibilities from which social care systems and people can select.

This occurs locally and internationally. We experience the social work done in this hospital or that community team as different from the social work done in that hospital or this community team. We experience child protection work as similar to but different from adult protection work. We experience organising long-term social care for elderly people as similar to and different from arranging appropriate placements for children being looked after by local authorities. Studies about different European systems of child protection (Cooper et al, 1995; Hetherington and Cooper, 2001) reveal major differences in social work practice and attitude that derive from different social ideas about intervening in parents' responsibilities and different approaches to managing the legal process.

In summarising texts about international social work above, I identified the following as the main areas of activity:

- International organisation of social work as a profession: the aim of this work seems to be mutual support and help in developing social work, and raising and maintaining commitment to the profession.
- Concern about education in the international context of social work: this work is also mainly about commitment to the profession, but permits understanding and a sense of humility about the possibilities and value of alternatives to our own system and social expectations.
- Concern and research to compare alternative welfare regimes and the role of social care within them: this work aims to identify the consequences for service and for practice of the opportunities and alternatives offered by different welfare regimes.
- Concern about cross-border work such as international adoption and work with asylum-seekers and refugees, to deal with the consequences of migration: this concern aims to develop a service and understanding of practice and social issues that will enable us to deal with the social needs that arise from globalisation.
- Responses to disasters and global movements that require and achieve an international response: these responses arise in the work of international organisations, and may incorporate local social

workers in the activity, as well as a cadre of international relief and development workers.

As with all social work, these activities reflect particular balances between the three perspectives. In particular, social development promotes individual and community development as part of economic development policies, and seeks particularly to be transformational. Social development in resource-poor countries has mainly helped village communities and economic development, particularly for oppressed groups such as women. However, Elliott (1993) points out that its methods and the situation in which it is used is just as relevant in rich countries where there are marked inequalities between rich and poor communities. It also has connections with Western community work, and its theoretical development has influenced Western community work, both in the colonial era and through UN agencies (Payne, 2005a: ch 10).

However, therapeutic and social order social work also exists in resource-poor countries. Adoption, dealing with offenders, responding to children's problems, for example with street children, providing residential care – these are all services that involve social workers in such countries.

A substantial amount of the research and knowledge development effort, however, has gone into comparative work trying to identify the alternative ways in which different countries organise their welfare regimes to deal with similar social problems. This is common in regional groupings of similar countries. For example, Jakobsson (1998) organised an extensive survey of services for elderly people in Nordic countries. In a more complex way, Chamberlayne's (Chamberlayne and King, 2001; Chamberlayne et al, 2002, 2004) narrative studies have tried to identify different experiences of poverty and childcare in European countries. This supports the position I have taken in this book, that there are a variety of ways in which welfare regimes may organise services, and arising from this variations in the way social work is constructed. Looking across different countries, therefore, we can identify a variety of different social works, with a range of roles. However, we can also identify continuities, and these continuities lie in the claim to connect the interpersonal with the social and the social with the interpersonal. We can understand the continuities by exploring the balance of the three perspectives within the diverse social professions created.

## Local UK social professions in international context

How does this analysis of diverse international social works help us to understand social work in any particular country, such as the UK? I suggested above that international diversity was only an extension of local diversity. Therefore, I argue that in any particular welfare regime, there are diverse social professions working alongside each other, as there are in other countries. Recently, we have tended to see UK social work as one entity, from which deviations are fragmentations. However, this is to accept that the 20th-century project to professionalise social work can only be declared complete with the recognition of one unified profession, and the question is where to draw the boundary. I argue that there always have been and always will be diversities, and the question is how to understand the movements and interactions.

As the professionalisation project moved towards completion, the analysis of varieties of social work became a discourse about the unification of specialisations. During the 1950s, for example, UK social workers debated, following North American colleagues who for political reasons had achieved unification in the 1950s (Leighninger, 1987), whether there was one form of 'generic' social work. The alternative was to accept that there were different forms of activity called childcare, probation, psychiatric and medical social work, which were fundamentally different activities. These different activities would rely on, for example different areas of knowledge such as child development, criminology, mental ill health and physical illness and disability. Part of the reasons for these differences were that workers worked in separate services, gained a commitment to their work and a focus on their particular specialised knowledge. When, during the 1970s, most of these services were merged into social services departments and the generic character of social work was accepted, it appeared that there was one social services system, of which social work was the dominant profession. The workforce appeared to be of social workers and less skilled, less educated paraprofessional staff.

Residential work in this scenario was placed in a difficult position. The proportion of staff that had received professional training was lower, in spite of continuing efforts from the 1960s onwards to improve it. So was this a paraprofessional service? However, it was clearly an important aspect of provision for the most seriously damaged children, and its social context and practice was noticeably different from field social work, requiring 24-hour, group-based work, involving long-term care, rather than fairly short-term assessment and problem solving.

There was a struggle to incorporate it into the conception of a unified social work. But the difference in its practice, and in its role in the welfare regime, has always resisted this. It is one of the UK social professions.

Probation and education welfare work also presented difficulties to the unified professionalisation project. Probation had long been regarded as (a very high-quality and well-established) part of social work, being concerned with the welfare and social integration and rehabilitation of offenders. However, an increasing focus on the punishment and retributive roles of the criminal justice system led to this role being seen as less relevant. Also, the welfare and rehabilitative focus of probation was seen as inimical to a professional focus on offending behaviour. In the end, this led to a shift in the welfare regime to treat probation as part of the criminal justice and offender management systems. Does it remain a social profession? Perhaps not in the conception of government ministers and the public who focus on retribution and offending behaviour. However, most offenders present substantial welfare and rehabilitative needs, and have families and communities affected by their offending behaviour. In Scotland, this work remains part of unified social work departments. It seems likely, therefore, that further rebalancing of the welfare regime around the social elements of dealing with offenders will occur, particularly since the British welfare regime is markedly out of line with the more socially oriented regimes of most other developed countries.

Since the Ralphs Report (1975), education welfare was seen as a form of social work; sometimes, as in Coventry, it was incorporated into social services departments. However, it mainly kept its base in education departments, and a focus on the problems that prevent regular school attendance rather than its wider welfare service functions and therapeutic work with children facing difficulties at school. Therefore, it has also been seen as a separate social profession. Will this change as the welfare regime incorporates child and family welfare functions into education departments?

Where does this analysis place the present position of 'social care', discussed towards the end of Chapter Two? My approach is to suggest that, as with youth and community work, residential work, probation, and education welfare, a social profession is being created, just as in many European countries social pedagogy exists alongside social assistance and social work, and in some, cultural social work and other social professions may be distinguished. The social professions of the UK have developed social care to operate alongside the others, to meet the requirements of its welfare regime, just as at one time they incorporated childcare and psychiatric social work as social professions to meet the welfare regime of the time.

Therefore, I propose that boundaries between occupational groups shift over time, and respond to changes in the welfare regime and social expectations in particular countries. This has clearly happened in the UK; we can see it happening in the diverse configurations of the social professions in any other country that we examine.

## Social work consequences of globalisation

If the West exploits resource-poor economies, then social work is part of the exploitation; if globalisation is beneficial, social work is part of the benefits. Alternatives to Anglo-American social work are less powerful in social work discourse, because they are not available in the major world language, English, and not promoted through the international system of knowledge dissemination, which is strongly dominated by English language journals published in the US. However, they are available and disseminated where they are particularly relevant and can have influence more widely through globalising mechanisms such as the internet. Also, a diversity of knowledge and understanding is available from richer countries, which may be reinterpreted for use in other countries that have not yet had the resources or the social need to develop all the different forms of social work.

Moreover, the Anglo-American practice discourse is, we saw in Chapter Three, a therapeutic one, deriving from 1950s' American casework, whereas many alternatives (for example, Silavwe, 1995; Chan et al, 2001) are more about social interdependence and cooperation. The Anglo-American discourse on values has led to ethical views being used in education and public discourse to represent social work, but we noted how difficult it was to apply rights-based approaches. Chapters Five and Six showed the impact of neoliberal managerialism and complex analyses of power that suggest an acceptance of professional uses of power. In Chapter Seven, we saw the incorporation of social work into the complex multiprofessional interactions of complex Western services. Consequently, if relations between Western and resource-poor nations are post-colonialist, instead of trying to achieve direct political power, social work is part of that. The spread of social work to many new nations, the conception that it is internationalist, the influence of Western social work literature, and in particular, the claim that there is one stream of rational knowledge based on universal evidence increases that post-colonialist use of cultural power. We may therefore see social work as part of the influential stream of Western cultural power.

This has consequences for the social work claim. If the social origins of the issues that face people in their lives are global, then the claim to have an impact through interpersonal work requires that social work must find ways of achieving and understanding global challenges in interpersonal interactions. If problems come from global change, then to have an interpersonal impact even on local problems, requires global understanding. This was probably always so, but if globalisation is occurring, the importance of global context is daily growing clearer. Three possible strategies exist for dealing with the problems presented by globalisation:

*Holistic strategies:* These involve trying to understand the conflicts, and make our own conceptions of the world, and the world of social work, more complex. Eventually, we should be able to encompass the whole, or create conceptions which, if not all-encompassing, are at least widely acceptable. Such an approach is potentially oppressive of particular cultures, or post-colonialist, since the attempt of overall conceptualisation inevitably comes from one set of cultural preconceptions. On the other hand, seeking a common conception may make it possible to give greater power to conceptions other than those of the West. It is not clear that all conceptions can be incorporated into one overall perspective.

*Partialising and comparative strategies:* Here we try to limit conceptions of social work so that they apply only to particular countries or to particular cultures. Once we accept that we cannot conceptualise different forms of social work as a whole, we can develop a related strategy of trying to compare different conceptions. Brown (1994), for example, argues that we can only learn about alternative approaches by confronting the differences between them, rather than asserting their wholeness. This approach denies the possibility of wholeness and implies that there is no social work. Rather, there is a collection of 'social works', and we can search for connections and differences between related ideas. As a consequence, we can understand and pursue our conception through understanding better the available alternatives.

*Discourse strategies:* These extend the approach I have taken throughout this book. We see the nature of social work as a collection of competing and interacting sets of ideas, presented as actions and concepts. The discourse about them forms social work. In this approach, we do not seek wholeness through one perspective. Instead, we value the discourse between perspectives as constructing a whole while exploring and valuing difference. Social work's universality does not come from the dominance of one conception of it or of one set of values. Rather, it comes from its engagement in a worldwide discourse about modes of social action in response to fundamental value objectives. The opportunities offered by globalisation broaden the discourse of social work. We must acknowledge the power of Western forms of knowledge through globalisation. Social works across the world do not have equal opportunities for influence. However, the situation internationally is just the same as the situation nationally and locally: the continuities are the claim and the interaction of perspectives. To meet the claim in each situation, workers rebalance the perspectives, creating a relevant social profession within the diversity of social work and increasing its offering of opportunities for flexibility in other welfare regimes.

## Conclusion: international social works

Therefore, the international dimension of social work is important to meeting its claim. If it is to incorporate the social into the local and interpersonal, it must respond in its practice not only to national social issues but also to international social movements. Also, if globalisation is a trend that affects the lives of people everywhere, social work must incorporate the interpersonal experience and needs of the people it serves into international movements. We cannot just intervene in national trends; we must understand and influence the context in which those trends are formed.

NINE

# Social work: (inter)personal, political and professional

One day, the social security office rang up. They had had a call from a neighbour complaining about social security being paid to the O'Gradys, when Sam O'Grady was such a fit and healthy man. He spent all his money on drink. Yesterday, he had been so drunk that he had fallen in the gutter. They should withdraw his social security at once and make him go to work. She had told him so in the street there and then. And he had terrible drunken rages. Neighbours often heard him shouting at his poor, uncomplaining wife. The officer asked for my opinion. I said I would go round and check what had happened.

Sam very definitely headed the O'Grady family. He was strong in physique and personality, a skilled, hard worker in a local factory and dominant but much loved by his wife and two daughters. They had been on their way up, having just bought a new house. Then there was an industrial accident. Sam was brain-damaged, lost his job and ended up at home all the time. The accident changed his dominant personality into aggression and violence. Money was tight, they lost their home because they could not pay the mortgage and had to move to a rented public sector house. The loss of a good lifestyle and the change of Sam's personality placed strains on the family. They limited the teenaged daughters' social lives and transferred the work of financial support and family management and leadership to Mrs O'Grady. I got involved because of the mental health problems, but also supported the family in a variety of ways, including helping to sort out their finances. It was not only Sam's personality that changed, however. Mrs O'Grady also suffered from depression arising from their change in lifestyle and the pressures of unaccustomed family responsibility in a very stressful situation.

I visited to find Mrs O'Grady in tears. She had received some nasty comments from two or three neighbours at the local shop. Apparently, Sam had been coming home from somewhere and had had a blackout. He fell over in the street, recovering to find himself being berated by two neighbours, but unable to reply because his speech was slurred and would not work properly. He felt totally humiliated. He had not been drinking, and rarely did. Although he often shouted at his wife and behaved aggressively, he never hit her or the girls. But he was not the man she had married. Mrs O'Grady did not want to tell the neighbours about their business or difficulties because Sam would feel even worse. I explained the position and agreed that I would let the social security office know enough to maintain their benefit. The local cultural expectations of marriage and male–female relationships, the assumed gender hierarchy in a marriage, where the male breadwinner leads the family, made it difficult for the wife and daughters to change their social roles, and all are relevant to understanding this situation.

This had taken place during one of the government's periodic campaigns about social security scroungers, eagerly supported by elements of the media, so no doubt people in the neighbourhood were particularly aware of the issue. The 'community' was not helpful to this family, but part of the reason for this was the family's wish for and right to privacy. Because of this, the ethical rule of confidentiality limited me from disclosing to others information that might help them deal with the family in a way that reflected more accurately their situation. This is an example of complexities in values (Chapter Four). Independence and respect for people and their ethical consequences came up against a need to act in the community in more open ways. Moreover, the way in which values are incorporated into the political and social roles of social institutions, such as the corner shop and the social security regime, affected what happened. The way institutions represent particular social perspectives on problems potentially placed social services and social security workers in conflict.

This account draws attention to some important issues about the public and private nature of social work:

- It is about personal and interpersonal experiences in people's private domains. The O'Grady family were anxious to keep their problems within the private domain. Social workers, entering private domains, bring private material into the public domain. This happens because they are from outside the private domain but have the right and privilege to intervene within it (Chapter Three). Also, they are part of an agency arrangement that gives a formal and public existence to their activity within clients' private domains (Chapter Five).
- Social work's access to private domains and the fact that it brings private issues into a public domain almost define it as a professional activity. Because of their public position, we accept that social workers have access to private issues. Thus, the social security office felt it right to ask me to investigate and enquire into the situation.

> Also, the family were prepared to allow me to be involved in their private concerns. However, this is a negotiated involvement: people have to agree to it and social workers have to behave in ways that are acceptable. We codify conventions about these acceptable forms of behaviour into conventions of practice, such as those we examined in Chapter Three, and of values (Chapter Four). These form the professional character of social work.

Social work becomes a political activity in two ways. First, because it is in the public domain and often serves the purposes of the state alongside the private concerns of its clients, its nature as a professional activity is a public concern as well as a professional one. Thus, the public and the state have interests in and influence on how social work is conceived and carried out. Second, it is concerned with issues that are often political, in two ways. For example, party political views on social security affected the O'Gradys. Power relations in their community also affected them and their family. At the human level, politics is concerned with the processes by which people and groups gain power over others, in social hierarchies. In their case, we might look at the importance of work, the sick role, gender relationships and expectations and community power.

I was asked to see various members of Mr Cartwright's family. He was an elderly man within a few weeks of dying. There were several daughters and a son; he had moved in with Julie, her three children and several pets a few weeks ago. The home was cheerful and chaotic. He said privately to his doctor that Julie was a bit rough when she helped him physically, but she meant well, but they refused all additional help. However, he had several falls. Another of his daughters complained to the social worker that Julie was stealing his disability living allowance, which was at the highest level because of his illness. Sometimes he was not being fed enough. A strategy meeting under the adult protection guidelines was called, because there was a fear that he, as a vulnerable adult, was being abused. I found out that Julie claimed Mr Cartwright's allowances and spent it on the family finances; there were no clear arrangements and neither wanted one.

As with the O'Gradys, all of these factors interact; the (inter)personal, political and professional are entwined. These three aspects of social work come together in two different ways. In one way, they represent broader or narrower conceptions of what social workers work on. They provide contexts for each other. So, dealing with an interpersonal problem, such as Mrs O'Grady's depression and Sam's humiliation, I could look up and see a broader political perspective of social security campaigns reflecting social attitudes. This helps to understand why they faced this aspect of the problem. Campaigning for better understanding of head injuries, I could look down during that work and realise the personal and interpersonal consequences of my work through that experience. The fact that I did comes from both from my conception of my profession that includes both social improvement and interpersonal work. In the other direction, adult protection guidelines reflect social expectations about how people should be treated and stimulated personal and interpersonal interventions in the Cartwright's private domain. However, this responded to interpersonal relationships and concerns within the family. We can analyse where the concerns come from, but these cases, and all social work cases, illustrate how the social role of social work brings the social and political into the personal and interpersonal.

## The claim and the discourse

Throughout this book, I have used the concepts of claims making and discourse to provide a framework for analysis of the links between social and interpersonal practice. At the outset, I identified the unique claim of social work to incorporate the interpersonal with the social in a professional practice. Chapters One and Two discussed how identity is constructed in social institutions and structures through the history of social relationships within them. Moreover, professional identity is intertwined with the personal identities of members of the profession, so that the collectivity of the profession represents its members and the members embody the identity of the profession. In embodying their profession, social workers incorporate social expectations. Social workers embody a complex of factors, values and political positions, which can be analysed in the discourse, in any practice, agency or welfare regime, between three views of social work: therapeutic, social order and transformational views.

Social work is apparently expressed primarily in its practice with individuals, groups, families and communities, but when examined, this interpersonal practice meets the claim of social work by incorporating the social. Chapters Three and Four explored how this occurs within the therapeutic narrative of interpersonal social work. Within it, the worker embodies the social through:

- their social pathway into social work practice, discussed in Chapter One;

- their incorporation of the social within their personal balance of the views of social work;
- the political and social values incorporated into social work through the process of working out values complexities.

By participation in the interpersonal practice, the client brings into the interpersonal their own social experience and context. However, the interpersonal narrative is not wholly therapeutic, because workers also incorporate the social through their profession and agency interactions. It is striking that in social work the two meanings of agency have great import. One meaning of agency is capacity to achieve an impact on the real world, the other is to refer to the organisational structure through which that impact is achieved and through which the real world has an impact on social workers in their interpersonal work.

Chapter Five discussed changes in the impact on professional social work of agency management. The traditional concern was that being part of managed agencies reduced the independent professional discretion implied by the interpersonal therapeutic narrative. This concern has been extended by the influence on social work of managerialism and enterprise as part of the neoliberal or economic rational political changes in the state in the 1980s and 1990s. This demonstrates the continuing, but changing, impact of how the state organises and provides social work on conceptions of social work. Thus, how social work is managed is a universal continuity in the discourse of social work, as is the debate about social work's power and authority in relation to its clients, discussed in Chapter Six. Agency management and power have both always been part of the discourse about how social work incorporates the social into its interpersonal work. Moreover, both discourses have incorporated current social and political ideas and changed the debate within social work. Also, both discourses have reflected increasingly complex analyses of agency management and discourse; simplifications, whether radical or neoliberal, have been rejected.

Chapters Seven and Eight examined how the discourses and structures within the social work profession help to incorporate the interpersonal into a social analysis. In the 20th century social work became involved in a discourse of professionalisation, but the understanding of the advantages and disadvantages of developing a profession changed. Thus, the discourse became less concerned with the formation of a professional status, but by ways in which knowledge and relationships with other professions are managed. Similarly, seeing social work as a universal has broken down with the evidence that its structures are various locally, nationally and internationally. The important thing is to analyse the discourses about what this particular profession is and how it interacts with others.

## Personal, political, professional

The triangular discourse about the extent to which and the ways in which social work is personal, political or professional have always been present in social work. I have interpreted them as being about the struggle to achieve social work's claim of bringing together the interpersonal and the social. We have seen that struggle in every chapter, in relation to achieving a professional identity, achieving an interpersonal practice, incorporating values, responding to agency management, dealing with professional, organisational and political power, operating in a profession among professions locally, nationally and globally.

Feminist ideas, which have influenced critical social work, see the personal as political: that is, individuals, or groups or categories of people experience it personally when others use power to oppress them. I can see and understand the experience of a woman whose voice is ignored in her otherwise male team, but I cannot experience it. Therefore, the action should focus on the experience – what does it mean to the person? What does it mean politically?

One of the ways of experiencing and understanding the world that we cannot experience personally is through the dialogue and reflexivity of the use of self in relationship as an integral part of interpersonal social work (Chapter Three). Thus, while I argued that this is a crucial characteristic of the nature of the interpersonal therapeutic narrative of social work, it is also integral to the political and transformational narrative. Our self experiencing the world of a client or service user creates an interaction between our political and social role and our interpersonal work. The use of self is potentially transformational, to the extent that we are prepared to be reflexive and incorporate into ourselves not only our personal and professional experience, but also the experience of our client or user's world, made personal by our interpersonal experiences with them. This is why traditionally the relationship has been so important in social work, and why this remains in transformational and social order social work.

Debate on the political in social work is a discourse about the focus on personal and interpersonal as against social explanations and actions in dealing with the problems that social workers face with their clients, but also on the incorporation of the personal into the political and social. Debate on the political and the professional is about the primacy of political as against professional decision making, but also how these influence the personal experience that stimulates the need for therapeutic work and for transformational action. What should the relationship be between democratic political decision making and managerial implementation of it, and professional discretion? The implication of social work's claim is that social work must embody and represent the social drawn from social institutions and structures that make practice and profession possible, while it must also embody and represent the interpersonal throughout the institutions and structures of the social in which it is incorporated. The social worker brings and represents the user's personal experience and incorporates it alongside an understanding of the political and social and allows each to influence the other. That is what they do in social assessment, which is what they do when they intervene, that is what they do when they campaign. They say, in effect: 'Listen to this personal experience, it should change our world, as it has changed me; see this political and social system and how it changes personal lives through me'.

However, these discourses do not construct social work the profession or social work the activity. They are the ideological context within which a local interpersonal construction takes place between workers who embody wider social work identities in a range of interacting social professions and clients who embody and represent other social experiences and structures. Service users and clients experience social workers as wise in the ways of the system, the system needs to experience social workers as wise in the ways of people, and to allow both to influence each other. In the UK, those professions include social work, social care, residential work, education welfare and a variety of specialisations. These wider social work identities are constructed through interaction between local, national and international social works and through interaction and practice with clients, families, groups and communities and their experience of the social. The experience of the user or client and the requirements of the social and political system sets the particular aspect of social care and the social professions that workers take up from the discourse about the three views of social work.

It is therefore only possible to understand social work from its local experience and personal embodiment, as in the narratives with which the chapters of this book start. In the reflexivity of therapeutic social work, the personal and local are incorporated into social work, and the sum of these incorporations of the local and personal become translated through agencies and the profession to have an impact on the social, locally, nationally and internationally. However, it is also only possible to understand social work through interacting politically among its various forms in multiprofessional and specialist practice. Is this a paradox? No, it is the struggle to meet the claim of the interaction of the interpersonal and the social. These two elements must be embodied in the worker's action and must also be incorporated into the local, national and international understanding referred to in Chapter Eight. A broad understanding that does not incorporate the variety of the local and interpersonal fails; an interpersonal action that does not embody the social will be inadequate to the needs that social workers must work with.

This is the source of the conflicts between academics, managers and practitioners in social work. They all struggle to embody and incorporate each other; they do so with variable skill and understanding. To the extent that they fail, they fail to be social workers.

## The construction of social work

Social work is socially constructed. To say that means that it is created in our everyday social relations, building on past social constructions. So, in every society, social work and related social professions have emerged as they are today from their various histories, and from the various social pressures and requirements that exist today. The brief picture of 'social work' contained in Table 1.1 (Chapter One) describes several elements that this book has expanded on:

- It is a service, a pattern of provision that offers services to a public; those who take it up become service users.
- It is a practice, a set of actions recognised in various ways as appropriate.
- It uses social and psychological sciences, not one or the other, but with both interacting together.
- It operates in interpersonal interactions with people.
- It works especially with people from deprived social groups and who are experiencing practical and emotional difficulties in social relationships. This means it is based on people's needs for the service and this particular practice in dealing with their difficulties. Therefore, it is not universally provided in the same way as education, health and social security. Wider use of the practice and wider availability of the service might be possible. However, needs-based provision is

the main social priority and how most people understand social work.

- It balances three objectives:
  - maintaining social order and providing social welfare services effectively;
  - helping people attain personal fulfilment and power over their lives;
  - stimulating social change.

Social work is one of a network of social services and professional practices that make up provision for welfare in most societies, their various welfare regimes. It is professional, not because it meets the specification of a list of characteristics of a profession, but because:

- its practice is recognised in law and the organisation of public services and society;
- it has developed knowledge and skills underlying the practice and organisation of service, not only possessed by social workers but unique in its particular combination of the social and the psychological with its values and objectives;
- its education is recognised as a professional specialism at every level by accredited universities throughout the world.

Because social work emerges from a particular place's history and social environment, we cannot specify a universal role for it in relation to other professions making up the field of welfare provision; this varies and changes over time (Chapters Seven and Eight). Every social worker embodies, as they practice, their particular pathway into the professional arena of social work. Their practice incorporates the legal, organisational and social expectations of social work conveyed through the impact on their practice of their agency's management and through their professional and personal relationships with service users and the communities that surround them and with other practitioners interacting with their practice. As they embody it, they represent it in relation to other professions. As they embody their enactment or performance of the culture of their locality and country, they change social work by interpenetrating social work and the local.

Therefore, social work is a social order, because it is a recognisable and recurrent pattern of activities in social relations, buttressed by the institutionalisation within social relationships of acknowledged (debated, yes, but recognisable) social values, social structures and organisations. Social workers are part of that order, by virtue of their pathway and the influences of the social environment of their professional service and practice. But they are also part of the cultural orders of their countries and social systems and of their locality. So, in each social worker, as they interact interpersonally with clients and those around them, they, as an incorporation of social work, become changed by their local, and their social work changes other social works by their impact on the discourse among social works across the world.

That is why the national and international organisation is crucial to social work, and consequently why the professionalisation project remains important. Agencies and professional power structure the incorporation into social work of the social (Chapters Five and Six) and also the interpersonal into the social (Chapters Seven and Eight). Understanding how this happens is crucial to understanding and setting objectives in the interpersonal and directing interpersonal change to influence the social.

# References


AASW (American Association of Social Workers) (1929) *Social Case Work: Generic and Specific*, New York, NY: AASW.

Adam, B., Beck, U. and van Loon, J. (2000) *The Risk Society and Beyond: Critical Issues for Social Theory*, London: Sage Publications.

Adams, A., Erath, P. and Shardlow, S.M. (eds) (2000) *Fundamentals of Social Work in Selected European Countries*, Lyme Regis: Russell House.

Adams, A., Erath, P. and Shardlow, S.M. (eds) (2001) *Key Themes in European Social Work: Theory, Practice, Perspectives*, Lyme Regis: Russell House.

Adams, R. (1992) *Prison Riots in Britain and the USA*, Basingstoke: Macmillan.

Adams, R. (2002) 'Social work processes', in R. Adams, L. Dominelli and M. Payne (eds) *Social Work: Themes, Issues and Critical Debates* (2nd edn), Basingstoke: Palgrave, pp 249-66.

Adams, R., Dominelli, L. and Payne, M. (eds) (2002) *Critical Practice in Social Work: Part 3: Managing and Organising Practice*, Basingstoke: Palgrave, pp 221-303.

Adams, R., Dominelli, L. and Payne, M. (2005) 'Transformational social work', in R. Adams, L. Dominelli and M. Payne (eds) *Social Work Futures: Crossing Boundaries, Transforming Practice*, Basingstoke: Palgrave Macmillan, pp 1-17.

Ainsworth, F. and Fulcher, L.C. (eds) (1981) *Group Care for Children: Concepts and Issues*, London: Tavistock.

Alcoff, L.M. and Mendieta, E. (eds) (2003) *Identities: Race, Class, Gender and Nationality*, Malden, MA: Blackwell Publishing.

Alden, P. (1929) 'I. Definition and progress of social work', *Proceedings: 1st International Conference of Social Work, Paris: July 8th-13th 1928*, Paris: International Conference of Social Work, pp 597-607.

Alexander, L.B. (1972) 'Social work's Freudian deluge: myth or reality?', *Social Service Review*, 46(4): 517-38.

Archer, M.S. (1995) *Realist Social Theory: A Morphogenetic Approach*, Cambridge: Cambridge University Press.

Archer, M.S. (2000) *Being Human: The Problem of Agency*, Cambridge: Cambridge University Press.

Askeland, G.A. and Payne, M. (2001a) 'What is valid knowledge for social workers?', *Social Work in Europe*, 8(3): 13-23.

Askeland, G.A. and Payne, M. (2001b) 'Broadening the mind: cross-national activities in social work', *European Journal of Social Work*, 4(3): 263–74.

Askonas, P. and Stewart, A. (eds) (2000) *Social Inclusion: Possibilities and Tensions*, Basingstoke: Macmillan.

Asquith, S., Clark, C. and Waterhouse, L. (2005) 'The role of the social worker in the 21st century: a literature review', Edinburgh: Scottish Executive (www.scotland.gov.uk/Resource/Doc/47121/0020821.pdf, accessed 26 January 2006).

Attlee, C.R. (1920) *The Social Worker*, London: Bell.

Bailey, R. (1980) 'Social workers: pawns, police or agitators?', in M. Brake and R. Bailey (eds) *Radical Social Work and Practice*, London: Arnold, pp 215–27.

Bailey, R. and Brake, R. (1975) 'Introduction: social work in the welfare state', in R. Bailey and R. Brake (eds) *Radical Social Work*, London: Arnold, pp 1–12.

Baker, R. (1976) *The Interpersonal Process in Generic Social Work: An Introduction*, Bundoora: PIT Press.

Banks, S. (2001) *Ethics and Values in Social Work* (2nd edn), Basingstoke: Palgrave.

Banks, S. (2004) *Ethics, Accountability and the Social Professions*, Basingstoke: Palgrave Macmillan.

Barclay Report (1982) *Social Workers: Their Role and Tasks*, London: Bedford Square Press.

Baron, S., Field, J. and Schuller, T. (eds) (2000) *Social Capital: Critical Perspectives*, Oxford: Oxford University Press.

Barry, M. and Hallett, C. (eds) (1998) *Social Exclusion and Social Work: Issues of Theory, Policy and Practice*, Lyme Regis: Russell House.

Bartlett, H.M. (1970) *The Common Base of Social Work Practice*, New York: National Association of Social Workers.

Bass, E. and Davis, L. (1988) *The Courage to Heal: A Guide for Women Survivors of Child Sexual Abuse*, New York: Harper and Row.

BASW (British Association of Social Workers) (1977) *The Social Work Task*, Birmingham: BASW Publications.

BASW (1980) *Clients are Fellow Citizens*, Birmingham: BASW Publications.

Bateman, N. (2000) *Advocacy Skills for Health and Social Care Professionals*, London: Jessica Kingsley.

Beck, U. (1992) *Risk Society: Towards a New Modernity*, London: Sage Publications.

Beckett, C. and Maynard, A. (2005) *Values and Ethics in Social Work: An Introduction*, London: Sage Publications.

Bell, D. (1974) *The Coming of Post-Industrial Society*, New York: Basic Books.

Berger, P.L. and Luckmann, T. (1971) *The Social Construction of Reality*, Harmondsworth: Penguin (original American publication, 1966).

Biestek, F.P. (1961) *The Casework Relationship*, London: Allen and Unwin.

Billis, D., Bromley, G., Hey, A. and Rowbottom, R. (1980) *Organising Social Services Departments: Further Studies by the Brunel Social Services Unit*, London: Heinemann.

Billups, J.O. (ed) (2002) *Faithful Angels: Portraits of International Social Work Notables*, Washington, DC: NASW Press.

Blakemore, K. and Boneham, M. (1994) *Age, Race and Ethnicity: A Comparative Approach*, Buckingham: Open University Press.

Bland, R. (2002) 'Independence, privacy and risk', in B. Bytheway, V. Bacigalupo, J. Bornat, J. Johnson and S. Spurr (eds) *Understanding Care, Welfare and Community: A Reader*, London: Routledge, pp 216-24.

Boehm, W.W. (1958) 'The nature of social work', in P.E. Weinberger (ed) (1969) *Perspectives on Social Welfare: An Introductory Anthology*, Toronto: Collier-Macmillan, pp 265-75.

Borel, K. (1997) 'Social knowledge and social change: a synthesis of styles', in EASSW (ed) *Social Work Education Advancing Human Rights*, Lisbon: Instituto Superior de Serviço Social, pp 309-18.

Bowers, S. (1949) 'The nature and definition of social casework', *Social Casework*, 30: 311-17.

Brandon, D. and Jordan, B. (1979) 'Introduction', in D. Brandon and B. Jordan (eds) *Creative Social Work*, Oxford: Blackwell, pp 1-6.

Brandon, D., Brandon, A. and Brandon, T. (1995) *Advocacy: Power to People with Disabilities*, Birmingham: Venture Press.

Braye, S. and Preston-Shoot, M. (1995) *Empowering Practice in Social Care*, Buckingham: Open University Press.

Braye, S. and Preston-Shoot, M. (2001) 'Social work practice and accountability', in L.-A. Cull and J. Roche (eds) *The Law and Social Work: Contemporary Issues for Practice*, Basingstoke: Palgrave, pp 43-53.

Brechin, A. and Sidell, M. (2000) 'Ways of knowing', in R. Gomm and C. Davies (eds) *Using Evidence in Health and Social* Care, London: Sage Publications, pp 3-25.

Brewer, C. and Lait, J. (1980) *Can Social Work Survive?*, London: Temple Smith.

Brint, S. (1994) *In an Age of Experts: The Changing Role of Professionals in Politics and Public Life*, Princeton, NJ: Princeton University Press.

Brown, A. (1977) 'Worker style in social work', *Social Work Today*, 8(29): 13–15.

Brown, H. and Smith, H. (eds) (1992) *Normalisation: A Reader for the Nineties*, London: Routledge.

Brown, K. (1994) 'A framework of teaching comparative social work', in G. Gehrmann, K.D. Müller and R. Ploem (eds) *Social Work and Social Work Studies: Co-operation in Europe 2000*, Weinheim: Deutscher Studien Verlag, pp 131–40.

Bull, R. and Shaw, I. (1992) 'Constructing causal accounts in social work', *Sociology*, 26(4): 635–49.

Butler, I. and Drakeford, M. (2005) *Scandal, Social Policy and Social Welfare* (2nd edn), Bristol: The Policy Press.

Butrym, Z.T. (1976) *The Nature of Social Work*, London: Macmillan.

Byrne, D. (1999) *Social Exclusion*, Buckingham: Open University Press.

Bytheway, B. (1994) *Ageism*, Buckingham: Open University Press.

Campbell, P. (1999) 'The service user/survivor movement', in C. Newnes, G. Holmes and C. Dunn (eds) *This is Madness: A Critical Look at Psychiatry and the Future of Mental Health Services*, Ross-on-Wye: PCCS Books, pp 195-209.

Campbell, T.D. (1978) 'Discretionary "rights"', in N. Timms and D. Watson (eds) *Philosophy in Social Work*, London: Routledge and Kegan Paul, pp 50–77.

Carkhuff, R.R. and Berenson, B.C. (1977) *Beyond Counseling and Therapy* (2nd edn), New York: Holt, Rinehart & Winston.

Causer G. and Exworthy, M. (1999) 'Professionals as managers across the public sector', in J. Reynolds, J. Henderson, J. Seden, J. Charlesworth and A. Bullman (eds) (2003) *The Managing Care Reader*, London: Routledge, pp 213–19.

CCETSW (Central Council for Education and Training in Social Work) (1975) *Education and Training for Social Work*, London: CCETSW.

CCETSW (1991) *Rules and Requirements for the Diploma in Social Work DipSW* (Paper 30, 2nd edn), London: CCETSW.

Chamberlayne, P. and King A. (2001) *Cultures of Care: Biographies of Carers in Britain and the Two Germanies*, Bristol: The Policy Press.

Chamberlayne, P., Bornat, J. and Apitzch, U. (eds) (2004) *Biographical Methods and Professional Practice: An International Perspective*, Bristol: The Policy Press.

Chamberlayne, P., Rustin, M. and Wengraf, T. (eds) (2002) *Biography and Social Exclusion in Europe: Experiences and Life Journeys*, Bristol: The Policy Press.

Chan, C.L.W., Ho, P.S.Y. and Chow, E. (2001) 'A body-mind-spirit model in health: an Eastern approach', *Social Work in Health Care*, 34(3/4): 261-82.

Charles, M. and Butler, S. (2004) 'Social workers' management of organisational change', in M. Lymbery and S. Butler (eds) *Social Work Ideals and Practice Realities*, Basingstoke: Palgrave Macmillan, pp 57-82.

Charlesworth, J. (2003) 'Managing across professional and agency boundaries', in J. Seden and J. Reynolds (eds) *Managing Care in Practice*, London: Routledge, pp 139-64.

Cheyney, A.S. (1926) *The Nature and Scope of Social Work*, New York: American Association of Social Workers.

Chilean Committee of Social Work (1961) 'Chilean Committee of Social Work', in ICSW (ed) 'The term "social work" as used throughout the world', *International Social Work*, 4(1): 7-8.

Clark, C. (2000) *Social Work Ethics: Politics, Principles and Practice*, Basingstoke: Macmillan.

Clark, C. (2002) 'Identity, individual rights and social justice', in R. Adams, L. Dominelli and M. Payne (eds) *Social Work: Themes, Issues and Critical Debates* (2nd edn), Basingstoke: Palgrave, pp 38-45.

Clarke, J. (1998) 'Doing the right thing? Managerialism and social welfare', in J. Reynolds, J. Henderson, J. Seden, J. Charlesworth and A. Bullman (eds) (2003) *The Managing Care Reader*, London: Routledge, pp 195-203.

Clarke, J. and Newman, J. (1997) *The Managerial State: Power, Politics and Ideology in the Remaking of Social Welfare*, London: Sage Publications.

Clausen, H., Kendall, M., Murray, S., Worth, A., Boyd, K. and Benton, F. (2005) 'Would palliative care patients benefit from social workers' retaining the traditional "casework" role rather than working as care managers? A prospective serial qualitative interview study', *British Journal of Social Work*, 35(2): 277-85.

Clough, R. (2000) *The Practice of Residential Work*, Basingstoke: Macmillan.

Compton, B.R. and Galaway, B. (1975-99) *Social Work Processes* (6th edn, 1999), Pacific Grove, CA: Brooks/Cole.

Conway, J. (2001) 'An Australian perspective on international fields of practice in social work', in M. Alston and J. McKinnon (eds) *Social Work: Fields of Practice*, Melbourne: Oxford University Press: 236-50.

Cooper, A., Hetherington, R., Baistow, K., Pitts, J. and Spriggs, A. (1995) *Positive Child Protection: A View from Abroad*, Lyme Regis: Russell House.

Cooper, M.G. and Lesser, J.G. (2002) *Clinical Social Work Practice: An Integrated Approach*, Needham Heights, MA: Allyn and Bacon.

Corby, B., Doig, A. and Roberts, V. (2001) *Public Inquiries into Abuse of Children in Residential Care*, London: Jessica Kingsley.

Cormack, U. and McDougall, K. (1950) 'Case-work in social service', in C. Morris (ed) *Social Case-Work in Great Britain*, London: Faber and Faber, pp 15–32.

Coulshed, V. and Orme, J. (1998) *Social Work Practice: An Introduction* (3rd edn), Basingstoke: Macmillan.

Craib, I. (1998) *Experiencing Agency*, London: Sage Publications.

CSWE (Council on Social Work Education) (2004) 'Education policy and accreditation standards', Alexandria, VA: Council on Social Work Education (www.cswe.org/, accessed 4 September 2005).

Cvetkovich, G. and Löfstedt, R.E. (1999) *Social Trust and the Management of Risk*, London: Earthscan,

Dalrymple, J. and Burke, B. (1995) *Anti-oppressive Practice: Social Care and the Law*, Buckingham: Open University Press.

Dalrymple, J. and Hough, J. (eds) (1995) *Having a Voice: An Exploration of Children's Rights and Advocacy*, Birmingham: Venture Press.

Davies, M. (1994) *The Essential Social Worker: A Guide to Positive Practice* (3rd edn), Aldershot: Arena.

Davies, M. (ed) (2000) *The Blackwell Encyclopaedia of Social Work*, Oxford: Blackwell Publishing.

Day, P. (1981) *Social Work and Social Control*, London: Tavistock.

Derezotes, D.S. (2000) *Advanced Generalist Social Work Practice*, Thousand Oaks, CA: Sage Publications.

de Schweinitz, E. and de Schweinitz, K. (1964) 'The place of authority in the protective function of the public welfare agency', in S.A. Yelaja (ed) (1971) *Authority and Social Work: Concept and Use*, Toronto: University of Toronto Press, pp 123–33.

Devine, E.T. (1922) *Social Work*, New York: Macmillan.

DH (Department of Health) (1998) *Partnership in Action (New Opportunities for Joint Working between Health and Social Services) A Discussion Document*, London: DH.

DH (1999) *The Children Act Report: 1995-1999*, London: The Stationery Office.

DH (2002) *The Requirements for Social Work Training*, London: DH. (www.dh.gov.uk/assetRoot/04/06/02/62/04060262.pdf).

DH (2005) 'Health and Social Care System' (www.dh.gov.uk/AboutUs/DeliveringHealthAndSocialCare/TheHealthAndSocialCareSystem/HealthAndSocialCareSystemArticle/fs/en?CONTENT_ID=4105339&chk=v/eD0Q, accessed 15 May 2005).

DHSS (Department of Health and Social Security) (1976) *Joint Care Planning: Health and Local Authorities*, London: DHSS Circular [HC(76)18, LAC976)6].

DHSS (1977) *Joint Care Planning: Health and Social Authorities*, London: DHSS Circular [HC(77)17, LAC(77)6].

Dominelli, L. (1997a) *Anti-Racist Social Work* (2nd edn), Basingstoke: Macmillan.

Dominelli, L. (1997b) *Sociology for Social Work*, London: Macmillan.

Dominelli, L. (2002) *Anti-Oppressive Social Work Theory and Practice*, Basingstoke: Palgrave Macmillan.

Dominelli, L. (2004) *Social Work: Theory and Practice for a Changing Profession*, Cambridge: Polity.

Dominelli, L. and McCleod, E. (1989) *Feminist Social Work*, Basingstoke: Macmillan.

Dorfman, R.A. (1996) *Clinical Social Work: Definition, Practice and Vision*, New York, NY: Brunner/Mazel.

Downie, R.S. and Telfer, E. (1969) *Respect for Persons: A Philosophical Analysis of the Moral, Political and Religious Ideas of the Supreme Worth of the Individual Person*, London: Allen and Unwin.

Drakeford, M. (2000) *Privatisation and Social Policy*, Harlow: Longmans.

Dubois, B. and Miley, K.K. (1999) *Social Work: An Empowering Profession*, Boston, MA: Allyn and Bacon.

Dutt, R. (2001) 'Racism and social work practice', in L.-A. Cull and J. Roche (eds) *The Law and Social Work: Contemporary Issues for Practice*, Basingstoke: Palgrave, pp 20-30.

EASSW (European Association of Schools of Social Work) (ed) (1995) *Social Work Education Advancing Human Rights*, Lisbon: Instituto Superior de Serviço Social.

Eddy, D.M. (1984) 'Variations in physician practice: the role of uncertainty', in J. Dowie and A. Elstein (eds) (1988) *Professional Judgement: A Reader in Clinical Decision-making*, Cambridge: Cambridge University Press.

Edwards, R.L. (ed) (1995) *Encyclopedia of Social Work* (19th edn, 2 vols), Washington, DC: NASW Press.

Elliott, D. (1993) 'Social work and social development: towards an integrative model for social work practice', *International Social Work*, 36(1): 1-36.

England, H. (1986) *Social Work as Art: Making Sense for Good Practice*, London: Allen and Unwin.

Esping-Andersen, G. (1990) *The Three Worlds of Welfare Capitalism*, Cambridge: Polity.

Etzioni, A. (1995) *The Spirit of Community: Rights, Responsibilities and the Communitarian Agenda*, London: Fontana.

Evans, D. and Kearney, J. (1996) *Working in Social Care: A Systemic Approach*, Aldershot: Arena.

Ezell, M. (1994) 'Advocacy practice of social workers', *Families in Society*, 75(1):36-46.

Fairclough, N. (1992) *Discourse and Social Change*, Cambridge: Polity.

Ferguson, N. (2003) *Empire: How Britain Made the Modern World*, London: Allen Lane.

Fink, A.E. (1961) 'Authority in the correctional process', in S.A. Yelaja (ed) (1971) *Authority and social work: Concept and Use*, Toronto: University of Toronto Press, pp 298-309.

Fischer, J. (1976) *The Effectiveness of Social Casework*, Springfield, IL: Thomas.

Fleet, F. (2000) 'Counselling and contemporary social work', in P. Stepney and D. Ford (eds) *Social Work Models, Methods and Theories: A Framework for Practice*, Lyme Regis: Russell House, pp 84-92.

Fook, J. (2002) *Social Work: Critical Theory and* Practice, London: Sage Publications.

Ford, P. and Postle, K. (2000) 'Task-centred practice and care management', in P. Stepney and D. Ford (eds) *Social Work Models, Methods and Theories: A Framework for Practice*, Lyme Regis: Russell House, pp 52-64.

Foren, R. and Bailey, R. (1968) *Authority in Social Casework*, Oxford: Pergamon.

Foster, P. and Wilding, P. (2000) 'Whither welfare professionalisation', in J. Reynolds, J. Henderson, J. Seden, J. Charlesworth and A. Bullman (eds) (2003) *The Managing Care Reader*, London: Routledge, pp 204-12.

Foucault, M. (1972) *The Archaeology of Knowledge and the Discourse on Language*, New York: Pantheon.

Freidson, E. (1970) *Profession of Medicine: A Study of the Sociology of Applied Knowledge*, New York: Dodd, Mead.

Freidson, E. (1994) *Professionalism Reborn: Theory, Prophecy and Policy*, Cambridge: Polity.

Garrett, M. (1980) 'The problem with authority', in M. Brake and R. Bailey (eds) *Radical Social Work and Practice*, London: Edward Arnold, pp 197-214.

Germain, C.B. (1970) 'Casework and science: a historical encounter', in R.W. Roberts and R.H. Nee (eds) *Theories of Social Casework*, Chicago, IL: University of Chicago Press.

Germain, C.B. and Gitterman, A. (1996) *The Life Model of Social Work Practice: Advances in Theory and Practice*, New York: Columbia University Press.

German Council on Social Welfare (1961) 'Use of the phrase "Social Work" in Germany', in ICSW (ed) 'The term "social work" as used throughout the world', *International Social Work*, 4(1): 8-9.

Gill, R. (1992) *Moral Communities: The Prideaux Lectures for 1992*, Exeter: University of Exeter Press.

Gilligan, C. (1982) *In a Different Voice: Psychological Theory and Women's Development*, Cambridge, MA: Harvard University Press.

Gilmore, S. (2001) 'A critical perspective on the welfare principle', in L.-A. Cull and J. Roche (eds) *The Law and Social Work: Contemporary Issues for Practice*, Basingstoke: Palgrave, pp 3-10.

Glasby, J. and Littlechild, R. (2004) *The Health and Social Care Divide: The Experiences of Older People*, Bristol: The Policy Press.

Glastonbury, B., Cooper, D. and Hawkins, P. (1980) *Social Work in Conflict: The Practitioner and the Bureaucrat*, London: Croom Helm.

Goffman, E. (1968) *The Presentation of Self in Everyday Life*, Harmondsworth: Penguin.

Goffman, E. (1972a) *Relations in Public: Microstudies of the Public Order*, Harmondsworth: Penguin.

Goffman, E. (1972b) *Interaction Ritual: Essays on Face-to-face Behaviour*, Harmondsworth: Penguin.

Goffman, E. (1972c) *Encounters: Two Studies in the Sociology of Interaction*, Harmondsworth: Penguin.

Goldstein, E.G. (1995) *Ego Psychology and Social Work Practice* (2nd edn), New York: Free Press.

Gomes, J. (1995) 'An overview of advocacy', in J. Dalrymple and J. Hough (eds) *Having a Voice: An Exploration of Children's Rights and Advocacy*, Birmingham: Venture Press, pp 19-30.

Gomm, R. and Davies, C. (eds) (2000) *Using Evidence in Health and Social Care*, London: Sage Publications.

Google UK (2005) 'Define "social work"' (www.google.co.uk/search?hl=en&lr=&oi=defmore&q=define:Social+Work, accessed 15 May).

Graham, M. (2002) *Social Work and African-centred Worldviews*, Birmingham: Venture Press.

Grant, G. (1997) 'Consulting to involve or consulting to empower?', in P. Ramcharan, G. Roberts, G. Grant and J. Borland (eds) *Empowerment in Everyday Life: Learning Disability*, London: Jessica Kingsley, pp 121-43.

Greenwood, E. (1957) 'Attributes of a profession', *Social Work*, 2(3): 45-55.

GSCC (General Social Care Council) (2005) 'Get copies of our codes' (www.gscc.org.uk/Good+practice+and+conduct/Get+copies+of+our+codes/, accessed 6 August).

Gutiérrez, L.M., Parsons, R.J. and Cox, E.O. (1998) *Empowerment in Social Work Practice: A Sourcebook*, Pacific Grove, CA: Brooks/Cole.

Halmos, P. (1965) *The Faith of the Counsellors*, London: Constable.

Halmos, P. (1970) *The Personal Service Society*, London: Constable.

Hämäläinen, J. (2003) 'The concept of social pedagogy in the field of social work', *Journal of Social Work*, 3(1): 69-80.

Hamilton, G. (1951) *Theory and Practice of Social Casework* (2nd edn), New York, NY: Columbia University Press.

Handler, J.F. (1974) *The Coercive Social Worker: British Lessons for American Social Services*, New York: Academic Press.

Hargie, O., Saunders, C. and Dickson, D. (1994) *Social Skills in Interpersonal Communication* (3rd edn), London: Routledge.

Harris, J. (2003) *The Social Work Business*, London: Routledge.

Hart, J. (1980) '"It's just a stage we're going through": the sexual politics of casework', in R. Bailey and R. Brake (eds) *Radical Social Work and Practice*, London: Arnold, pp 43-63.

Healy, K. (2000) *Social Work Practices: Contemporary Perspectives on Change*, London: Sage Publications.

Healy, K. (2005) *Social Work Theories in Context: Creating Frameworks for Practice*, Basingstoke: Palgrave.

Healy, L.M. (1995) 'International social welfare: organizations and activities', in R.L. Edwards (ed) *Encyclopedia of Social Work* (19th edn, vol 2), Washington, DC: NASW Press, pp 1499-510.

Hearn, J. (1982) 'Radical social work – contradictions, limitations and political possibilities', *Critical Social Policy*, 2(1): 19-34.

Hetherington, R. and Cooper, A. (2001) 'Child protection: lessons from abroad', in L.-A. Cull and J. Roche (eds) *The Law and Social Work: Contemporary Issues for Practice*, Basingstoke: Palgrave, pp 97-104.

Hockey, J. and James, A. (2003) *Social Identities across the Life Course*, Basingstoke: Palgrave Macmillan,

Hokenstad, M.C. and Kendall, K.A. (1995) 'International social work education', in R.L. Edwards (ed) *Encyclopedia of Social Work* (19th edn, vol 2), Washington, DC: NASW Press, pp 1511-20.

Hollis, F. (1970) 'The psychosocial approach to the practice of casework', in R.W. Roberts and R.H. Nee (eds) *Theories of Social Casework*, Chicago, IL: University of Chicago Press, pp 33-75.

Horner, W.C and Whitbeck, L.B. (1991) 'Personal versus professional values in social work: a methodological note', *Journal of Social Service Research*, 14 (1/2): 21-43.

Hough, G. (1999) 'The organisation of social work in the customer culture', in B. Pease and J. Fook (eds) *Transforming Social Work Practice: Postmodern Critical Perspectives*, London: Routledge, pp 40-54.

Hough, G. and Briskman, L. (2003) 'Responding to the changing socio-political context of practice', in J. Allan, B. Pease and L. Briskman (eds) *Critical Social Work: An Introduction to Theories and Practices*, Crows Nest, NSW: Allen and Unwin.

Howarth, D. (2000) *Discourse*, Buckingham: Open University Press.

Howe, D. (1987) *An Introduction to Social Work Theory*, Aldershot: Wildwood House.

Hudson, B. (2000) 'Inter-agency collaboration – a sceptical view', in A. Brechin, H. Brown and M.A. Eby (eds) *Critical Practice in Health and Social* Care, London: Sage Publications, pp 253-74.

Hugman, R. (1991) *Power in Caring Professions*, London: Macmillan.

Humphries, B. (1996) 'Contradictions in the culture of empowerment', in B. Humphries (ed) *Critical Perspectives on Empowerment*, Birmingham: Venture Press, pp 1-16.

Hunt, A.W. (1964) 'Enforcement in probation casework', in E. Younghusband (ed) (1966) *New Developments in Casework*, London: Allen and Unwin, pp 155-66.

Husband, C. (1980) 'Culture, context and practice: racism in social work', in R. Bailey and R. Brake (eds) *Radical Social Work and Practice*, London: Arnold, pp 64-85.

Husband, C. (1991) '"Race", conflictual politics, and anti-racist social work: lessons from the past for action in the 90s', in CD Project Steering Group, *Setting the Context for Change*, London: CCETSW, pp 46-73.

IASSW (International Association of Schools of Social Work) (2001) 'About IASSW: International Definition of Social Work' (www.iassw-aiets.org/, accessed 20 March 2006).

Ife, J. (1997) *Rethinking Social Work: Towards Critical Practice*, South Melbourne: Longman.

Ife, J. (2001) *Human Rights and Social Work: Towards Rights-based Practice*, Cambridge: Cambridge University Press.

IFSW (International Federation of Social Workers) (2000) 'International Federation of Social Workers: definition of social work' (www.ifsw.org/en/p38000017.html, accessed 6 August).

IFSW (2004) 'Ethics in Social Work: statement of Principles' (www.ifsw.org/en/p38000324.html, accessed 24 March 2006).

IFSW (2005) 'National Codes of Ethics' (www.ifsw.org/en/p38000194.html, accessed 24 March 2006).

Jakobsson, G. (1998) 'The politics of care for elderly people in Scandinavia', *European Journal of Social Work*, 1(1): 87-93.

James, R.K. and Gilliland, B.E. (2001) *Crisis Intervention Strategies* (4th edn), Belmont, CA: Wadsworth.

Japanese National Committee on Social Welfare (1961) 'How the term "social work" is used in Japan', in ICSW (ed) 'The term "social work" as used throughout the world Part II', *International Social Work*, 4(3): 29-32.

Jenkins, R. (1996) *Social Identity*, London: Routledge.

Jordan, B. (1975) 'Is the client a fellow-citizen?', *Social Work Today*, 15: 471-5.

Kamerman, S.B. (2002) 'Fields of practice', in M.A. Mattaini, C.T. Lowey and C.H. Meyer (eds) *Foundations of Social Work Practice: A Graduate Text*, Washington, DC: NASW Press, pp 319-39.

Kendall, K.A. (1978) 'The IASSW 1928-1978: a journey of remembrance', in K.A. Kendall, *Reflections on Social Work Education 1950-1978*, New York: International Association of Schools of Social Work, pp 170-91.

Kendall, K.A. (2000) *Social Work Education: Its Origins in Europe*, Alexandria, VA: CSWE.

Kennard, D. (1998) *An Introduction to Therapeutic Communities*, London: Jessica Kingsley.

Kennett, C. (2001) 'Psychosocial day care', in J. Hearn and K. Myers (eds) *Palliative Day Care in Practice*, Oxford: Oxford University Press, pp 59-78.

Krill, D. (1990) *Practice Wisdom: A Guide for Helping Professionals*, Newbury Park, CA: Sage Publications.

Laczko, F. and Phillipson, C. (1991) *Changing Work and Retirement*, Buckingham: Open University Press.

Langan, M. and Lee, P. (1989a) 'Whatever happened to radical social work?', in M. Langan and P. Lee (eds) *Radical Social Work Today*, London: Unwin Hyman, pp 1-18.

Langan, M. and Lee, P. (eds) (1989b) *Radical Social Work Today*, London: Unwin Hyman.

Lee, J.A.B. (2001) *The Empowerment Approach to Social Work Practice: Building the Beloved Community* (2nd edn), New York: Columbia University Press.

Lee, P.R. (1929) 'Social work: cause and function', in F. Lowry (ed) (1939) *Readings in Social Case Work 1920-1938: Selected Reprints for the Case Work Practitioner*, New York: Columbia University Press, pp 22-37.

Lees, R. (1971) 'Social work 1925-50: the case for a reappraisal', *British Journal of Social Work*, 1(4): 371-80.

Leighninger, L. (1987) *Social Work: Search for Identity*, New York: Greenwood.

Leighton, N. (1985) 'Personal and professional values – marriage or divorce?', in D. Watson (ed) *A Code of Ethics for Social Work: The Second Step*, London: Routledge and Kegan Paul, pp 59-85.

Lewis, H. (1982) *The Intellectual Base of Social Work Practice: Tools for Thought in a Helping Profession*, New York: Haworth Press.

Lewis, J. (2002) 'The boundary between health and social care for older people', in B. Bytheway, V. Bacigalupo, J. Bornat, J. Johnson and S. Spurr (eds) *Understanding Care, Welfare and Community: A Reader*, London: Routledge, pp 313-20.

Lewis, J. and Glennerster, H. (1996) *Implementing the New Community Care*, Buckingham: Open University Press.

Loch, C.S. ([1883]1977) *How to Help in Cases of Distress*, Plymouth: Continua.

Lukes, S. (1974) *Power: A Radical View*, London: Macmillan.

Lurie, H.L. (1935) 'Re-examination of child welfare functions in family and foster care agencies', in F. Lowry (ed) (1939) *Readings in Social Case Work 1920-1938: Selected Reprints for the Case Work Practitioner*, New York: Columbia University Press, pp 611-19.

Lynn, E. and Muir, A. (1996) 'Empowerment in social work: the case of CCETSW's Welsh language policy', in B. Humphries (ed) *Critical Perspectives on Empowerment*, Birmingham: Venture Press, pp 131-44.

McDermott, F.E. (ed)(1975) *Self-determination in Social Work: A Collection of Essays on Self-determination and Related Concepts by Philosophers and Social Work Theorists*, London: Routledge and Kegan Paul.

Malherbe, M. (1982) *Accreditation in Social Work: Principles and Issues in Context: A Contribution to the Debate*, London: CCETSW.

Marcus, G.F. (1935) 'The status of social case work today', in F. Lowry (ed) (1939) *Readings in Social Case Work 1920-1938: Selected Reprints for the Case Work Practitioner*, New York: Columbia University Press, pp 122–35.

Martin, V. and Henderson, E. (2001) *Managing in Health and Social Care*, London: Routledge.

Mattaini, M.A. (2002) 'Practice with individuals', in M.A. Mattaini, C.T. Lowery and C.H. Meyer, *Foundations of Social Work Practice: A Graduate Text* (3rd edn), Washington, DC: NASW Press, pp 151–83.

Mayadas, N.S., Watts, T.D. and Elliott, D. (eds) (1997) *International Handbook on Social Work Theory and Practice*, Westport, CT: Greenwood Press.

Mayer, J. E. and Timms, N. (1970) *The Client Speaks*, London: Routledge and Kegan Paul.

Midgley, J. (1981) *Professional Imperialism: Social Work in the Third World*, London: Heinemann.

Midgley, J. (1995) 'International and comparative social welfare', in R.L. Edwards (ed) *Encyclopedia of Social Work* (19th edn, vol 2), Washington, DC: NASW Press, pp 1490–9.

Midgley, J. (1997) *Social Welfare in Global Context*, Thousand Oaks, CA: Sage Publications.

Midgley, J. (2000) 'Globalization, capitalism and social welfare: a social development perspective', *Canadian Social Work*, 2(1): 13–28.

Milligan, D. (1975) 'Homosexuality: sexual needs and social problems', in R. Bailey and R. Brake (eds) *Radical Social Work*, London: Arnold, pp 96–111.

Mondros, J.B. and Wilson, S.M. (1994) *Organizing for Power and Empowerment*, New York: Columbia University Press.

Morales, A.T. and Sheafor, B.W. (2001) *Social Work: A Profession of Many Faces* (9th edn), Boston, MA: Allyn and Bacon.

Moreau, M.J. (1990) 'Empowerment through advocacy and consciousness-raising: implications of a structural approach to social work', *Journal of Sociology and Social* Welfare, 17(2): 53–68.

Morgan, S. and Payne, M. (2002) 'Managerialism and state social work in Britain', *Hong Kong Journal of Social Work*, 36(1/2): 27–44.

Morris, J. (1993) *Independent Lives: Community Care and Disabled People*, London: Macmillan.

Mullaly, B. (1997) *Structural Social Work: Ideology, Theory, and Practice* (2nd edn), Don Mills, Ontario: Oxford University Press.

Mullender, A. and Ward, D. (1991) *Self-Directed Groupwork: Users Take Action for Empowerment*, London: Whiting and Birch.

Munro, E. (1998) *Understanding Social Work: An Empirical Approach*, London: Athlone.

NASW (National Association of Social Workers) (1973) *Standards for Social Service Manpower*, Washington DC: NASW, pp 4-5.

NASW (1981) 'Working statement on the purpose of social work', *Social Work* 26(1): 6.

Ng, S.M. and Chan, C.L.W. (2005) 'Intervention', in R. Adams, L. Dominelli and M. Payne (eds) *Social Work Futures: Crossing Boundaries, Transforming Practice*, Basingstoke: Palgrave Macmillan, pp 68-82.

Nokes, P. (1967) *The Professional Task in Welfare Practice*, London: Routledge and Kegan Paul.

Ohlin, L.E., Piven, H. and Pappenfort, D.M. (1956) 'Major dilemmas of the social worker in probation and parole', in S.A. Yelaja (ed) (1971) *Authority and Social Work: Concept and Use*, Toronto: University of Toronto Press, pp 206-24.

Oliver, M. (1990) *The Politics of Disablement*, London: Macmillan.

Oliver, M. (ed) (1991) *Social Work: Disabled People and Disabling Environments*, London: Jessica Kingsley.

Orcutt, B.A. (1990) *Science and Inquiry in Social Work Practice*, New York: Columbia University Press.

Parad, H.J. (1965) 'Introduction', in H.J. Parad (ed) *Crisis Intervention: Selected Readings*, New York, NY: Family Service Association of America, pp 1-2.

Parker, R. (1990) *Safeguarding Standards: A Report on the Desirability and Feasibility of Establishing a United Kingdom Independent Body to Regulate and Promote Good Practice in Social Work and Social Care*, London: National Institute for Social Work.

Parton, N. and O'Byrne, P. (2000) *Constructive Social Work: Towards a New Practice*, Basingstoke: Macmillan.

Patten, S.N. (1906) *The New Basis of Civilisation*, New York, NY: Macmillan.

Pawson, R., Boaz, A., Grayson, L., Long, A. and Barnes, C. (2003) *Types and Quality of Knowledge in Social Care*, London: Social Care Institute for Excellence.

Payne, M. (1989) 'Open records and shared decisions with clients', in S. Shardlow (ed) *The Values of Change in Social Work*, London: Tavistock/Routledge, pp 114-34.

Payne, M. (1993) *Linkages: Effective Networking in Social Care*, London: Whiting and Birch.

Payne, M. (1995) *Social Work and Community Care*, Basingstoke: Macmillan.

Payne, M. (1999) 'The moral bases of social work', *European Journal of Social Work*, 2(3): 247–58.

Payne, M. (2000) *Anti-bureaucratic Social Work*, Birmingham: Venture Press.

Payne, M. (2005a) *Modern Social Work Theory* (3rd edn), Basingstoke: Palgrave Macmillan.

Payne, M. (2005b) 'Social work process', in R. Adams, L. Dominelli and M. Payne (eds) *Social Work Futures: Crossing Boundaries, Transforming Practice*, Basingstoke: Palgrave Macmillan, pp 21–35.

Payne, M. (2005c) *The Origins of Social Work: Continuity and Change*, Basingstoke: Palgrave Macmillan.

Payne, M., Adams, R. and Dominelli, L. (2002) 'On being critical in social work', in R. Adams, L. Dominelli and M. Payne (eds) *Critical Practice in Social Work*, Basingstoke: Palgrave, pp 1–12.

Pease, B. and Fook, J. (eds) (1999) *Transforming Social Work Practice: Postmodern Critical Perspectives*, London: Routledge.

Percy-Smith, J. (ed) (2000) *Policy Responses to Social Exclusion: Towards Inclusion?*, Maidstone: Open University Press.

Perkin, H. (1989) *The Rise of Professional Society: England since 1880*, London: Routledge.

Perlman, H.H. (1957) *Social Casework: A Problem-solving Process*, Chicago, IL: University of Chicago Press.

Pinker, R. (1990) *Social Work in an Enterprise Society*, London: Routledge.

Pittock, M.G.H. (1999) *Celtic Identity and the British Image*, Manchester: Manchester University Press.

Pollitt, C. (1993) *Managerialism and the Public Services: Cuts or Cultural Change in the 1990s?*, Oxford: Blackwell.

Pray, K.L.M. (1942) 'The role of professional social work in the world today', in K.L.M. Pray (1949) *Social Work in a Revolutionary Age and Other Papers*, Philadelphia, PA: University of Philadelphia Press, pp 17–36.

Pugh, R. (1996) *Effective Language in Health and Social Work*, London: Chapman and Hall.

Putnam, R.D. (2000) *Bowling Alone: The Collapse and Revival of American Community*, New York, NY: Simon and Schuster.

QAA (Quality Assurance Agency for Higher Education) (2000) *Social policy and administration and social work*, Gloucester: QAA (www.qaa.ac.uk/academicinfrastructure/benchmark/honours/socialwork.pdf, accessed 9 May 2005).

Race, D.G. (ed)(2003) *Leadership and Change in Human Services: Selected Readings from Wolf Wolfensberger*, London: Routledge.

Ralphs Report (1975) *Report of the Working Party on the Role and Training of Education Welfare Officers*, London: Local Government Training Board.

Rapoport, L. (1970) 'Crisis intervention as a mode of brief treatment', in R.W. Roberts and R.H. Nee (eds) *Theories of Social Casework*, Chicago, IL: University of Chicago Press, pp 265-311.

Reamer, F.G. (1999) *Social Work Values and Ethics* (2nd edn), New York, NY: Columbia University Press.

Rees, S. (1975) 'How misunderstanding occurs', in R. Bailey and M. Brake (eds) *Radical Social Work*, London: Edward Arnold, pp 62-75.

Rees, S. (1991) *Achieving Power: Practice and Policy in Social Welfare*, Sydney: Allen and Unwin.

Reith, M. (1998) *Community Care Tragedies: A Practice Guide to Mental Health Inquiries*, Birmingham: Venture Press.

Reynolds, B.C. (1935) 'Social case work: What is it? What is its place in the world today?', in F. Lowry (ed) (1939) *Readings in Social Case Work 1920-1938: Selected Reprints for the Case Work Practitioner*, New York, NY: Columbia University Press, pp 136-47.

Richmond, M.E. (1917) *Social Diagnosis*, New York, NY: Free Press (1965 facsimile of the 1917 edn, Russell Sage Foundation).

Richmond, M.E. (1922) *What is Social Case Work?*, New York, NY: Russell Sage Foundation.

Roberts, A.R. (ed)(2000) *Crisis Intervention Handbook*, New York, NY: Oxford University Press.

Rogers, C.R. (1951) *Client-Centred Therapy: Its Current Practice, Implications and Theory*, London: Constable.

Rogers, C.R. (1961) *On Becoming a Person: A Therpists's View of Psychotherapy*, London: Constable.

Rogers, C.R. (1980) *A Way of Being*, Boston, MA: Houghton Mifflin.

Rose, S.M. (1990) 'Advocacy/empowerment: an approach to clinical practice for social work', *Journal of Sociology and Social Welfare*, 17(2): 41-52.

Rosenfeld, J.M. (1984) 'The expertise of social work: a cross-national perspective', in C. Guzzetta, A.J. Katz and R.A. English (eds) *Education for Social Work Practice: Selected International Models*, Vienna: International Association of Schools of Social Work, pp 111-18.

Rowbottom, R., Hey, A. and Billis, D. (1974) *Social Services Departments: Developing Patterns of Work and Organisation*, London: Heinemann.

Sainsbury, E. (1980) 'A professional skills approach to specialisation', in T. Booth, D. Martin and C. Melotte (eds) *Specialisation: Issues in the Organisation of Social Work*, Birmingham: BASW Publications.

Saks, M. (1995) *Professions and the Public Interest: Medical Power, Altruism and Alternative Medicine*, London: Routledge.

Satyamurti, C. (1979) 'Care and control in local authority social work', in N. Parry, M. Ruston and C. Satyamurti (eds) *Social Work, Welfare and the State*, London: Edward Arnold, pp 89–103.

Schneider, R.L. and Lester, L. (2001) *Social Work Advocacy: A New Framework for Action*, Belmont CA: Brooks/Cole.

Schön, D.A. (1983) *The Reflective Practitioner: How Professionals Think in Action*, New York, NY: Basic Books.

Schriver, J.M. (1987) 'Harry Lurie's critique: person and environment in early casework practice', *Social Service Review*, 61(3): 514–32.

Schwartz, B. (1993) 'Why altruism is impossible ... and ubiquitous', *Social Service Review*, 67(3): 314–43.

Seden, J. and Reynolds, J. (eds) (2003) *Managing Care in Practice*, London: Routledge.

Seebohm Report (1968) *Report of the Committee on Local Authority and Allied Personal Social Services*, Cmnd 3703, London: HMSO.

Shardlow, S. and Payne, M. (1998) *Contemporary Issues in Social Work: Western Europe*, Aldershot: Arena.

Shaw, J. (1974) *The Self in Social Work*, London: Routledge and Kegan Paul.

Shepherd, G.J., St John, J. and Striphas, T. (eds) (2006) *Communication as ...: Perspectives on Theory*, Thousand Oaks, CA: Sage Publications.

Sheppard, M. and Ryan, K. (2003) 'Practitioners as rule using analysts: a further development of process knowledge in social work', *British Journal of Social Work*, 33(2): 157–76.

Sheppard, M., Newstead, S., di Caccavo, A. and Ryan, K. (2000) 'Reflexivity and the development of process knowledge in social work: a classification and empirical study', *British Journal of Social Work*, 30(4): 465–88.

Silavwe, G.W. (1995) 'The need for a new social work perspective in an African setting: the case of social casework in Zambia', *British Journal of Social Work*, 25(1): 71–84.

Simey Report (1947) *Salaries and Conditions of Work of Social Workers: Report of a Joint Committee of the British Federation of Social Workers and the National Council of Social Service*, London: NCSS.

Simpson, J.A. and Weiner, E.S.C. (eds) (1989) *The Oxford English Dictionary* (2nd edn), Oxford: Clarendon House.

Solomon, B.B. (1976) *Black Empowerment: Social Work in Oppressed Communities*, New York, NY: Columbia University Press.

Stalley, R.F. (1978) 'Non-judgemental attitudes', in N. Timms and D. Watson (eds) *Philosophy in Social Work*, London: Routledge and Kegan Paul, pp 91–110.

Steiner, C. (ed) (1975) *Readings in Radical Psychiatry*, New York, NY: Grove Press.

Studt, E. (1954) 'An outline for the study of social authority factors in casework', in S.A. Yelaja (ed) *Authority and Social Work: Concept and Use*, Toronto: University of Toronto Press, pp 111–22.

Tan, N.-T. and Dodds, I. (eds) (2002) *Social Work Around the World II*, Berne: International Federation of Social Workers.

Tan, N.-T. and Envall, E. (eds) (nd, 2000) *Social Work Around the World*, Berne: International Federation of Social Workers.

Taylor, C. and White, S. (2000) *Practising Reflexivity in Health and Welfare: Making Knowledge*, Buckingham: Open University Press.

Taylor, M. and Vigars, C. (1993) *Management and Delivery of Social Care*, Harlow: Longman.

Teare, R.J. and McPheeters, H.L. (1970) *Manpower Utilization in Social Welfare: A Report based on a Symposium on Manpower Utilization in Social Welfare Services*, Atlanta, GA: Social Welfare Manpower Project, Southern Medical Education Board.

Thompson, N. (2001) *Anti-Discriminatory Practice* (3rd edn), Basingstoke: Palgrave.

Thompson, N. (2003) *Communication and Language: A Handbook of Theory and Practice*, Basingstoke: Palgrave Macmillan.

Thompson, N. (2005) *Understanding Social Work: Preparing for Practice*, Basingstoke: Palgrave Macmillan.

Timms, N. (1983) *Social Work Values: An Enquiry*, London: Routledge and Kegan Paul.

TOPSS UK Partnership (2002) 'National Occupational Standards for Social Work', Leeds: TOPSS England (www.topssengland.net/files/SW%20NOS%20doc%20pdf%20files%20edition%20Apr04.pdf).

Toren, N. (1969) 'Semi-professionalism and social work: a theoretical perspective', in A. Etzioni (ed) *The Semi-Professions and their Organization: Teachers, Nurses, Social Workers*, New York, NY, NY: Free Press, pp 141–95.

Trevithick, P. (2005) *Social Work Skills: A Practice Handbook*, Buckingham: Open University Press.

Trevithick, P., Richards, S., Ruch, G. and Moss, B. (2004) *Teaching and Learning Communication Skills in Social Work Education*, London: Social Care Institute for Excellence.

Truax, C.B. and Carkhuff, R.J. (1967) *Toward Effective Counseling and Psychotherapy: Training and Practice*, Chicago, IL: Aldine.

Tufts, J.H. (1923) *Education and Training for Social Work*, New York, NY: Russell Sage Foundation.

Turner, B.S. (1987) *Medical Power and Social Knowledge*, London: Sage Publications.

Wagner Report (1988) *Residential Care: A Positive Choice*, London; HMSO.

Wakefield, J.C. (1993) 'Is altruism part of human nature? Toward a theoretical foundation for the helping professions', *Social Service Review*, 67: 406-58.

Walker, S.H. (1928) *Social Work and the Training of Social Workers*, Chapel Hill, NC: University of North Carolina Press.

Watts, T.D., Elliott, D. and Mayadas, N.S. (eds) (1995) *International Handbook on Social Work Education*, Westport, CT: Greenwood Press.

Weale, A. (1978) *Equality and Social Policy*, London: Routledge and Kegan Paul.

Weisman, I. and Chwast, J. ([1960]1962) 'Control and values in social work treatment', in C. Kasius (ed) *Social Casework in the Fifties: Selected Articles 1950-1960*, New York, NY: Family Service Association of America, pp 252-62.

White, S. (2003) 'The social worker as moral judge: blame, responsibility and case formulation', in C. Hall, K. Juhila, N. Parton and T. Pösö (eds) *Constructing Clienthood in Social Work and Human Services: Interaction, Identities and Practices*, London: Jessica Kingsley, pp 177-92.

Wilding, P. (1982) *Professional Power and Social Welfare*, London: Routledge and Kegan Paul.

Wilensky, H.L. and Lebeaux, C.N. (1965) *Industrial Society and Social Welfare*, New York, NY: Free Press.

Wilkes, R. (1981) *Social Work with Undervalued Groups*, London: Tavistock.

Wilkes, R. (1985) 'Social work: what kind of profession?', in D. Watson (ed) *A Code of Ethics for Social Work: The Second Step*, London: Routledge and Kegan Paul, pp 40-58.

Williams, F. (1992) 'Somewhere over the rainbow: universality and diversity in social policy', in N. Manning and R. Page (eds), *Social Policy Review 4*, Canterbury: Social Policy Association.

Wilson, E. (1980) 'Feminism and social work', in R. Bailey and R. Brake (eds) *Radical Social Work and Practice*, London: Arnold, pp 26-42.

Wilson, J. (1995) *How to Work with Self-help Groups: Guidelines for Professionals*, Aldershot: Arena.

Wistow, G. (1982) 'Collaboration between health and local authorities: why is it necessary?', *Social Policy and Administration*, 16(1): 44-62.

Wistow, G. (1990) *Community Care Planning: A Review of Past Experiences and Present Imperatives*, Leeds: Nuffield Institute for Health.

Wood, G.G. and Middleman, R.R. (1989) *The Structural Approach to Direct Practice in Social Work*, New York, NY: Columbia University Press.

Wootton, B. (1959) *Social Science and Social Pathology*, London: Allen and Unwin.

Yelaja, S.A. (1965) 'The concept of authority and its use in child protective service', in S.A.Yelaja (ed) (1971) *Authority and Social Work: Concept and Use*, Toronto: University of Toronto Press, pp 229-42.

Yelaja, S.A. (ed) (1971) *Authority and Social Work: Concept and Use*, Toronto: University of Toronto Press.

Yelloly, M.A. (1980) *Social Work Theory and Psychoanalysis*, Wokingham: Van Nostrand Reinhold.

# Index


## A

academic literature 166-7, 169, 170, 175
acceptance and value complexities 95
accountability 105, 137-8
  and professionalisation 141-2, 147-8, 148-9, 151-2
Adams, R. 76, 116, 117-18
advocacy services 45, 48, 132-3, 150
ageing and ageism 133
agency 24-5, 85, 125-6, 185
  *see also* self-determination
agency base of social work 103-8, 185
  and power 124, 125-8, 182
  and professionalisation 104, 120, 127, 144-5, 190
agent-focused ethics 92
Ainsworth, F. 47
Alcoff, L.M. 24
altruism and professionalism 143-4, 149-50
American Association of Social Workers (AASW) 33, 34
Anglo-American social work discourse 178-9
anti-discriminatory approach 90-1, 112
  and power 131-2, 133
  value complexities 95, 97, 98
anti-racist practices 133
Archer, M.S. 24, 69
Attlee, C.R. 32
authority 109, 124, 125-8, 129

## B

Bailey, R. 42, 127, 129
Baker, R. 75
Banks, S. 86, 87-8, 91-2
Barclay Report (1982) 46, 74
Bartlett, H.M. 37, 70
Beckett, C. 92-3
Bell, D. 146
Berger, P.L. 3
Biestek, F.P. 65, 126
Billups, J.O. 168-9
*Blackwell Encyclopaedia of Social Work* 165-6
Blakemore, K. 134
Bland, R. 47
Boehm, W.W. 37, 40
Boneham, M. 134
Borel, K. 78
Bowers, S. 36, 39
Brake, R. 42
Brandon, D. 43-4
Brewer, C. 42, 60
Brint, S. 146
British Association of Social Workers (BASW) 40, 41, 75
British Federation of Social Workers 35, 38
Brown, H. 68
Brown, K. 179
bureau-professionals 111, 112, 119
bureaucracy 111, 115
Butler, S. 160
Butrym, Z.T. 38
Byrne, D. 134

## C

Campbell, T.D. 96-7
Care Councils 86, 87, 149
carers 108, 133
case-based ethics/casuistry 92
casework *see* social casework
Central Council for Education and Training in Social Work (CCETSW) 40, 41
Chamberlayne, P. 175
Chan, C.L.W. 59
charities 106-7, 146, 171
Charity Organisation Society (COS) 84
Charles, M. 160
Charlesworth, J. 152
Cheyney, A.S. 33
child protection work 23, 135-6
Children Acts 45, 153-4
Chilean Committee of Social Work 37
Chwast, J. 126
citizenship sharing view of welfare 93
claim of social work 1-2, 10, 31, 184-6, 187
  and agency base 126
  and diversity 173-4, 175, 180
  and globalisation 179
  and interpersonal practice 58, 60-1, 80
  and values 83-4, 85, 98, 100
  and welfare regimes 48-51
Clark, C. 93
Clarke, J. 109, 111
Clausen, H. 162

Clough, R. 47
codes of ethics 83, 84, 85, 86-8, 89, 94, 100-1
communication 55, 61-6
communist resistance to social work 168
communitarianism 92, 93
community work 67-8, 164, 171
community-based ethics 92
competences of social workers 74, 75-6
complexity 44-5, 151-2, 161-2
  value complexities 94-100, 182, 185
Compton, B.R. 59, 65, 74
confidentiality 94, 95, 96, 182
conflicts of interest 85, 98, 100, 182
consensus management 108
consent and power relations 124, 125, 183
consumerist view of ethics 93
contractarian view of ethics 91
Conway, J. 169, 171
Cooper, A. 136
Cormack, U. 36, 39
Coulshed, V. 74
Council on Social Work Education (CSWE) 40, 166
counselling 46, 145
counselling theory and communication 62
Craib, I. 24
creativity/creative social work 43-4, 78
criminal justice professionals 48, 177
crisis intervention 60
critical discourse analysis 11-12
critical social work 44-5, 65, 135-6, 186
critical thinking 69
cultural power and post-colonialism 178-9
cultural social work 50
cultural theory 62

## D

Davies, M. 14, 42, 78
Department of Health 28-9, 30, 31
deprofessionalisation 120, 159-60
Derezotes, D.S. 66, 85
Devine, E.T. 33, 34
diagnostic casework *see* social diagnosis
'direct care' 47
disabled living approaches 133
discourse-based ethics 92
discourses of social work 8-20, 40-4, 184-6
  and globalisation 179-80
  and identity 23-52
  and knowledge 71
  and management 109
discrimination *see* anti-discriminatory approach
distributive justice 90
'disvalues' 84-5
diversity 173-5, 176-8, 179-80, 186
division of labour in families 111
Dodds, I. 170
Dominelli, L. 14, 59, 61, 65-6, 68-9, 79, 120, 131, 132
Dorfman, R.A. 59, 64
Drakeford, M. 113-14
Dutt, R. 137

## E

economic rationalism 110, 185
education welfare work 177
Elliott, D. 175
embodiment 51, 55, 80, 85, 184-5, 187-8, 189
empowerment 45-6, 59, 67-8, 125, 132-6, 150
  definitions of social work 28, 29, 37
*Encyclopedia of Social Work* 166
England, H. 42-3, 78
enterprise 113, 114-16, 119, 185
Envall, E. 170
equality *see* inequalities
Esping-Andersen, G. 49
ethics *see* values of social work
ethnic minorities 90, 91, 112, 131-2
Etzioni, A. 92
Evans, D. 59-60
evidence-based practice 72-3, 148
excluded groups 45, 134, 135
expertise and neutrality 149

## F

Fabian socialism 84
failures of social work 148-9
Fairclough, N. 10, 11
false consciousness 44
families: power relations 11, 111, 130
feminism 42, 44, 92, 93, 131, 186
Ferguson, N. 173
Fleet, F. 125
flexibility 56, 78-9, 111, 162
Flexner, Abraham 144
Fook, J. 44, 69
Ford, P. 76
Foren, R. 127
Foster, P. 119
Foucault, M. 10, 11

Freidson, E. 146
Fulcher, L.C. 47

## G

Galaway, B. 59, 65, 74
Garrett, M. 129
gender issues 90-1, 112, 131
General Social Care Council (GSCC) 87
generalist view of management 109-10
'generic' social work debate 176
Germain, C.B. 146
German Council on Social Welfare 37
gestalt approach 39
Gill, R. 97
Gilligan, C. 92
Gilliland, B.E. 60
Gilmore, S. 137
Glasby, J. 152
globalisation issues 172-5, 178-80, 186
Goffman, E. 56-7
Goldstein, E.G. 77
Greenwood, E. 144
'group care' 47
group work 67-8

## H

Halmos, P. 145
Hamilton, G. 36, 39
Handler, J.F. 129
Harris, J. 108, 115
Health Act (1999) 153
Health and Social Care Act (2001) 153
healthcare: joint working 152-9
Healy, K. 44-5, 69, 70, 71, 135-6, 158, 166
Hearn, J. 130
Henderson, E. 116, 117-18
hierarchy 130
Hockey, J. 24
Hokenstad, M.C. 166, 171
Hollis, F. 39
Horner, W.C. 82
hospice social workers 3, 8, 48
hospitals and social work 106, 107
Hough, G. 119
Howarth, D. 10
Howe, D. 77-8
Hudson, B. 152
Hugman, R. 146
human communication 55, 61-6
human rights approach *see* rights-based approach
Humphries, B. 134-5

## I

identity of social work 23-4, 26-52, 184
Ife, J. 76, 90, 110
individual problem solving 10, 28, 29, 35, 36, 37, 41
individualisation and value 95, 96, 151, 182
individuality and use of self 78
inequalities 90-1, 111, 112, 131-2
intake and assessment (I&A) teams 23
intergovernmental activities 168
International Association of Schools of Social Work (IASSW) 28, 167, 171
International Council on Social Welfare (ICSW) 40, 42, 167
International Federation of Social Workers (IFSW) 88-90, 167, 169
  definitions of social work 28, 70, 83-4, 86
  problem areas of practice 88, 89, 98
international organisations 167-8, 174-5
  social work organisations 167, 174, 190
international social work 163-72, 174-5, 186
'international view' 171
interpersonal practice 53-80, 183-4, 184-5, 186-8
  and power 124-5
  and professionalisation 150-1
interpretivist view of knowledge 145-6, 150
intervention 55, 58-61, 182
intuition and use of self 78, 79

## J

Jakobsson, G. 175
James, A. 24
James, R.K. 60
Japanese National Committee on Social Welfare 37
Jenkins, R. 24
joint working 152-9
Jordan, B. 43-4
journals of social work 167

## K

Kamerman, S.B. 155
Kant, Immanuel 91
Kearney, A. 59-60
Kendall, Katherine A. 166, 171
Kennett, C. 50

knowledge
  and discourse 71
  and practice 44, 55, 70–4
    types of knowledge 71–4
  and professionalisation 145–6, 147, 149, 189
    multiprofessional working 156–7
Krill, D. 42

## L

Lait, J. 42, 60
language 4–6, 10–11
  *see also* communication; discourse
law and power 136–8
learning disabilities: development of term 6
learning theory 62
Lee, J.A.B. 64, 66
Lee, Porter R. 34
legal decision making 136–7
Leighton, N. 97
Lewis, J. 152–3
Littlechild, R. 152
local authorities 108, 152–3
local diversity in social work 176–8, 186
Loch, C.S. 70
long-term teams 23
Luckmann, T. 3
Lukes, S. 128–9
Lurie, H.L. 38–9, 40

## M

McCleod, E. 131
McDougall, K. 36, 39
McPheeters, H.L. 75
Malherbe, M. 148
managed relationship approach 104, 105
management of social work 103–20, 148–9, 185
managerialism 48, 109–20, 137, 138, 148–9, 185
Marcus, G.F. 34–5
marketisation 112–14, 115–16, 119, 150, 153
Martin, V. 116, 117–18
Mattaini, M.A. 59, 72–3
Maynard, A. 92–3
Mendieta, E. 24
mental hygiene movement 34
'mentally handicapped': use of term 6
Middleman, R.R. 68
Midgley, J. 166–7
Milford Conference Report (1929) 33, 34
Mill, John Stuart 91
Mondros, J.B. 67–8
moral communities 97–8
Morales, A.T. 74
Mullaly, B. 69, 135
Mullender, A. 130
multiprofessional working 50–1, 142, 154–9, 162
Munro, E. 64

## N

National Association of Social Workers (NASW)(US) 40, 41, 144
National Occupational Standards for Social Work 74, 165
needs-based provision 188–9
neutrality and expertise 149
New Labour
  partnership working 153–4, 155
  Third Way policies 111
new Right policies 109, 110–12, 114
Newman, J. 111
Ng, S.M. 59
NHS Act (1973) 152–3
NHS and Community Care Act (1990) 46, 153
Nokes, P. 145
non-governmental organisations (NGOs) 167–8
non-judgementality and value complexities 95
normalisation 133

## O

O'Byrne, P. 61–2
oppression 44, 98, 131, 132–6, 149
Orcutt, B.A. 146
organisation of social work 103–6, 152–9, 190
organisations *see* international organisations
Orme, J. 74
other-based ethics 92
*Oxford English Dictionary* 4, 27–8, 32

## P

Parad, H.J. 60
Parker, R. 148
participation 45–6, 48, 65–6
partnership 46, 47–8, 51, 65–6
partnership working 153–4

Parton, N. 61-2
pathways in social work profession 6-8, 9, 184
patriarchy 131
Patten, S.N. 32
Pawson, R. 71-2, 73
Payne, M. 152, 172
performance in social work practice 56-8, 104-5
Perlman, H.H. 36, 126
personal capacities of social workers 74-5
  use of self 55, 76-9
personal identity 24-6
personal social services: use of term 4
personal values of social worker 82, 97-8
personality 26
Pinker, R. 115
policy managerialism 110
political interactions 183-4, 184-5, 186-8
political philosophy and ethics 93-4
Pollitt, C. 110
positivism 44, 145, 146
post-colonialism 172, 173, 178-9
Postle, K. 76
postmodernism 42-3, 44, 65, 71
power 11, 69-70, 71, 77, 121-39, 185
  and post-colonialism 173, 178-9, 180
  and professionalisation 149, 190
practice *see* interpersonal practice
Pray, K.L.M. 35, 38
preventive/interventive distinction 60
principle-based values 91-2
private domain and social work 182-3
privatisation 112-14, 115-16, 119
probation work and unified profession 177
procedural justice 90
process 55, 66-70
professional power 123, 124, 131, 148-50
professional–organisation approach 104-5
professionalisation of social work 141-62, 182-3, 185-6, 189, 190
  and agency base 104, 120, 127, 144-5
  and knowledge 70, 145-6
  and local diversity 176-8
  and managerialism 120, 148-9
  and politics of values 83, 100-1, 183
  and power 127, 138-9
  social work and other professions 50-1, 152-9, 161-2
  worker style and use of self 78-9
psychoanalysis 34-5, 38
psychological understanding 28, 29
psychology and communication 62
public inquiries 137-8
public interest and professionalisation 147-8
public values 82, 97-8
public/private domains 182-3
publications on social work 165-7, 169, 170
Pugh, R. 62

## Q

QAA Benchmark for Social Work Degrees 74-5, 165-6
quasi-markets 113

## R

radical social work 42, 44-5, 48, 84, 128-32
Ralphs Report (1975) 177
Rapoport, L. 60
rational management 109, 110
Rawls, John 91
Reamer, F.G. 98, 99
Rees, S. 110
reflective practice 150
reflexiveness 12-13, 42
regulation of social workers 148-9
relatedness 66
relational/cultural theory 62
relationship with client 55, 61-6, 76-9
relationship-based ethics 92
religion 71, 92-3
residential work 47, 176-7
resource-poor countries 91, 171-2, 173, 175, 178-9
'respect for persons' 91, 95, 98, 182
Reynolds, B.C. 35, 38
Reynolds, J. 116, 117-18
Richmond, Mary E. 32, 33, 34, 39
rights-based approach 28, 29, 83-4, 88-91, 92, 93-4, 96-7
  neglect of rights 149
risk avoidance 138
Roberts, A.R. 60
Rogers, C.R. 62, 65
role theory 56-7
Rosenfeld, J.M. 76

## S

Sainsbury, E. 145
Saks, M. 147
Salomon, Alice 171
Satyamurti, C. 127, 129

Schön, D.A. 150
Schwartz, B. 150
'scientific charity' 146
Seden, J. 116, 117-18
Seebohm Report (1968) 4, 107, 144, 160
self: use of self and practice 55, 76-9, 186
self-actualisation 77-8
self-determination 45-6, 48, 95, 125-6
service ideal 149-50
shared practice 50-1
Shaw, J. 77
Sheafor, B.W. 74
Shepherd, G.J. 63
Sheppard, M. 67, 69
Silavwe, G.W. 96
Simey Report (1947) 35, 38
skills for social work 55, 70-1, 74-6, 189
Smith, H. 68
social action work 67-8
social assistance 4, 50
social capital 134
social care 4-5, 29, 30, 31, 46-8, 49-50
  in unified profession 177-8
Social Care Councils 86, 87, 149
social casework 33, 34-5, 36, 39, 107
social change 10, 28, 29, 36, 42, 45
social construction approach 2-3, 4, 188-90
social control 124, 125-8, 130-1, 135, 164
social democratic welfare 93
social development 171-2, 175
social diagnosis 32, 33, 39, 84
social governance *see* social control
social justice 28, 83-4, 134
social movements 111
social order views of social work 14, 15-20, 28, 29, 51-2, 80, 189-90
  and communication 62
  and early views of social work 32, 34, 42
  and international social work 175
  and intervention 59-61
  and knowledge 71, 73
  and management 105-6, 119
  and power 136, 138
  and process 68
  and professionalisation 149-50, 151
  and social care 47
  and values 83, 84, 90, 101
social pedagogy 5, 50, 163-4, 168, 171
social practice and discourse 10, 11
social security 5, 49
social services 5, 30, 49, 176-7
social understanding 28, 29
social welfare: use of term 5
social work
  aims and nature of profession 1-2
  definitions 4-6
    and identity 26-44
  international development 170-2
  origins and evolution of term 32-40
  terminology 4-6
social work education 189
  international aspects 165-6, 168-9, 170, 171, 174
specialisation issues 176
Stalley, R.F. 97
state
  and definitions of social work 28-9
  management context 106-7, 108, 110-11, 148-9
    privatisation and marketisation 112-14
  politics of professionalisation 147, 183
  and values 93-4
substantive equality 90-1

## T

Tan, N.-T. 170
TAPUPA framework 73
Taylor, C. 135
Taylor, M. 117-18
Taylorism 109, 110
Teare, R.J. 75
'technical rationality' 150
Thatcherism 111
therapeutic relationships 65
therapeutic view of social work 12-13, 14-20, 28, 51-2, 79-80, 187-8
  and communication 62
  critique of 40, 42
  definitions and identity of social work 34-5, 38, 42-4
  and international social work 175
  interpersonal practice 184-5
  and intervention 59, 61
  and knowledge 71, 73-4
  and management 105-6, 119
  and power 125-6, 136
  and professionalisation 150
  and self-determination 45-6
  and skills 76
  and social care 47, 48
  and use of self 79
  and values 83, 84, 101
thinking processes 67, 69
Third Way policies 111

Thompson, N. 62, 64, 124, 132
Timms, N. 84-5, 86
Toren, Nina 144-5
Towle, Charlotte 39
transformational views of social work 13-20, 28, 51-2, 79-80
  and communication 62
  and definitions 42
  and early views of social work 32, 38
  and intervention 59, 61
  and knowledge 71, 74
  and power 136
  and process 68, 69
  and professionalisation 150, 151
  and skills 76
  and use of self 79
  and values 83, 84, 101
transparency 149, 150
Trevithick, P. 62, 75
Tsang, N.M. 6-7
Tufts, J.H. 32
Turner, B.S. 146

## U

unification of social work profession 176-7
utilitarianism 91

## V

values of social work 55, 71, 81-101
  complexities of 94-100, 182, 185
Vigars, C. 117-18
virtue-based view of ethics 85, 86

## W

Wakefield, J.C. 150
Walker, S.H. 33
Ward, D. 130
Watson, D. 100
Weisman, I. 126
welfare 5, 93-4, 110-12
welfare benefits/rights 5
welfare regimes 48-51, 164, 174, 177
Whitbeck, L.B. 82
White, S. 135
Wilding, P. 119, 148
Wilkes, R. 42, 92
Wilson, S.M. 67-8
'wise person' role 58, 187
Wood, G.G. 68
Wootton, B. 40, 42, 50
worker style 78-9

## Y

Yelaja, S.A. 127
Younghusband, Dame Eileen 171
youth work 50, 164